D1488572

WE COULD
PERCEIVE
NO SIGN
OF THEM

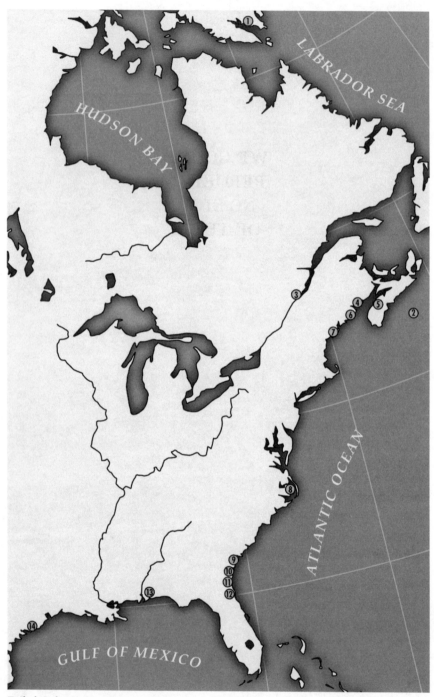

Failed Colonies: 1. Meta Incognita; 2. Sable Island; 3. Charlesbourg-Royal; 4. Ste.-Croix; 5. Port Royal; 6. St.-Saveur; 7. Popham; 8. Roanoke; 9. Charlesfort/Santa Elena; 10. Spanish Mission colonies; 11. San Miguel de Gualdape; 12. Fort Caroline/San Mateo; 13. Santa Maria de Ochuse; 14. Fort St. Louis.

WE COULD PERCEIVE NO SIGN OF THEM

Failed Colonies *in* North America 1526–1689

David MacDonald *and* Raine Waters

WESTHOLME
Yardley

Westholme Publishing, LLC
904 Edgewood Road
Yardley, Pennsylvania 19067
Visit our Web site at www.westholmepublishing.com

ISBN: 978–1–59416–347-0
Also available as an eBook.

Printed in the United States of America.

Land in a swamp, march through the woods, and in some inland post feel the savagery, the utter savagery, had closed round him—all that mysterious life of the wilderness that stirs in the forest, in the jungles, in the hearts of wild men. There's no initiation either into such mysteries. He has to live in the midst of the incomprehensible, which is also detestable. And it has a fascination, too, that goes to work upon him. The fascination of the abomination—you know, imagine the growing regrets, the longing to escape, the powerless disgust, the surrender, the hate.
—Joseph Conrad, *Heart of Darkness*

[F]rom thence we returned by the water side, round about the Northpoint of the Iland, untill we came to the place where I left our Colony in the yeere 1586. . . . [W]e passed toward the place where they were left in sundry houses, but we found the houses taken downe, and the place very strongly enclosed with a high palisado of great trees . . . and one of the chiefe trees or postes at the right side of the entrance had the barke taken off, and 5. foote from the ground in fayre Capitall letters was graven CROATOAN without any crosse or signe of distresse. . . . From thence wee went along by the water side, towards the poynt of the Creeke to see if we could find any of their botes or Pinnisse, but we could perceive no signe of them.
—John White on his return to the colony on Roanoke Island, "The fifth voyage of M. John White into the West Indies and parts of America called Virginia, in the yeere 1590," in Richard Hakluyt, *Voyages, Navigations, Traffiques and Discoveries of the English Nation*, published 1598–1600

CONTENTS

Illustrations

Introduction

THE NATIONS OF THE MODERN AMERICAS began as successful colonies, but not all colonies succeeded, and the difference between colonies that survived and those that failed was small. Both contribute to our understanding of the ordeals of the Europeans who first settled in the New World and of the Native Americans who had to interact with them, but with the exception of the famous lost Roanoke colony, the failed colonies of North America remain largely unknown except to specialists in colonial history.

A colony is a community established by people in a new land who remain politically connected to their country of origin, although not all colonial communities were alike. The Abbè Joseph de La Porte, writing in the eighteenth century, recognized this when referring to the establishment of the French in Illinois: "The Chevalier de La Salle . . . entered the Illinois area . . . and constructed a fort there; the Spanish would have built a church, the English a tavern."* Behind this typically Gallic bon mot is a basic truth. The French often began a colony by establishing a military outpost, the Spanish a mission, and the English a civilian community. There were exceptions, of course, and some scholars argue that one or another type was not a true colony, but such particularism seems unjustified. If successful, colonies of every nation-

*L'Abbe Delaporte, *Le Voyageur François*, t. 10, Paris: Chez L. Cellott, 1769, 6.

ality soon incorporated military, religious, and civilian elements. Here we consider European settlements in North America to have been colonies whatever their initial character.

Not every unsuccessful colony is mentioned here, and some, such as the Scottish colony near Charleston, are touched on only incidentally. Those treated at length were selected as significant, illustrative of the varieties of colonization, and important to the evolution of settlement in North America.

The sixteenth and seventeenth centuries were the "great" age of colonization, and all colonies founded during this period faced challenges dictated by the limitations of contemporary European culture. Shared challenges involved finance, food, leadership, knowledge of the area colonized, behavior of colonists, and relations with the people already inhabiting the land, but each colony was also unique in the intensity of the shared challenges and its responses to them, as well as in trials and tribulations particular to each colony.

Although the age of colonization was a period of expanding national economies, emerging European national monarchies seldom had sufficient income to meet all needs. Even the Spanish monarchy was chronically in debt and repeatedly declared bankruptcy despite the enormous wealth generated from the New World and Far Eastern trade. Generally, little royal funding was available for colonization, and colonial schemes were frequently financed by a combination of merchants, wealthy gentlemen, aristocrats, and the monarch, the royal contribution often a modest fraction of the total. Financiers sought short-term gains, such as the discovery of a quick route to the trade of the Far East, hoards of precious metals, mines, or at least valuable trade goods such as furs and spices. Few had the patience or resources to support long-range goals.

The greatest problem faced by every colony during its initial years was the supply of food. European technology during the age of colonization had not yet developed the ability to preserve and transport large quantities of wholesome food over long distances. Initial colonial expeditions usually carried insufficient quantities of mediocre food, and accidents often deprived them of a substantial portion of even those provisions. Colonists found to their dismay that promised support from Europe was often delayed, inadequate, and of poor quality, and they routinely turned to the indigenous people to supply them without understanding the realities of the Native economy.

Inadequate leadership plagued many colonies. Early modern Europe was highly hierarchical, and the early leadership of most colonies was vested in a single individual; seldom did any individual possess the knowledge, temperament, and experience to deal effectively with all the challenges that confronted a new colony. Colonial commandants often came from the ranks of the minor gentry. They had some education and were literate, which placed them above the commonality, yet they were not part of the economic or intellectual elite. Little was given to them, and they pursued position and wealth vigorously. Most had military backgrounds, and it was not unusual for them to have been privateers and even pirates earlier in their careers. They were generally hard men, physically brave and daring, but often also authoritarian, violent, and rapacious. It was customary that a council of senior officers advised the commandant, but the commandant made the decisions, and councils seldom played a major role in changing or significantly modifying a course of action.

Colonists who migrated willingly were often naively optimistic about opportunities in the new land and understood little about the difficulties. They frequently embarked for their new homes knowing nothing beyond the superficial report of overly enthusiastic explorers who spent little time in North America. Like the investors in colonial schemes, many colonists sought short-term gains, searching for precious metals or seeking advantageous trade with the Native peoples rather than investing time in the plodding work of raising crops. Those who did endeavor to farm simply, and sometimes incorrectly, assumed that familiar crops would prosper in foreign climes, and colonists often arrived in North America too late to plant crops during their first year, when the need for food became most acute.

Not all colonists went to the New World voluntarily. The European population increased significantly during the age of colonization, and at the same time, economic developments dispossessed many people. Frequently characterized as vagrants and sturdy beggars, the unemployed and homeless were regarded as dangers to society, defined as innately criminal, and subject to arrest and prosecution. Some theorists felt colonies could serve as dumps for such undesirable individuals, while others, perhaps more charitably inclined, thought colonies could provide the dispossessed with new opportunities to lead respectable lives. Many colonies included a contingent of such people, some of whom may have been willing to emigrate for a chance at a new life, but others, whether convicted merely of begging or of serious crimes, were forcefully conscripted or given the choice to go to a colony or face a worse fate, the galleys or the hangman's noose. Beggars and convicts seldom proved useful additions to colonizing efforts. At best they were often unhealthy and lacked skills to cope successfully with their new environment. At worst they were poorly motivated, undisciplined, ill adjusted, disorderly, disruptive, and sometimes homicidal.

Europeans of all nations were abysmally ignorant of the people they met in America and explicitly or implicitly shared a common attitude toward them. With few exceptions, colonists condescendingly regarded Native Americans as simple savages and had little understanding or appreciation of their customs, manners, and mores. Europeans saw themselves as benevolently dispensing the advantages of civilization and true religion, and they were both puzzled and angered when Indians were not grateful and did not submit subserviently. Europeans were willing to live in peace and harmony if Indians were cooperative, submissive, provided the colonists with food and resources, offered no resistance to the colonists' intrusion into and takeover of their territory, and accepted Christianity willingly. If not, colonists of every nationality were prepared to make war against Native peoples, conquer, subjugate, kill, and even massacre whole communities. Individual colonists and soldiers, undisciplined, ignorant, or in desperate circumstances, often stole food and goods, callously insulted and maltreated Indians, abused women, and even committed murder. Usually Indians soon realized that it was against their long-term interests to aid colonists, and those who did not come quickly to that realization came to regret it. Colonists' behavior invoked a variety of responses from indigenous people, ranging from withholding aid and leaving the area to retaliatory violence and endemic warfare.

The European attitude toward Native people was manifest in the kidnapping of Indians to train as translators. During Christopher Columbus's first voyage, he abducted more than a dozen Indians from several tribes for that purpose, and the practice was almost universal among later explorers and colonists of all nations. Most of the kidnapped soon died of European diseases to which they had no immunity. Europeans expected gratitude and loyalty from the few captives who survived and usually trusted them implicitly, failing to realize they may have resented their captivity, yearned to return to their families, and continued to identify with their Native cultures rather than those of their captors. Native translators, despite years of indoctrination and acculturation, routinely deserted at the first opportunity to return to their indigenous cultures, much to the baffled outrage of Europeans.

European explorers and colonists of all nations used translators to interrogate Indians about sources of precious metal and other sorts of wealth and understood translated replies to indicate that nearby lands contained vast riches. Typically, the locations of these rich lands were a little vague, although supposedly within reach, not immediately but in the foreseeable future. Europeans seldom suspected that Indians were capable of fashioning their answers to serve their own purposes and hinder their interrogators. The translators and informants may have hoped that the Europeans would depart to search for the fabled wealth, although some stories may have resulted from Europeans' own wishful misunderstanding of Native informants or from the willful exaggeration of explorers or colonists to impress investors and retain their support.

Europeans did not understand the economics of Native American life. Typically, Indians generously gave food to newly arrived colonists, but the colonists failed to understand that food came from the Indians' own sustenance and such generosity could not long endure. Indians grew sufficient crops for their own consumption and a small reserve, beyond which there was no demand or use for excess food production until colonists arrived. Indigenous chiefdoms in exceptionally fertile areas did produce sufficient food surpluses to support ruling hierarchies and could have aided colonists significantly, but generally such chiefdoms were far from the coastal areas where Europeans established early colonies. Many Indians left their villages during the winter months to live in small family groups while they hunted for game, leaving behind the colonists when their provisions were at their lowest. Colonists also failed to understand that the large animals of North America could not be domesticated and attributed the Indians' supposed failure to do so, like the moderate size of their fields, to indolence and lethargy.

Here we limit ourselves to failed North American colonies founded during the sixteenth and seventeenth centuries in the United States and Canada. Not all colonies were founded at that time. The Norse colonized Greenland late in the tenth century, and about the year 1000 they also attempted to settle in North America, but they were quickly discouraged by the presence of indigenous people whose enmity they aroused. They survived in Greenland until about 1450; their eventual disappearance there remains imperfectly understood. John Jacob Astor sponsored a commercial colony on the Pacific coast during the first years of the nineteenth century, an unsuccessful venture yet significant in the emergence of the United States and Canada as nations.

Colonies, of course, were also founded throughout Central and South America, and the colonial efforts that failed in those areas offer stories as compelling and even stranger than anything in North America, such as German knights in armor in the jungles of Venezuela, Dutch burghers in Brazil, and Scots in Panama. But those are stories for another day.

A Note about Names

In recent years, attempts to find an acceptable term of general reference for the indigenous people of the Americas have produced no good resolution. Native people, of course, are best designated as members of a specific tribe, band, or community. Many familiar names for tribes, however, are not those used by members themselves, but rather imposed by other, frequently hostile groups, while the proper names often remain unrecognizable to modern readers.

The term "Indian" is, of course, an absurdity, based on Columbus's mistaken belief that he had reached the Far East, but it remains in general use, even among Native people who generally do not find it pejorative. Russell Means, who became a prominent member of the American Indian Movement, accepted and used "Indian" in preference to "Native American." Both, however, obscure basic differences among groups. Nevertheless, "Native American" has gained some currency, as opposed to "Amerindian," which enjoyed brief popularity but has faded, as have a number of other usages. The terms "Native" and "indigenous person" are useful in cases of ambiguity, uncertainty, or to avoid repetition. We capitalize Native in respect, as in Paul Kelton, *Epidemics and Enslavement: Biological Catastrophe in the Native Southeast, 1492–1715.*

Most Indian tribal, band, and community names are mass nouns, and as such, one form serves as singular and plural. So, for example, we write "Guale" rather than "Guales" and "Etchemin" rather than "Etchemins."

Similar problems arise in referring to people of African origin or descent. Here we have conformed to the general current consensus, "black."

PART ONE

The Spanish *and* French *in* the Southeast

ONE

The First Spanish Colony *in* North America: San Miguel de Gualdape (1526)

Background

In 1526, Lucas Vásquez de Ayllón founded San Miguel de Gualdape, the earliest colony in North America. The experiences of the San Miguel de Gualdape colonists were archetypical. The colony was rationally planned and set forth well equipped with every prospect of success, but the colonists quickly encountered almost every challenge that later colonists would face.

While the events associated with the founding and failure of San Miguel de Gualdape are fairly well attested, the geographic setting of the events is the subject of intense debate. The river that Ayllón and his companions called the Jordan, a central feature of the accounts, has been identified by modern researchers as far north as the Cape Fear River and as far south as the Savannah River. The Spanish accounts record that Ayllón and the colonists moved roughly forty-five leagues from the place of their initial landing to where they established the colony, but they neglect to indicate whether they went north or south. As a result, commentators have argued that San Miguel de Gualdape was located as far north as Virginia near the later site of Jamestown and as far south as Sapelo Island on the mid-coast of Georgia. Efforts of archaeologists to locate remains of the colony have been unsuccessful to date. Rather than attempting to reconcile irreconcilable views, we follow what is closest to a current consensus.

Lucas Vásquez de Ayllón was born in Spain about 1475. His father was a lawyer, and he followed the same profession. He first came to the New World, landing at Santo Domingo, the capital of Española (Hispaniola, the modern Dominican Republic), in 1502 along with the new governor, Nicolás de Ovando y Cáceres. There Ayllón served as *alcalde*, a post combining the offices of mayor and judge, for the interior and northern part of the island. He was deeply involved in the factional politics of the Spanish West Indies and ignored no opportunity to build his own wealth. In 1509, he was recalled to Spain and subject to a *residencia*, a review of his conduct in office. There were accusations that Ayllón had enriched himself unjustly, but he seems to have avoided heavy censure and went on to hold higher offices in the West Indies. While in Spain, Ayllón studied at the University of Salamanca, earning the honorific title *licenciado*, indicating he was learned in law. In 1511, the Spanish king, Ferdinand II, established an *audiencia*, or tribunal, for the West Indies to protect royal prerogatives and provide supervision of the governor's exercise of power. The audiencia consisted of three *oidores*, or judges, one of whom was Ayllón. He continued his involvement in factional politics and building his fortune, acquiring the half-ownership of a large sugar plantation and sugar mill, both worked by Indian slaves.

By 1520, the Native peoples of the Caribbean—the Arawak, Taíno, Carib, and others—had been reduced to a fraction of their original population by slavery, disease, and warfare against the Spanish. In the quest for slaves, even the Bahamas, not yet settled by Europeans, had been depopulated, and yet the quest for slaves continued, despite the growing protest by the Dominican Fathers Antonio de Montesino, Bartolomé de las Casas, and their followers.

In 1521, Juan Ponce de León set forth to establish a colony on the southwest coast of Florida. Ponce de León had officially discovered Florida eight years earlier, in 1513, although Spanish slave hunters had preceded him to the peninsula (then presumed to be an island), poisoning relations with the Indians. Ponce de León encountered fierce hostility from the indigenous Calusa during his initial exploration, despite which he intended to plant a colony in their territory. The Calusa attacked before the settlement could be established, and Ponce de León was among the casualties, struck by a poisoned arrow. The expedition retreated to Cuba, where he died of his wound.

Also in 1521, two ships set forth independently to capture slaves. Vásquez de Ayllón and Diego Cavallero, secretary of the audiencia, hired Francisco Gordillo, an experienced slave raider, to command the expedition, and Alonso Fernández Sotil as sailing master and pilot. Diego Colón, son of Cristopher Columbus and governor of Española, granted a license for the voyage that also permitted new exploration. Ayllón's interest in exploration was due to the report that about five years previously, Pedro de Salazar had captured Indians of unusually large stature northwest of the Bahamas. It is uncertain whether Salazar had landed on one of the northern-most Bahamas or on the coast of North America.

About the same time, Sancho Ortiz de Urrutía, a prosperous merchant, in partnership with Juan Ortiz de Matienzo, hired Pedro de Quxós, whom he had often employed in the past, to pilot a ship carrying merchandise from Hispaniola to Cuba, after which he was to go slave hunting in the Bahamas. Quxós's name is also written Quejo, Quijos, Quexo, and Quexós. Urrutia and Matienzo too had a license from Diego Colón to transport merchandise, but it did not mention permission to explore. Neither Quxós nor Gordillo realized initially the extent to which the Bahamas had already been depopulated.

While unproductively searching for slaves, the two ships met by chance in the Bahamas, and the commanders agreed to join forces. They sailed north for eight days and then turned west before sighting a low-lying coast. They landed on the feast day of John the Baptist near the mouth of a river that was later called the Jordan and explored the area for several days. The Spanish encountered indigenous people whom they befriended with gifts of brightly colored cloth and clothing and who reciprocated with gifts of food. The Spanish spent a few days exploring the area, and then Gordillo and his men claimed the newly found land in the name of Ayllón and Cavallero. This outraged Quxós who then claimed the land for Urrutía and Matienzo. Despite the disagreement, the two groups spent the next two weeks gaining the trust of the Natives, trading trifles chiefly for freshwater pearls, and continuing to explore the vicinity. The Spanish questioned the Indians, but as the two groups had no language in common, it is questionable how much the Spanish really understood. The Spanish encountered a village, the name of which they comprehended as Chicora; the Spanish came to apply the name to the entire area. The Indians mentioned Duhare, which the Spanish understood as an inland chiefdom ruled by a king called Datha who was the overlord of a number of areas including much of the coast. This excited the interest of the Spanish, who well remembered the inland kingdoms of Mexico and Peru and the wealth they held.

After about three weeks on the coast, the Spanish lured sixty of the Indians aboard their ships, took them prisoner, and sailed away with their cargo of slaves. On the return voyage, Gordillo had a serious disagreement with his sailing master, Sotil, as the result of which Gordillo transferred to Quxós's ship along with a few of the crew and his share of the captive Natives. Sotil's ship failed to reach port and was never heard from again. At Santo Domingo, the sponsors of the expedition divided the slaves and set them to work on their properties.

Preparations

When official duties required Ayllón to travel to Spain, the associates in the discovery decided to have him carry a petition to the royal court granting them sole permission to exploit the new land. Conscious of the developing royal disapproval of enslaving Indians, the petitioners indicated their intention to return the slaves to their homeland.

One young captive of quick wit and engaging disposition learned Spanish and converted to Christianity. Baptized as Francisco, he was called Francisco de Chicora, Francisco Chicorano, or *el Chircorano*. The young man ingratiated himself to Ayllón and became his frequent companion, traveling with him to Spain, where their relationship is described as like that of father and son. Francisco filled Ayllón's ear with fanciful stories of his homeland and the kingdom of Duhare, which he said were fruitful lands, where there were many large pearls and gems. He told of herds of domesticated deer that grazed in forests during the day and returned to their stables in the evening, where they were milked like Spanish cows and their milk made into cheese. The king of Duhare and his wife were of gigantic stature, the result of an herbal concoction given them when young that softened their bones so they could be stretched and their height increased. Ayllón and at least one other listener were completely taken in by these and other tales. Another expressed disbelief but did not record his skepticism until many years later.

Ayllón's petition to the crown has not survived, but its content can be largely reconstructed on the basis of conversations he had with friends, particularly the ethnographer and historian Pietro Martire d'Anghiera. Ayllón, who of course had not seen the newly discovered territory, depicted Chicora and the adjacent areas as ideal for colonization. Although the initial discovery had been made at about 33°30′ north, Ayllón fraudulently represented the land discovered as in the range of 35° to 37° north, parallel to Andalucia in Spain, and claimed its climate was much the same and similar crops would prosper there. Ayllón's exaggerated and dishonest description of the newly discovered territory owed much to his desire to persuade the crown to license the project, to Francisco Chicorano's tales of the wealth of the country, and to contemporary geographic theory that lands on the same latitude had similar climates and similar flora and fauna. Chicora, thus, would be a New Andalucia, the perfect habitation for Spanish colonists. Moreover, Duhare, an organized kingdom, could be approached rationally and civilly, unlike dealing with wild savages whose lives lacked structure and discipline. No conquest would be required, and the Indians would be treated benevolently. Ayllón argued that as a man of law, he could be relied on to scrupulously observe royal policies and decrees, unlike military commanders, who too often demonstrated a lack of subordination. The allusion to Cortes and those like him was readily apparent. Moreover, Ayllón's resources were sufficient to finance the entire project. Charles V, Holy Roman emperor and king of Spain, had merely to approve to gain a new and valuable province.

The emperor's secretary, Lope de Concillos, supported Ayllón's petition, and the emperor granted the *asiento y capitulación*, permission to establish the colony, on June 12, 1523, with one particularly striking provision. Ayllón alone was to be the *adelantado*, literally the one who goes before, the initiator of the colony, solely responsible to bear the burdens and to enjoy the benefits of the enterprise. Ayllón's associates in the discovery were all omitted from the grant. It is not apparent whether Ayllón betrayed his associates and contrived to have them excluded or whether Charles V felt more comfortable placing the responsibility and accountability in the hands of one individual. In any event, Ayllón does not seem to have been distressed by the exclusion of the others. The royal permission also contained other specific instructions. The colony was to be founded within the area of 35° to 37° north. The emperor ordered that Natives were to be treated fairly and not enslaved, with the exception of any captives taken in the case of war.

Ayllón was ordered to bring priests to attend to the spiritual needs of the colonists and convert the Indians, and monks to found a monastery of St. Francis. Ayllón was also required to take silkworms and develop a silk industry to exploit the many mulberry trees that Ayllón claimed grew in the area. Finally, Ayllón was to launch his colonizing effort no later than summer 1524 and have the colony fully established by 1527. In addition to granting permission, Charles V arranged Ayllón's induction as a knight of the Order of Santiago, a purely honorary appointment. Ayllón was not a military man, but the award signaled the emperor's support and elevated Ayllón's status.

Ayllón arrived back in the Caribbean to a host of difficulties. He found his official duties many, pressing, time consuming, and requiring travel, and shipments of supplies from Spain for the colony were delayed. The delays were so great that Ayllón had to petition for a time extension, which was granted. He now had until 1525 to begin the project. Ayllón retained the service of Quxós since the return of the first voyage so he would be readily available and so no one else could hire him and benefit from his knowledge. Early in 1525, Ayllón sent an exploratory expedition of two caravels commanded by Quxós. In addition to about sixty sailors, the ships carried several of the Chicora captives who had learned enough Spanish to be useful translators. Ayllón instructed Quxós to explore at least 200 leagues of the coast, the equivalent of 640 miles, carefully taking bearing and soundings. The royal permission stated that Ayllón had the right to explore 800 leagues or until he found land already discovered, and that he should explore any strait he might discover. An exploration of 200 leagues would be at least a start. Quxós was also instructed to claim the land he explored in the name of Charles V and Ayllón, to place stone markers with the name of Charles V and the date, and to sow European edible plants.

Ayllón also ordered that Quxós, in accord with the royal decree, should treat the Indians kindly, give gifts to them, and establish peaceful relations. Quxós was also supposed to obtain a number of Indians to train as translators. The only practical way to do this, commonly employed by all European nations, was to kidnap them. Europeans seldom seem to have understood that this was not conducive to establishing friendly, peaceful relations.

While Quxós was piloting the two ships along what is now the South Carolina coast, Ayllón was busy defending himself against a lawsuit instituted by Matienzo, who claimed that Ayllón had obtained

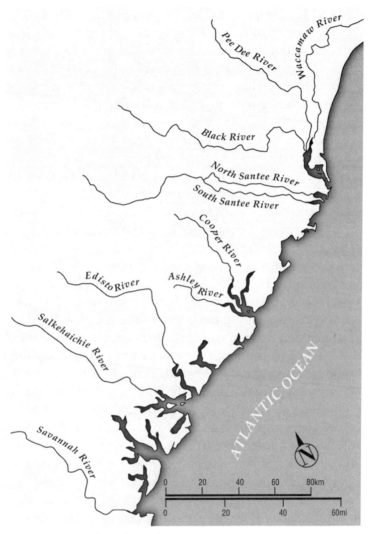

Principal coastal rivers of South Carolina.

the permission to colonize through fraud and that he, Matienzo, was equally entitled to the newly discovered lands. Matienzo initially filed suit late in 1524, but it was not soon resolved. The trial continued through 1525 and well into 1526. Ayllón was able to show that he had a license to explore but Matienzo did not, and that Matienzo had no real interest in colonization but was merely trying to extract a monetary settlement. Matienzo received no satisfaction.

Quxós and his companions sighted land early in May 1525, at the mouth of the Savannah River. There he discovered that his Chicoran translators could not understand the language of the local people. The Chicoran language is most often considered to be a dialect of Catawba, a branch of the Siouan language family, while the people living on the lower Savannah River were probably related to the Guale, who lived mainly to the south. The Guale language is generally described as unclassified, though some think it was a dialect of Muskogean or at least significantly influenced by Muskogean. Quxós took several of the local men, probably kidnapping them, to be trained as translators, his consistent practice when the expedition encountered a new language. Quxós then sailed north until he came to the area discovered in 1521. The local tribesmen, well remembering the kidnapping of sixty of their people, were naturally hostile, but the Spanish appeased them at least for the time by promising to return the kidnapped people and a liberal distribution of gifts, especially brightly colored clothing.

The sources are not clear where Quxós went next. It is possible he proceeded northwest along the coast to the neighborhood of Cape Fear, where he may have encountered persistently adverse winds that led him to return to the south for more exploration along the coast, then turning north again when winds proved favorable. Or he may have sailed south initially and only later turned north. During the southernmost leg of the voyage, he encountered yet another new language, Timucuan, various dialects of which were spoken over much of northeastern and north-central Florida. There is vigorous debate about the affinities of Timucuan. Some hold it is distantly related to Muskogean, while others suggest it is related to languages originating in northern South America that spread through the Caribbean to Florida. Quxós again took men to be trained as translators.

Quxós now turned north. Somewhere north of Cape Fear, he encountered Algonkian speakers and again took several to be translators. He penetrated as far as the Delmarva Peninsula in the modern state of Delaware and briefly entered the mouth of the Chesapeake Bay but explored little there. He sailed along a total of about 215 leagues, a little less than 700 nautical miles, before turning homeward, but there were several disappointments. There was no strait leading to the Pacific, and the section of the coast that Ayllón promised would be a New Andalucia actually consisted of barrier islands separated by shallow sounds from a discouraging coast of swamps and sandy pine barrens.

Quxós's expedition returned to Santo Domingo before the end of July, bringing his involuntary translators-in-training.

Despite the discouraging report about the fantasy of a New Andalucia, Ayllón was fully committed to founding a colony. In all probability he had never intended to establish his settlement as far north as 35° to 37°; the rhetoric about New Andalucia served mainly to encourage the award of the royal license. Ayllón would aim first for the area of initial discovery in 1521 and from there explore until a suitable spot was located for a permanent colony, after which he could investigate Duhare, reported by Francisco de Chicora to be a wealthy, organized kingdom, the only one then reported in eastern North America.

Colonization

Ayllón seems to have begun organizing the colonizing expedition almost immediately on the return of Quxós. Under his command he gathered six ships with their crews and about five hundred men as colonists, among whom were gentlemen, professionals such as doctors, skilled artisans, and farmers. Women, children, and black slaves were also part of the expedition, probably not counted among the five hundred. Dominicans also took part; we know the names of only three: the famed champion of the Indians Father Antonio de Montesinos, Father Antonio de Cervantes, and a lay brother Luis. Pedro de Quxós served as chief pilot, and Francisco de Chicora and the other Native interpreters gathered by Quxós formed an important element of the expedition. Ayllón intented to establish a fully functional community immediately that would soon become agriculturally self-sufficient and a center for profitable trade with the indigenous people.

Ayllón stocked the ships with provisions from his own estates, as well as with food and supplies he purchased in the Caribbean and from Spain. Cattle, sheep, and pigs were loaded onto the ships as food for the voyage and breeding stock for the colony, along with eighty-nine horses. The expenses were enormous, and by the time the expedition sailed, Ayllón had sold or mortgaged virtually all his resources and invested his entire wealth in the venture. If the colony succeeded, he could realize great rewards under the terms of the royal grant, but if it failed he and his family would be ruined.

The expedition left Puerto Plata on the northern coast of Santo Domingo in mid-July 1526 and arrived at the coast in the vicinity of the South Santee River and Winyah Bay on August 9. As the largest ship attempted to approach an anchorage, it ran aground and the pounding sea broke it open. The crew and passengers were saved, but the contents, a large portion of the provisions to support the colony, were lost. Moreover, Ayllón and the others soon realized the area was unsuitable for colonization. Most of the region consisted of infertile sand, too poor for farming or pasturage. Some of the land bordering rivers had good soil, but that was confined to small, discontinuous plots, and often swampy. There was so little fertile ground that few Indians lived in the area, and they had little to trade. Those kidnapped in 1521 were probably members of a village who came temporarily to the coast every year to catch and dry fish.

During the first days ashore, Ayllón ordered a small ship built to compensate in part for the lost major ship, and he sent out scouting parties by sea and land. Also during the first days ashore, Ayllón's trusted friend and adviser, Francisco de Chicora, slipped away from the camp, taking the other Native translators with him. The Spanish never saw a trace of any of them again. All that *el Chircorano* had done—learning Spanish, converting to Christianity, befriending Ayllón, and entrancing the Spanish with fantastic tales—served to gain the opportunity to escape and return to his home. Ayllón and the colonists were left with no way to communicate effectively with Indians.

The scouting parties that went inland returned with discouraging reports. They do not seem to have gone far enough to pass through the pine barrens into the more fertile areas where they would have encountered numerous Native villages. Ayllón also sent out three expeditions by sea, one after another, before finally deciding to move the colonists far to the south. The exact location Ayllón chose remains a subject of debate but is very likely to have been near the mouth of the Sapelo River by Sapelo Island. Our best source, Gonzalo Fernandez de Oviedo y Valdes, generally known as Oviedo, describes it as flat with areas of marsh, substantial forests, and a powerful river, the Gualdape, the name an indication of its location in Guale territory. The Guale resided mainly in scattered homesteads and villages wherever the soil would support the growth of their three essential crops—corn, beans, and squash—and they hunted and fished in a flourishing estuarine ecosystem. A chief, a few other notables, their families, and servants resided in a loosely organized village that contained a large council building and a charnel house where the remains of former

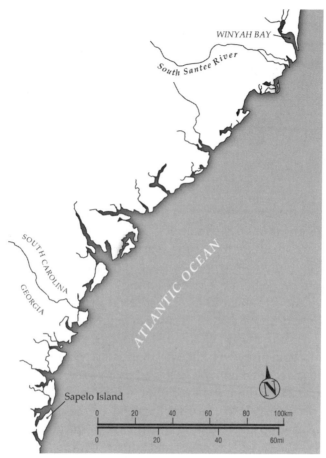

Winyah Bay, South Carolina, to Sapelo Island, Georgia.

chiefs were preserved. Other dependent villages and homesteads were scattered through the surrounding territory. They were the most numerous, prosperous, and organized people Ayllón had encountered, and they were friendly, at least initially.

Even before Ayllón decided to move the expedition south in early September, illness began to spread among the colonists. Ayllón sent the sick, women, and children on the ships to the new destination, along with the remaining provisions, equipment, and presumably enough healthy men to aid and protect them. The ships probably required only a few days to travel the forty to forty-five leagues, roughly 120 to 135 miles, to the new location on Sapelo Sound.

Ayllón and other healthy men capable of bearing arms took the horses and possibly other livestock and moved south by land. It would have been difficult and probably dangerous to both men and beasts to embark horses on ships in the absence of piers or wharfs. On land the men could also explore the countryside, and they could hunt and forage to some degree as they moved. The journey by land probably took several weeks. The men had to skirt swampy areas and search for fords at every river and considerable creek. The horses could not be ridden or driven all day every day but required time to graze. By late September, both groups had reunited and began to build the colony.

The colony was named San Miguel de Gualdape. The Feast of the Archangels Michael, Gabriel, and Raphael was celebrated on September 29, an indication of the founding date. Gualdape probably reflects the Spanish understanding of the Native name of the area or of the river by which the colony was located and incorporates the name of the Guale among whom they were settling. The sources contain no description of the settlement, but almost certainly it was built according to the standard Spanish plan, houses arranged in an orderly pattern around a central plaza where the colonists erected a Dominican church. Subsequent events indicate that at least some of the houses, those built for gentlemen who had the labor of servants to command, were somewhat substantial. In addition to buildings, the official founding of a colony involved the establishment of the municipal governmental institutions, consisting of the appointment of alcaldes, magistrates who served as judges and administrators, and a municipal council. Ayllón's chief deputy, Captain Francisco Gómez, headed the local militia.

Despite the apparent progress, the colonists faced severe problems. Provisions brought from the Caribbean were nearly exhausted, it was much too late to plant crops, and the Guale had no substantial surplus to trade to the Spanish. Fish were abundant, at least for those who could catch them, but the diet was unbalanced even for the able. Ayllón sent scouts inland in the hope of finding Native settlements where they could obtain food, but again they failed to penetrate far enough to encounter prosperous villages in the Piedmont. Disease continued to spread among the colonists. A near-contemporary Spanish source indicates that the colonists were suffering from malaria. An Old World disease, malaria may have been carried to the American coast by infected colonists or slaves and transmitted to mosquitoes that retransmitted the disease to other colonists. This same scenario took place among French colonists on the coast of the Gulf of Mexico during the first years of the eighteenth century. Malaria usually becomes a chronic disease among otherwise healthy people, but among individuals weakened by hunger it can fatally overwhelm bodily defenses. Modern writers have suggested that contaminated water may have also contributed to the problem. The colonists are unlikely to have taken drinking water from the river, brackish so near the coast, but rather they were probably using shallow barrel wells to tap the underground lens of fresh water that sits on top of the deeper salt water along the Georgia coast. In an age before the knowledge of germs, such shallow wells could have been easily contaminated, leading to dysentery or typhoid. To compound the problems of hunger and disease, the colonists suffered from cold. Area temperatures in the autumn are usually moderate and mild, but occasionally weather fronts drop temperatures below freezing. All these factors combined to kill colonists in significant numbers.

Ayllón was among those who fell ill, and on October 18, 1526, only about three weeks after the official founding of the colony, he died. Ayllón designated his nephew, Juan Ramirez, to lead the colony after him, but Ramirez was at Puerto Rico where he was serving as royal treasurer. Immediate command passed to Captain Francisco Gómez, but he and the alcaldes were unable to control the disintegration of order and the emergence of factions.

Gómez and the alcaldes ordered that a ship be readied to carry the news of Ayllón's death to Ramirez and return with orders and supplies, but another group, headed by Pedro de Bazán and Ginés Doncel, wanted to abandon the colony immediately and return to the Caribbean. After gathering supporters, Bazán and Doncel arrested Captain Gómez and the alcaldes, whom they imprisoned in Doncel's house. Monesterio and Oliverso, two *hildalgos*, or gentlemen, became the leaders of yet another faction demanding the release of Gómez and the alcaldes. Bazán and Doncel refused and decided to make a preemptive attack on Monesterio and Oliverso. At night, Bazán went armed to Monesterio's house, where there was a confrontation. Oliverso came to Monesterio's aid, and Oliverso and Bazán engaged in a sword fight, in which Bazán was laid low with a cut to the leg.

About this time, black slaves set fire to Doncel's house or perhaps some subsidiary buildings. Fire, of course, was a major danger to the village of highly flammable buildings thatched with straw, and the colonists quickly rallied to put out the flames before they spread. While the colonists were busy fighting the fire, the black slaves escaped to join the Guale. Much has been made of this event in recent years, labeling it as the first slave rebellion in North America. Monesterio and Oliverso freed Gómez and the alcaldes and restored them to power. The alcaldes had Bazán beheaded and Doncel arrested.

While this was taking place at San Miguel, a third group of Spanish abandoned the colony and imposed themselves on a Guale village about nine miles from the colony. It did not take the Guale long to grow weary of the imperious demands of the Spanish. They rose and killed the interlopers. The Guale, now reinforced by the escaped slaves, became openly hostile to the Spanish, whom they harassed with deadly effect.

Confronted with all these difficulties, which transpired in just two weeks after Ayllón's death, Gómez and the alcaldes decided to abandon the colony, but their tribulations were not over. Storms so scattered the returning ships that no two were able to make the same port and so prolonged the voyage that the colonists exhausted their scant supply of food and water. Weakened by disease and further assailed by unusual cold, many died during the voyage. Of the seventy on one ship, no more than twenty survived.

San Miguel de Gualdape failed for a variety of reasons. The early loss of the principal ship with most of the provisions was important and perhaps ultimately fatal, but other factors contributed. The defection of Francisco de Chicora and the other translators, the illness that ravaged the colonists, the dissolution of law and order after the death of Ayllón, and the abuse of the Guale all contributed. Oviedo, the official chronicler of the Indies, friend of Ayllón, and important source for the history of the colony, attributed the failure to a fundamental flaw greater than all others: Ayllón was ignorant of the conditions into which he led the colonists, and so his preparations were inappropriate for what they encountered. The same challenges that faced Ayllón and the colonists of San Miguel de Gualdape also faced later colonists, who often proved unable or unwilling to learn from past failures.

Aftermath

Despite promises, no effort was ever made to return those kidnapped in 1521 to their homes. Of the over 500 colonists who sailed with Ayllón, only about 150 lived to return to the Caribbean four months later.

The Dominican Fathers Antonio de Montesinos and Antonio de Cervantes, and the lay brother Luis were among the survivors. When Charles V granted Venezuela as a concession to his creditor, the Welser banking house, Montesinos accompanied the German expedition in his role as protector of the Native people. There Montesinos died about 1545, said to have been a martyr, although details of his death are unknown. Father Cervantes continued to serve in Española for at least fifteen years and eventually retired to a monastery in Spain, where he was still living in 1561. Nothing is later heard of Luis. Captain Gómez and Pedro de Quxós were also among the survivors, as was Doncel, who, after all the misery and death, seems to have been let off easily. Later he is known to have become a ship owner. Ayllón left a young widow, five children, and debts that his widow and his son and heir were still struggling to settle decades later.

Perhaps Ayllón's strangest legacy was his vision of Chicora as a land of plenty, a New Andalucia, a land that never really existed. Still, the vision continued to captivate imaginations and influenced later Spanish and French explorations and colonizing expeditions.

Sources

Matienzo's lawsuit against Ayllón preserved material relevant to the 1521 exploration. David Beers Quinn, trans. and ed., *New American World: A Documentary History of North America in 1612* (New York: Arno Press, 1979), 1:254-260, contains in translation the statement of issues in the case before the court, Ayllón's declaration to the king, Ayllón's replies to Matienzo's interrogatories, Pedro de Quxós's replies to Matienzo's interrogatories, and Quxós's further testimony concerning claiming the newly found land. In addition, Martín Fernández de Navarrete, *Colección de los viages y descubrimientos que hicieron por mar los españoles* (Madrid: En la Imprenta Real, 1829) 3, no. 46, 153-160, contains the *asiento y capitulación*, the royal permission for Ayllón to establish a colony. A translation is available in Quinn, *New American World*, 1:249-254, and Paul Quattlebaum, *The Land Called Chicora* (Gainesville: University of Florida Press, 1956) 135-141. Quattlebaum so attempts to present Ayllón in a heroic mode that he unconvincingly tries to acquit him of involvement in slave raiding, and he argues that San Miguel de Gualdape was on the eastern coast of Winyah Bay, rather than far to the south near Sapelo Island, one of many different attempts by different people to locate the colony.

Pietro Martire d'Anghiera, often referred to as Peter Martyr in English, was born in Italy in 1457. While in Rome he became acquainted with the Spanish ambassador with whom he went to Spain in 1487, where he was quickly recognized as a leading member of the cadre of Italian scholars bringing the ideas and ideals of the Renaissance to Spain. Although the fully developed Real y Supremo Consejo de las Indias (Royal and Supreme Council of the Indies) was not officially established until 1524, a nascent form of the council existed from 1511, when Pietro Martire became its official chronicler, an association he continued until his death in 1526. Pietro Martire's most important historical work is *De Orbe Novo Petri Marturis Mediolanensis Protonotarij Senatoris Decades* (Compluti [i.e., Alcalá de Henares, Spain]: Apud Nichaele[m] d[e] Eguia, 1530). The standard English translation is Francis Augustus MacNutt, ed., intro., and notes, *De Orbe Novo: The Eight Decades of Peter Martyr D'Anghera*, 2 vols. (New York: G. P. Putnam's Sons, 1912). Quinn, *New American World*, 1:264-271, also contains a translation of Pietro Martire's account of Ayllón's voyages and the customs of the indigenous people. The *Decades* were composed and published over many years, from as early as 1493 until 1525, shortly before the author's death. The full eight *Decades* did not appear together until 1530. They take the form of letters addressed to eminent people describing Spanish discoveries and activities as well as the customs of the Native peoples throughout Spanish America. When Ayllón was in Spain, Pietro Martire invited him and Francisco de Chicora to dine at his table. Pietro Martire's rambling, discursive account in the second, third, and fourth books of his seventh decade contain an early report of the exploration of 1521, information about incredible tales told by Francisco de Chicora and others, and ethnography information about the indigenous people of the coast.

Gonzalo Fernández de Oviedo y Valdés, known generally as Oviedo, was born in Spain in 1478. A member of an aristocratic family and well connected at court, he served in a variety of posts, going to Santo Domingo in 1514 as the royal controller of gold mining and smelting, a post he held for almost twenty years. He traveled to Spain in 1515 to convey the royal share of gold and to complain about the misrule of the governor, Pedro Arias Dávila. While there he came into conflict with Father Bartolomé de las Casas, the great defender of the Native American peoples. Las Casas, a man who saw matters in absolute terms, maintained that the indigenous people of America were inherently mild and friendly and could be won over to Christianity by kindness. Oviedo replied that while some were docile and could be treated kindly, others were aggressive cannibals and not suitable for conversion. The enmity long persisted between the two, Las Casas harshly denouncing Oviedo's writings and even hindering publication.

In 1519, Charles V vested Oviedo with additional offices, and during the following decades, Oviedo served in a variety of governmental posts in addition to supervising gold production, traveled across the Atlantic twelve times, and at the same time wrote works of fundamental importance. Oviedo's *De la natural hystoria de las Indias* (Toledo: Remón de Petras, 1526) describes the Native peoples encountered by the Spanish, their customs and religion, and the flora and fauna of the region. An English translation is available: Sterling A. Stoudemire, trans. and ed., *Natural History of the West Indies: Gonzalo Fernández de Oviedo y Valdés* (Chapel Hill: University of North Carolina Press, 1959). The book virtually ignores political matters, though it is often described as a summary of Oviedo's greatest work, *La historia general y natural de las Indias*, in which politics play a major role. The first part of that work appeared in 1535 as Gonzalo Fernández de Oviedo y Valdés *Primera parte de la historia natural y general y de las indias yslas y tierra firme de mar oceano* (Sevilla: Juan Cromberger, 1535). The second part, the publication of which was probably delayed by Bartolomé de las Casas, finally appeared shortly after Oviedo's death in 1557 as Gonzalo Fernández de Oviedo y Valdés, *Libro XX. De la segunda parte de la general historia de las Indias* (Valladolid: Francisco Fernández de Córdoba, 1557). The entire work, consisting of fifty-five books (i.e., chapters), was first published in its entirety as Gonzalo Fernández de Oviedo y Valdés, *Historia General y Natural de las Indias, Islas y Tierra Firme del Mar Océano*, 4 vols., ed. José Amador de los Rios (Madrid: Imprenta de la Real Academia de la Historia, 1851–1855).

Oviedo knew many of the people who played important roles in Spanish America in the early sixteenth century, and his *Historia General* is a record of events interspersed with discursive anecdotes. He discusses Ayllón and the colony mainly in Book 37 (in the Rios edition, vol. 2, pt. 2, 624-633) with additional material in Book 50 (in the Rios edition, vol. 4, 537-538) on the troubled return of the colonists to Santo Domingo and the other Spanish colonies in the Caribbean after they abandoned San Miguel de Gualdape. There is no English translation of the entire *Historia General*, but Book 50 is available in English: Gonzalo Fernández de Oviedo y Valdés, *Misfortunes and Shipwrecks in the Seas of the Indies, Islands, and Mainland of the Ocean Sea (1513–1548): Book Fifty of the General and Natural History of the Indies,* trans. and ed. Glen F. Dille (Gainesville: University Press of Florida, 2011). The material relevant to Ayllón is on pp. 101-102. Quinn, *New American World,* 1:260-264, contains a translation of Oviedo's account of Ayllón's colonization effort.

Oviedo first met Ayllón when he was on his way with Francisco de Chicora to the royal court in Spain. Many years later, he wrote that he thought Francisco was a fraud, disbelieved his tales, and tried to warn Ayllón against him, but Ayllón trusted Francisco implicitly and gave credit to no word against him. Oviedo's account may have been colored by later events, just as Ayllón may have been moved to accept Francisco's tales at least in part because of their usefulness in his petition to the crown. Oviedo provided the fullest account of Ayllón and the San Miguel de Gualdape colony, but even that account is often infuriatingly superficial. For example, he provides little about the revolt and escape of the black slaves and Guale warfare against the colonists after Ayllón's death.

Paul E. Hoffman, *A New Andalucia and a Way to the Orient* (Baton Rouge: Louisiana State University Press, 1990) gives the best overview of Ayllón's activities and San Miguel de Gualdape. In a valuable appendix, "Alonso de Chaves' Rutter and the Locations of Ayllon's Explorations and Colonies," 315–328, Hoffman provides a history of the various attempts to locate Ayllon's activities from the sixteenth century to date and employs for the first time Alonso de Chaves's "Navigators' Mirror," the manuscript of which bears the date 1537, in the attempt to clarify the location of the colony. Hoffman demonstrates that Chaves relied on a number of rutters, sailing directions, to construct his overview of the coast, which strongly supports the southern location of San Miguel de Gualdape. The original is published in Castañeda Delgado, Paulino, Mariano Cuesta, and Pablo Hernández, eds., *Alonso de Chaves y el libro IV de su "Espejo de navegantes"* (Madrid: [P. Castaneda], 1977).

TWO

The First Pensacola: Santa Maria de Ochuse (1559–1561)

Background

The discovery of the Americas was soon followed by the conquest and looting of the rich cultures of Mexico and Peru, the discoveries of the immense silver deposits in South America and Mexico, the emeralds of Colombia, the pearls of Venezuela, and the importation of spices from the Philippines. The wealth transformed Spain from a recently and incompletely unified country of no particular distinction to the greatest power of Europe in control of an empire consisting of the Caribbean, South America, Central America, claims to North America, conquests in the Philippines, control of the Spanish Netherlands, and holdings in the Mediterranean. The wealth that flowed into Spain flowed out again just as quickly. During the long reign of the Spanish monarch Philip II (1556–1598), Spain fought wars against France, England, Portugal, the Netherlands, the Ottoman Empire, and in Italy, all vastly expensive, and at the same time supported a costly court and luxury among the aristocratic class. Philip borrowed extensively from bankers to meet obligations, and the interest on the loans created further debt. The government declared bankruptcies repeatedly, and each scheme to refinance the government drove it deeper into debt and further weakened Spain.

As a result of unbridled expenditures in Spain, the Spanish Empire in the Americas, the chief source of Spanish wealth, was itself poorly financed, weakly defended, and vulnerable. English, French, Dutch, and Jewish buccaneers of various nationalities plundered Spanish shipping and looted towns, but the Spanish still left strategic locations underdeveloped and poorly defended. The threat of foreign colonization within territory claimed by Spain could, however, motivate the Spanish to act, and nowhere was this truer than in the Florida Straits.

During the age of sailing ships, currents and wind patterns dictated that the Straits of Florida, also known as the Bahama Passage, was the only good exit from the Caribbean. Through this area the Spanish treasure fleets and virtually all other Spanish shipping sailed, vulnerable to hurricanes and the predations of pirates, but the Spanish were slow to develop the area until the late 1550s, when Philip II's extensive network of spies reported that France, England, and even Scotland were independently contemplating planting colonies in Florida that could threaten the treasure fleets and challenge Spanish holdings in the Americas. In the sixteenth century, the term "Florida" included the northern coast of the Gulf of Mexico, the Florida Peninsula, and the Atlantic coast of North America at least as far north as Chesapeake Bay. Juan Ponce de León made the first official landing on the Florida peninsula in 1513, although Spanish slave traders had almost certainly raided it earlier and others continued to kidnap Indian slaves after 1513. Many tribes and chiefdoms on the Florida Peninsula became fiercely hostile to Spanish incursions, and when Ponce de León returned in 1521 to establish a colony, the Calusa attacked the expedition, which withdrew before anything significant was accomplished. An Indian wounded Ponce de León with a poison arrow, and he died shortly after returning to Havana, Cuba. In 1526, Lúcas Vázquez de Ayllón actually founded a colony on the coast of what is now Georgia, but it failed quickly. Florida gained a reputation as a dangerous, swampy, fever-ridden expanse with few resources along the coast to support colonists. Despite all, Florida's position on the straits was so vital that Spain could not permit any other nation to colonize there, so in 1559, the Spanish sought again to colonize the region to forestall others.

Preparations

Often missionaries began Spanish colonies by establishing themselves in an Indian settlement, the first step in a slow process of acculturation that over the course of decades gradually created a typical Spanish colonial *pueblo* (community). The Spanish perception of an imminent threat of foreign intrusion into Florida allowed no such gradual approach. The expedition of 1559 was an ambitious attempt to import all the elements of Spanish communities at once and to establish not just one but three colonies in quick succession: one settlement at the best harbor on the shore of the gulf coast, a second deep in the interior to supply the coastal settlements with food, and the third on the Atlantic to guard the Florida Straits. Several Spanish explorers had visited the great harbor on the gulf coast decades before 1559, but due to the crude navigation techniques of the era its location was only approximately known. A member of explorer Hernando de Soto's expedition called the harbor the Bahía de Ochuse, Bay of Ochuse, after the name of a local Native village. Today it is known as Pensacola.

Don Luis de Velasco y Ruiz de Alarcón, señor de Salinas, viceroy of New Spain. (*Museo Nacional de Arqueologia, Historia y Etnografia, Ciudad de México*)

From Ochuse, colonists were to move inland to found a second settlement at the chiefdom of Coosa in northwest Georgia, which Soto and his men had visited. Survivors of Soto's expedition (1539–1543) described Coosa as a land of plenty filled with fertile gardens tended by friendly Indians.

From Coosa some colonists were supposed to move to the Atlantic coast to build a third settlement, a fortified military colony at a good harbor reported by Spanish mariners and called Santa Elena. At the beginning of the colonization project, Santa Elena's exact location was not known, and the name seems to have been applied to several locations. The name was eventually localized at today's Port Royal on the South Carolina coast. The colony at Coosa was to supply Ochuse and Santa Elena with food, and shipping from Spain and the Caribbean would carry other supplies to the colonies.

The project was magnificently begun. King Philip II, despite his many financial pressures, supported the venture with 300,000 pesos (also called pieces of eight), a vast sum, and charged the viceroy of New Spain, don Luis de Velasco y Ruiz de Alarcón, señor de Salinas, with oversight of the project. Velasco chose Tristán de Luna y Arellano, a close friend, as commander of the effort. Luna was a man of excellent reputation, experienced, brave, and determined. He had accompanied Francisco Vázquez de Coronado y Luján in his futile exploration of the American southwest in 1540–1542 in a quest for the legendary Seven Cities of Gold. There he served initially as captain of the horse (cavalry commander), then as *maestre de campo* (master of the camp, chief of staff and second in command), and earned the rank of lieutenant general. Late in the expedition, he was badly wounded. His bravery and competence as an officer were greatly admired, and he was one of the few to emerge from the trek with an enhanced reputation. Luna married twice and was twice widowered, inheriting wealth from both wives. He so believed in the colonization project that he invested in the effort by selling some of his properties and mortgaging others, including properties he managed for his minor children. Many of the others who went on the expedition also used their own money to equip themselves.

Expedition

The personnel of Luna's expedition consisted of two hundred cavalry, a little over three hundred infantry, six Dominican clergy, a hundred skilled artisans, many servants of various origins, Spanish and Hispanicised-Indian families, and Indian and black slaves, all totaling about fifteen hundred people. The expedition even included several women from Coosa, kidnapped by Soto seventeen years earlier, who were to serve as interpreters. Viceroy Velasco told Luna to be cautious about the number of people included in the expedition who would consume provisions but produce nothing, but the plan to establish full-formed Spanish communities required wives and children, and the military culture of the period dictated that every soldier had a servant, sometimes two. Luna seemed not to be alarmed at the burden of these many unproductive mouths, and he must have taken comfort in the enormous amount of supplies and provisions packed aboard the fleet, totaling more than a million pounds. Preparations also included a set of instructions detailing precisely how the initial settlement was to be constructed. Lots for a hundred family homes were to be arranged in a grid pattern around a central square containing government and religious buildings.

An armada of thirteen ships, ranging in size from enormous galleons of about six hundred tons to small barks of fifty to seventy

The Straits of Florida and Santa Maria de Ochuse, modern Emanuel Point, in Pensacola Bay, Florida.

tons, carried the expedition. People, provisions, and about 240 horses embarked at San Juan de Ulúa, the naval fortress by Veracruz on the Mexican coast, and set sail on June 11, 1559, northeast toward the Florida coast. The fleet encountered a storm that blew them to the southeast for six days. The horses fared poorly in the pitching ships, and during the voyage more than a hundred died and were heaved overboard. After the storm abated, the fleet continued toward the northeast, sighting the Florida coast to the east of Pensacola Bay. They anchored briefly, taking on water, wood, and grass for the surviving horses, and then sailed along the coast toward the west. They passed the mouth of Pensacola Bay unaware but realized their mistake when they reached the more easily identifiable Mobile Bay. There Luna unloaded the surviving horses and some men to manage them with the instructions to move by land to the east to Pensacola Bay while the ships sailed there, arriving on August 14, 1559. Luna and the ships' pilots were greatly impressed by the bay, its size and apparently safe anchorage. One ship was dispatched to carry the news of the expedition's safe arrival to the viceroy, a second seems to have sailed for Spain to inform the king, and a third left for New Spain, probably to fetch material that could not be accommodated on the original fleet.

The next five weeks were occupied in choosing a site for the permanent settlement, which Luna named Santa Maria de Ochuse. There on the western side of the bay at the modern Emanuel Point, the colonists began setting up a camp and unloading supplies from the ships.

The colonists left much of the food on the ships until a good, waterproof storehouse could be built. In the meantime, Luna sent out two exploration parties, one to investigate the hinter ground of the settlement and the other to sail up the Escambia River near the head of the bay. The land expedition found few resources, and the river proved too winding and narrow for deep penetration into the interior. The two detachments returned to discover that a disastrous hurricane had struck the bay.

Hurricane

The event is best described by Tristán de Luna himself in his letter of September 24, 1559, to King Philip II:

> On Monday, during the night of the nineteenth of September, there came up from the north a fierce tempest, which, blowing for twenty-four hours from all directions until the same hour as it began, without stopping but increasing continuously, did irreparable damage to the ships of the fleet, with great loss by many seamen and passengers, both of their lives as well as of their property. All ships which were in this port went aground although it is one of the best ports in these Indies, except only one caravel and two barks, which escaped. This has reduced us to such extremity that unless I provide soon for the need in which it left us, for we lost on one of our ships that went aground a great part of the supplies that were collected in it for the maintenance of this army, and what

we had on land was damaged by the heavy rains, I do not know
how I can maintain the people.

Luna's restrained, factual description of the hurricane masks the
real horror. Seven ships were destroyed by the storm, including the
flagship and vice flagship of the fleet and all the other large ships in
the harbor. The three that survived were small. None of the sources
give a precise number of those who perished, but it must have been
substantial. Fray Agustín Dávila Padilla, who included an account of
the Luna expedition in a broader history published in 1596, provides
more graphic details. Dávila did not take part in the expedition but
relied on the reminiscences of a fellow Dominican who had been there
over thirty years earlier. Dávila records that one ship broke open in
the midst of the storm and sank with all aboard. Another was carried
some distance inland and deposited intact among a grove of trees.
Dávila did not believe the sea could have moved the ship so far and
thought it rather the work of demons. He assures the reader that several people saw them in the air during the storm. Luna continued in
his letter to the king, explaining his course of action after the storm:

> I shall be forced lest all perish to go into the interior with all the
> people to some place where there are resources making it possible
> to maintain them. I shall leave the few supplies which I have at
> present for the people who will remain settled in the town at this
> port, so they may have something to eat during the interval before
> don Luis de Velasco provisions them from New Spain. However,
> if I am able, and have anything with which to do it, I shall not fail
> to send them help down a river which flows into the Bahía Filipina
> [i.e., Mobile Bay] and up which I shall have to go.

The Struggle to Succeed

Luna dispatched two ships to Mexico to inform the viceroy, carry his
letter to the king, and bring supplies back to the colony. When Viceroy
Velasco received news of the disaster, he immediately began to gather
food for the colony, but Mexico had not yet developed significant commercial agriculture or efficient transport. Scarce food had to be transported by pack mule from the interior. Moreover, the annual sailing
of the fleet to Spain took priority and required most all of the large
vessels and food. Velasco was at least able to send sufficient food to
relieve hunger at Ochuse for the moment. The small supply ships ar-

rived in December 1559, and Velasco promised more shipments as soon as possible.

Meantime, Luna took decisive action, sending a detachment to the interior to locate the Native town Nanipacana, of which he had reports and where he expected to find supplies of food. After a difficult march across country, the detachment located the town, consisting of about eighty houses, north of Mobile Bay on what is now called the Alabama River. The inhabitants fled at the approach of the Spanish but left behind some stores of corn and beans, which the Spanish seized. After some negotiations, the people returned to the town, and the Spanish camped on the opposite side of the river. They grandly named the camp Santa Cruz de Nanipacana. The Spanish observed many ruined houses at Nanipacana, the result of the passage of Soto through the area seventeen years earlier, leaving a wake of death, disease, and a diminished town. Enough still remained so that the detachment at Nanipacana sent a message to Luna urging him to bring the colonists there.

Luna sat at Ochuse until the middle of February, hoping that more provisions would come from Mexico. As the colonists waited, a contagious disease broke out in the camp, and Luna was one of the victims. For days he raged in delirium, calling for his long-dead wife and talking nonsense. His recovery was slow, and those around him felt it was incomplete. As the expedition continued, Luna seemed to alternate between an iron determination to make the colonies succeed and periods of indecision, and he increasingly resisted consulting with his officers, able men whose opinions he previously respected. Luna's responsibility to the king, the viceroy, soldiers, colonists, and to his family, whose future he had mortgaged to help finance the expedition, must have also weighed heavily on his mind.

Finally it became apparent that the great majority of colonists had to move to Nanipacana or starve on the seashore. Luna left a small group, less than one hundred men, at Ochuse to wait for the supplies from Mexico. Ideally, ships would have carried colonists from Ochuse to the head of Mobile Bay and then up the Alabama River to Nanipacana. Artisans among the colonists managed to construct several small ships and boats, but they were too few and too small to carry everyone. Many, including some women and children, had to make the long, exhausting journey on foot. The detachment at Nanipacana sent food to the trekkers, but it was not sufficient. The colonists arrived exhausted and starving to find that the Indians, evidently alarmed at the increasing Spanish demands, had fled, taking their stores of corn and beans with them. The Spanish, camped on the far side of the river from the village and lacking a boat, had been unable to prevent the Indians' flight. Enough food remained in the Spanish camp for the moment, but it was apparent that the arduous trip to Nanipacana had done nothing to improve the colonists' long-term prospects.

The Struggle to Survive

At this point, the question of Luna's leadership became paramount. It seemed apparent to the friars and the military officers that Luna was not well, and they called for him to step down and yield to his second in command, the highly respected *maestre de campo*, Jorge Cerón Saavedra. Cerón followed proper procedure, calling a council with Luna, officers, and treasury officials in attendance, and there he worked out a compromise. Luna would retain nominal leadership, but while he recuperated, Cerón would exercise direct control.

The compromise broke down after only two days. Luna called another council, informed the officers he had recovered, and resumed command. He ordered Cerón to assemble a party to proceed up the Alabama River in a couple of small boats in search of food. Cerón's party traveled over 150 miles north but found nothing but a few deserted villages and fields, both emptied of anything the Spanish could eat. By the time Cerón returned, the colonists at Nanipacana had exhausted the meager stores of corn and were reduced to eating acorns.

In mid-April, Luna dispatched a second expedition consisting of fifty horsemen, a hundred footmen, and a number of servants, commanded by the third-ranking officer, the Sargento Mayor Mateo del Sauz. They marched north seeking the chiefdom of Coosa, in modern northwest Georgia, about which Soto's men had made glowing reports. They moved slowly, hoping to find caches of corn on the march, but for over forty days they found none and subsisted on acorns, berries, and leaves; they even boiled and ate leather straps, shield linings, and their boots. When they finally found a stash of corn, they sent a portion back to Nanipacana, where it prevented starvation but only alleviated hunger for a short time.

When at last the expedition reached Coosa, Sauz and his command were disappointed. Soto's men had described Coosa as a prosperous chiefdom filled with flourishing gardens. Sauz reported Coosa had a larger population and more food than the territory through which they had passed on the journey, but it was no paradise. The population and food supply were much less than they had expected, and much of the land was uninhabited forest. Sauz brought several Indian women slaves on the expedition who had been kidnapped by Soto seventeen years earlier. They had learned Spanish during their captivity and were now supposed to serve as translators, but they slipped away at the first opportunity, leaving Sauz to contend with problems of communication.

Sauz saw little possibility of establishing a sustainable Spanish colony at Coosa, much less a base that could supply provisions to Ochuse and Santa Elena. He reported the discouraging situation to Luna but suggested that he should come to Coosa to see the situation for himself. Sauz clearly wished to avoid blame for failing to colonize Coosa, which many still believed to be a land of plenty.

There are several possible explanations for the disparity between the accounts about Coosa by Soto's men and Sauz's report. Soto and his men may have found a prosperous land but left behind disaster. The people of Coosa had greeted Soto cordially, but he abused their hospitality, took over their dwellings, held their chief captive, confiscated food, and carried men and women away in chains as bearers and slaves. Soto's brutality was long remembered, and many modern commentators have suggested that Soto's men left behind an even more devastating legacy, European epidemic diseases such as smallpox and measles. However, P. Kelton has argued that the epidemiological characteristics of these highly lethal diseases are inconsistent with their spread by Soto's expedition or other early Spanish expeditions. Kelton points out that such diseases would have run their course among the troops early in an expedition and then died out, leaving no source for further transmission. Rather than quickly and highly lethal diseases such as smallpox, Soto's men may have spread malaria, a chronic debilitating disease, and ordinary but potentially deadly diseases associated with poor sanitation and crowded conditions such as typhoid and dysentery. The lethal epidemic diseases appeared later when Native populations were concentrated in slave plantations and mission settlements, where interactions with disease-carrying Europeans were much more frequent. Also, the stories Soto's men told about Coosa's prosperity may have been grossly exaggerated. Stories tend to grow with

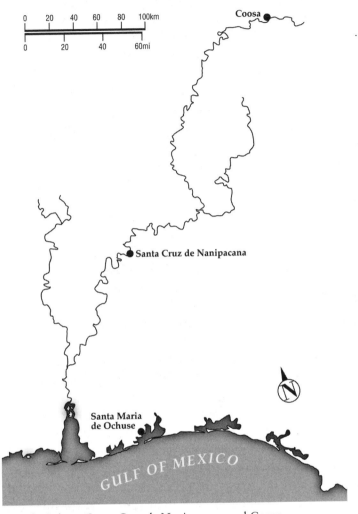

Santa Maria de Ochuse, Santa Cruz de Nanipacana, and Coosa.

retelling. It is even possible that Sauz exaggerated the poverty of Coosa as an excuse for his failure to establish a settlement. Coosa was a sufficiently powerful chiefdom at the time of Sauz's visit to extract tribute from a number of villages, although one former dependency was in revolt, and Coosa remained strong enough a few years later to deter a Spanish expedition led by Juan Pardo from entering its territory. Sauz and most of his party returned to Nanipacana after a few months, leaving a small detachment behind.

Meanwhile, at Nanipacana conditions had grown increasingly bleak. Married soldiers and colonists, gripped by unremitting hunger, repeatedly petitioned Luna to send them back to Mexico and abandon the attempt to colonize Florida. Luna initially resisted, but as the number of deaths mounted, he relented somewhat, allowing a small ship to sail to Veracruz, carrying some of the married men along with their wives, children, and a number of friars. In Mexico, the evacuated colonists and clergy were critical of Luna's leadership, undermining Velasco's confidence in his old friend.

As conditions continued to deteriorate, Luna finally, reluctantly decided to evacuate Nanipacana, moving down the Alabama River to the head of Mobile Bay. The trip downriver proved more difficult than anticipated, supplies were lost, people died, and hunger increased. From Mobile Bay, the colonists returned to Ochuse, where, eight days after their arrival in late June, relief ships sailed into the port. The ships, however, carried little food; Velasco, assuming the colonists had found abundant supplies at Nanipacana and Coosa, had not included much in the shipment.

The ships also brought new orders from King Philip II in Spain, instructing Luna to proceed to the harbor of Santa Elena on the Atlantic side of the Florida Peninsula and establish a colony to forestall an anticipated attempt by France to establish its own colony there. The king, of course, had no knowledge of the desperate condition of Luna's expedition at the time. Luna nevertheless ordered some fifty or sixty men to sail to Havana, there to resupply and then sail to Santa Elena, the location of which remained imperfectly known. The men were to establish a temporary camp to hold the site until a permanent colony could be established, but the expedition never got beyond Cuba, stymied by bad weather. It is hard to imagine that the men, exhausted by over a year of deprivation, were enthusiastic about the proposed new adventure.

During the months after the return to Ochuse, Luna's command of the remaining soldiers and colonists in Florida virtually collapsed amid complaints, quarrels, and mutual recriminations. Luna argued with his officers, whom he threatened with fines, confiscations of their estates, and even death sentences. In reply, officers wrote petitions and complaints and even filed lawsuits against Luna. Religious officials sided with the officers, and even common soldiers wrote to Luna demanding evacuation to Mexico and refused to obey his orders. Velasco wrote to Luna, instructing him to work cooperatively with his subordinates and maintain a presence at both Ochuse and Coosa until yet another effort could locate Santa Elena and occupy the site. Velasco still hoped success could be salvaged from the effort, but a torrent of complaints about Luna's incapacity to command continued in the form of letters from the officers and officials at Ochuse and from clerics and others who had returned from there.

At Coosa, the remaining troops attempted to strengthen their relation with the local Indian leaders, even accompanying warriors on a raid against those who had ceased to yield tribute. Nevertheless, about November 1560, the last of the Spanish troops withdrew from Coosa to Ochuse, claiming the food supply was insufficient for them to remain. This was yet another blow to Luna's determination.

End of the Effort

Finally, in April 1561, another relief fleet arrived at Ochuse, with orders from Velasco relieving Luna of command and appointing in his place Angel de Villafañe, an experienced and respected officer. Villafañe took about 230 of the surviving colonists to Havana, leaving fifty men with supplies to hold the camp at Ochuse until a final decision about the colony was made. Then Villafañe sailed north with four ships and about seventy-five of the men evacuated from Ochuse. As the small fleet sought the port of Santa Elena a hurricane struck, destroying two ships. Villafañe sailed the two remaining storm-battered ships first to Hispaniola (modern Haiti) and then to Havana. There many of his men deserted, ending yet another unsuccessful Spanish attempt to establish a colony on the Atlantic coast. In August 1561, Villafañe sailed to Ochuse and evacuated the fifty men remaining there, and so ended the attempt to colonize Pensacola Bay that had begun so magnificently two years earlier.

The Santa Maria de Ochuse colony failed for many reasons. Obvious factors were the hurricane that ravaged the colony and the debilitating illness that affected Luna's leadership. The colony included many unproductive people, but it would have required major changes in the military and civilian culture of the time to exclude them, and the initial expedition was well supplied. It can be argued that the attempt to establish three settlements simultaneously was simply too ambitious, and that New Spain, which was overexploited by the royal government and underdeveloped, simply did not have the resources to support such an effort. Of perhaps greater importance was ignorance of the area the Spanish attempted to colonize. They did not know that the hinterland of Pensacola Bay offered few resources, they had only an approximate indication of the location of Coosa, and they assumed too readily that the reports of Coosa's prosperity were accurate. The Spanish did not realize the distance from Coosa to the Atlantic coast and had only a general idea of the location of Santa Elena. Despite all, had there been no hurricane and had Luna not fallen ill, at least the colony at Pensacola Bay might have survived.

Aftermath

The sources offer little specific information about the number of colonists who perished during the two-year effort, but counting the number known to have been evacuated at various times, it seems apparent that only a little over a third of the original fifteen hundred survived. The Spanish decided that the gulf coast of Florida was unsuitable for colonization and ignored the area until the late seventeenth century, when the threat of another foreign colonization venture forced them to take action. In 1562, just a year after Ochuse was abandoned, King Philip II's fear became fact—the French established a colony on the Florida Straits. That colony too would fail, but for much different reasons.

Luna traveled to Spain to explain the failure of the colony, but the royal government showed no sympathy or appreciation of his efforts. He returned to Mexico about 1567, ill and impoverished. An old friend, Luis de Castilla, took Luna into his household and even paid for his funeral when he died in 1573.

In recent years, spectacular archaeological discoveries by personnel of the Florida Bureau of Archaeological Research and the Anthropology Department of the University of West Florida have greatly enhanced understanding of the written sources and illuminated the life of the colonists. In 1992, the bureau located the remains of a ship off of Emanuel Point and, along with the University of West Florida underwater archaeological program, excavated the ship, proving it dated to the mid-sixteenth century. In 2006, University of West Florida archaeologists and students discovered a second mid-sixteenth century shipwreck in the same vicinity, confirming that both were part of the fleet devastated by the hurricane in 1559. In 2016, University of West Florida archaeologists and students discovered a third of the hurricane wrecks, close to the other two.

In 2015, local historian Tom Garner alertly spotted sixteenth-century pottery fragments in the dirt at a construction site at Emanuel Point. He informed archaeologists of the University of West Florida who, with the cooperation of the landowners, conducted a salvage excavation, recovering Spanish, Aztec, and Native American Florida pottery, glass trade beads, nails, and other metal fragments. The site had long been regarded as one among several possible sites of the Luna colony, but earlier archaeological surveys had not found definitive evidence. Garner's discovery and the excavation, led by Professor John Worth, the eminent archaeologist and historian of Spanish colonies in the southeastern United States, have solved the question of the colony's location. Excavation continues.

Sources

Primary documents are conveniently gathered in Herbert Ingram Priestly, *The Luna Papers: Documents Relating to the Expedition of Don Tristán de Luna y Arellano for the Conquest of La Florida in 1559–1561*, 2 vols. (Deland: Florida State Historical Society, 1928). The work contains transcriptions of the original Spanish manuscripts and English translations. An electronic version is available at books.google.com, and the book was reprinted in 1971 by Books for Libraries Press, Freeport, NY, but much to be preferred is the 2010 reprint by the University of Alabama Press, which contains an excellent new preface by John Worth.

In 1596, the Dominican Augustín Dávila Padilla published *Historia de la Fundación y Discurso de la Provincia de Santiago de México de la Orden de Predicadores, por las vidas de sus varones insignes y casos Notables de Nueva España* (Madrid: Pedro Madrigal, 1596), though the best and most-often-reprinted edition was published in Brussels by Iuan de Meerbeque in 1625. Dávila's work is not a history in the modern sense but rather a glorification of the Dominicans' role in early colonial Mexico, enlivened by romantic and sometimes fantastic anecdotes. Dávila's account of the Luna expedition (pp. 189-229), largely based on a Dominican who related his reminiscences to Dávila thirty years after the events, varies from contemporary documents in a number of details and includes some dubious elements. Dávila's account cannot, however, simply be dismissed. It contains some important observations and the fullest account of the conflicts between Luna and his subordinate officers during the last months of the expedition.

The work of archaeologists of the University of West Florida is continuing and has already contributed significantly to the understanding of the colony at Pensacola. The faculty homepage of Professor John Worth provides convenient access and links: ages.uwf.edu/jworth/jw_research.html (accessed May 5, 2020).

THREE

The French *and* Spanish Struggle *in* Florida: Charlesfort/San Mateo *and* Fort Caroline/Santa Elena (1562–1587)

The French Initiative

Between 1495 and 1559, the French kings fought a series of wars against the Hapsburgs of Spain and the Holy Roman Empire for ascendancy in Italy. Ultimately Spain triumphed, and France lost almost all influence on the peninsula. Deep suspicion and animosity subsequently continued to dominate relations between the two nations. In Spain, the conflict had contributed to the monarchy's chronic shortage of money, despite all the wealth from its New World empire. Following the end of the Spanish wars, Calvinism grew rapidly in France, leading to a series of intermittent civil wars between 1559 and 1598 pitting conservative Catholic forces against Protestant.

Conflicts between Protestants and Catholics vastly complicated the efforts of Admiral Gaspard de Coligny, the guiding figure behind French colonization, to establish settlements in the New World. Coligny openly embraced the Protestant cause shortly after the end of the last war between France and Spain, but as a moderate he pleaded for freedom of religious observation, asserted the loyalty of Huguenots (French Protestants) to the French crown, and argued that political allegiance was not subject to religious belief. These were ideas ahead of their time, and although a few moderate Catholics and Protestants were attracted to his position, Catholic and Protestant extremists opposed him.

Spain and Portugal reaped riches from their colonies, and Coligny was committed to establishing French colonies that might bring similar wealth to France, prestige to the French monarchy, and a modicum of tolerance to the Huguenots. In 1555, Coligny was instrumental in the effort to establish a colony in Brazil at Rio de Janeiro Bay. Protestants were prominent in the attempt, but there were also Catholics among the colonists. The colony was not a success for a variety of reasons, and the Portuguese destroyed it violently in 1560. Coligny then turned his attention to the establishment of a French colony on the southern Atlantic coast of North America.

The Spanish had long dreaded the establishment of a foreign colony in Florida, the term then loosely applied to all southeastern North America. Trade and treasure fleets vital to the Spanish government and economy sailed from the Caribbean to Spain through the Florida Straits. Any foreign colony in the area threatened those fleets, could serve as a base for the conquest of the great silver mines in northern Mexico, and potentially endangered all Spanish America. Tristán de Luna y Arellano (1559–1561) and Angel de Villafañe (1561) tried unsuccessfully to establish Spanish colonies in Florida largely to preclude any such attempt. Spain could not ignore an attempt by another nation to establish a colony there.

Coligny was an intelligent and skilled politician, not one to blunder into a situation unaware, but he did not explicitly articulate his reasons for establishing a colony specifically on the Florida coast. This has led to much speculation, some of it ill founded. Modern commentators often claim that Coligny founded the colony as a refuge for Huguenots, who made up about 10 percent of the French population, but the colonial venture was small and could not accommodate more than a few hundred people in the foreseeable future. Nor can it reasonably be assumed that Coligny sought to bring about a war between Spain and France in the New World or more generally. If Coligny's action provoked a war, it would have alienated Huguenot and moderate Catholic allies, strengthened radical Catholic enemies, and resulted in his own political ruin. Coligny strongly cautioned the colonists to avoid all provocations and conflicts with the Spanish.

Coligny's motives seem to have been much more subtle. His chief opponents were the noble Guise family, leaders of the radical Catholic faction, and they were supported by the Spanish who saw themselves as the leaders of the opposition to Protestant heresy. Coligny felt the establishment of a colony would increase tensions between France and Spain insufficient to lead to war but sufficient to discredit the Guise's alliance with Spain in the eyes of the court and all loyal Frenchmen. Moreover, France, like the other Atlantic European countries, saw colonies as necessary for the growth of national wealth, power, and prestige. The great harbor ports of Le Havre and Dieppe in Normandy and La Rochelle to the south

Gaspard de Coligny, ca. 1560. Attributed to "l'Anonyme Lécurieux." (*Bibliothèque nationale de France*)

were the centers of the Huguenot movement in France, and by 1560, the French maritime community was largely Protestant. Any French colony would necessarily include many Huguenots. The establishment of a successful French colony would redound to the credit of the French crown, Coligny, and the Huguenots, demonstrating that they would work, sacrifice, and encounter danger to advance French national interests. Catholics were also to take part in Coligny's proposed colony, and he may have hoped to show that the two groups could work and coexist in harmony. The rewards of success could be great, but much could go wrong with Coligny's plan, and whatever his ideals, Coligny was taking chances with other peoples' lives.

Coligny chose Jean Ribault of Dieppe to lead an expedition preliminary to the establishment of a colony. Ribault, born about 1515, was a member of a minor aristocratic Norman family long engaged in seafaring. He had a varied career, privateering under French license against Spanish and Portuguese shipping and later working in England under Sebastian Cabot as a naval adviser, planner, recruiter, and teacher of navigation. He probably converted to Calvinism before his return to France in 1555 and then went on to serve the French monarchy with distinction at sea against the Spanish and English in 1557 and 1558. Ribault also worked for France and perhaps England as an intelligence agent and may have even been a double agent at times. By

1560, he was well known internationally and regarded as one of the most important naval experts of his age, although he had never traveled across the Atlantic. Ribault's second in command was René Goulaine de Laudonnière, a successful merchant and experienced mariner, and like Ribault a member of an aristocratic Norman family.

The Charlesfort Colony

In 1562, Coligny sent Ribault and Laudonnière on a preliminary exploratory expedition in two large ships. During the sixteenth century, the usual ocean route to North America from Europe was to sail far south to the Canary Islands, where ships could take on fresh provisions and water and then ride the trade winds west across the Atlantic. Had Ribault followed that course, the Spanish might have discovered his presence. Rather, Ribault made the bold move of sailing well north of the usual route directly across the Atlantic on a west-southwest course. Conventional wisdom maintained that a ship on such a course would likely be becalmed between the southern and northern trade winds, but Ribault made a rapid and successful crossing. Navigators sailing from France, England, and northern Europe came to use the new route commonly, although the southern route also remained in use.

Ribault and Laudonnière made landfall in late April near where St. Augustine now stands and then sailed north. On the first of May, they reached the mouth of a large river they called the River May (modern St. Johns River), where they met friendly Native Timucua and announced the French claim to the land by setting up a stone column with the French royal arms carved on it. They then sailed farther north, arriving at an excellent harbor they named Port Royale. There the Native Guale were also friendly, so the French erected another column bearing the royal arms. Although his was supposedly an exploratory expedition, Ribault took a step of far-reaching consequence, establishing a tiny colony he hoped to soon reinforce and expand. He had constructed a small wooden fort, christened Charlesfort after King Charles IX, and left men (sources differ about the number—thirty, twenty-eight, or twenty-six) with supplies to support them until he could return. Ribault appointed Captain Albert de la Pierria to lead the colony in his absence.

Ribault departed Port Royal for home on June 11, 1562. The voyage was swift and problem free, but he returned to a France wracked by religious civil war. Coligny and the Prince of Condé, the main Huguenot leaders, were much too occupied to be concerned immedi-

Anonymous portrait, left, often described as Jean Ribault. Le musée Condé, inventory no. MN 316. Right, René Laudonnière, from Crispin de Passe, *Effigies regum ac principum, eoreum scilicet, quorum vis ac potentia in re nautica, seu marina, prae caeteris spectabilis est* (Colonia Agrippina, 1598).

ately with Ribault. The French Huguenots were allied with England, so Ribault turned to England for aid. There he met and befriended Thomas Stucley, who had connections among the English aristocracy and at court. Stucley was a dubious character, described by those he amused as "the lusty Stucley" and by his critics as a "decayed gentleman." During his life he played many roles, among them pious Catholic, mercenary, privateer, pirate, counterfeiter, wastrel, spy, rebel, and traitor. Ribault regaled Stucley and his associates with stories of the riches of Florida and the opportunities for colonists there, and Stucley encouraged his English friends to win support for an expedition to Florida. Even Queen Elizabeth quietly provided some backing, although she was reluctant to offend the Spanish openly. Ribault and Stucley prepared five ships to relieve the small French colony, but Stucley proved duplicitous. He gave the details of the proposed relief mission to Bishop Álvaro de la Quadra, the Spanish ambassador to England, and schemed to take charge of the expedition for his own purposes.

The deterioration of the alliance between England and France was more immediately destructive to Ribault's plans. When Ribault attempted to return to France, the English arrested him and threw him into the Tower of London. Stucley took the five ships, but rather than sailing to the French colony, he raided in the Bay of Biscay, attacking Spanish, Portuguese, and French ships even while secretly offering his services as a spy to Spain.

In Florida, the men at Charlesfort expected Ribault to return swiftly with additional provisions, but fourteen months passed without the appearance of a support fleet. While the French colonists waited for relief ships, the Spanish ambassador to France, relying on spies, reported to his king that the French had established a settlement in Florida and were outfitting a second fleet to support the colony. The Spanish royal government sent orders to the governor of Cuba to investigate the reports and deal with any French encroachment.

As the months passed, the French at Charlesfort ran short of food and became increasingly dependent on the Guale for sustenance. Their requirements taxed the local Indians' resources, and the colonists had to range farther afield to gather supplies from friendly villages. When a fire consumed most of the food the French had collected, the situation became grave. The commander, Albert de la Pierria, showed himself to be an abrasive martinet. When he hanged one man and expelled another from the colony over a trivial matter, the colonists revolted and killed him. They then elected a new leader, Nicolas Barré, a ship's pilot, under whose direction they built a small boat and abandoned the colony, sailing for France in August 1563. The refugees from Charlesfort endured a long and terrible passage across the Atlantic. When the men ran out of food they ate their leather shoes and jerkins and finally resorted to cannibalism. Ironically, the survivors were finally rescued by one of Stucley's ships patrolling the Bay of Biscay in search of prizes.

After some inevitable delays, the Spanish governor at Havana dispatched a ship to search the coast of Florida and question Indians about the French settlement. They found a French cabin boy, Guillaume Rouffin, living with the Guale. Rouffin claimed he had stayed behind because he had no confidence in the small ship and inexperienced crew, and he told the Spanish that the French had abandoned the settlement just days before. With Rouffin's aid, the Spanish found Charlesfort, burned it, and took the stone pillar that Ribault had erected. By mid-June 1563, the Spanish had returned to Havana and dispatched a report to Spain that the French threat was no more, at least for the time being. The Spanish interrogation of the cabin boy, however, revealed disturbing information. He confirmed that the majority of Ribault's men were Huguenots and said many had talked enthusiastically about hopes of looting Spanish treasure ships in the Florida Straits. Any future French intrusion would be doubly feared.

The end of the first French war of religion in 1563 gave Coligny the opportunity to renew his concern for the Florida colony. Since Ribault was still imprisoned in England, Coligny turned to Ribault's second in command, Laudonnière, to lead a relief expedition to Charlesfort, but the situation changed in 1564 when news reached France that the colony had been abandoned, followed shortly by the arrival of the survivors. Laudonnière was now charged with establishing a new French colony in Florida.

The French Second Effort: Fort Caroline

Laudonnière's expedition left France in April 1564, arrived on the Florida coast in June, and landed at the River May that had been discovered by the previous French expedition. In counsel with his officers, Laudonnière decided not to reoccupy Port Royal and Charlesfort, where the soil was poor and food scarce. They would plant the new colony on the banks of the River May, a few miles upriver from the mouth. The consensus of opinion is that the River May is the modern St. Johns River, although recently several investigators have argued that the River May was rather a river to the north in modern Georgia. That hypothesis disregards much early evidence and has found little acceptance.

The bar at the mouth of the St. Johns made it difficult for large ships to enter, and the anchorage was less protected from hurricanes than Port Royal, but the Timucua chief Saturiwa had greeted the French enthusiastically two years earlier, and he was equally pleased to receive them again. The lush plant life of the area also seemed to promise abundant crops. The colonists consisted of about three hundred men, mostly Huguenots, but included some Catholics and a number of so-called Moors, African slaves who were to serve as laborers. The colonists and slaves set to work to build a triangular defense work, named Fort Caroline. The fort consisted of earthworks on the two sides facing the land, and a wooden wall on the third side facing the river. There were bastions at each corner, and a narrow, shallow, water-filled moat offered some additional protection on the land sides. Saturiwa sent eighty men to aid the construction, and the colonists also built storehouses, shops, and cabins within the fort and more dwellings in the surrounding area, but once the basic fortification and housing were established, Laudonnière found it difficult to keep the colonists on task to strengthen the fort further and otherwise improve the colony.

The colonists, like those everywhere, were eager to search for precious metals, and in Florida such dreams were encouraged by the ornaments of gold and silver worn by Indians. While exploring, the French encountered two Spanish sailors who had been marooned by shipwreck fifteen years earlier and who had been living among the Indians. They told the French that the Indians salvaged gold and silver from Spanish wrecks cast up on the shores and there were no deposits of precious metals in the area, but they added that they had heard of a chiefdom where gold and silver were abundant, although they were not quite certain where this bonanza was located. The French explored ever farther afield rather than work on improving the colony.

Some colonists complained that Laudonnière relied too heavily on a few cronies and paid too little attention to the majority. Others protested that conditions were not what they had been led to expect, and the most religious colonists grumbled that there was no ordained minister in the colony, although there was a lay preacher. Those who were compelled to work on the fort, which was not completed until autumn, were bitterly resentful that they were not able to explore for riches. Laudonnière fell ill with a recurring fever, further weakening his administration of the increasingly unhappy colony.

Fueled by fundamental misunderstanding of the region and the Native economy, the French relations with the Timucua began to deteriorate. The colonists, misled by the lush vegetation, thought the soil of the St. Johns region was fertile, assumed that the Timucua could and would supply them with provisions indefinitely, and so made no effort to grow their own food. Despite superficial appearances, the soil was not much better than that at Port Royal, and the Timucua actually had little surplus and could not continue to feed the colonists.

The colonists also misunderstood the nature of the Timucua's initial generosity. When the French accepted hospitality, gifts of food, and aid in building their settlement, Saturiwa felt the French entered into an alliance, but when he came to the French for military aid to attack an enemy, Laudonnière refused, stating he would not purchase the

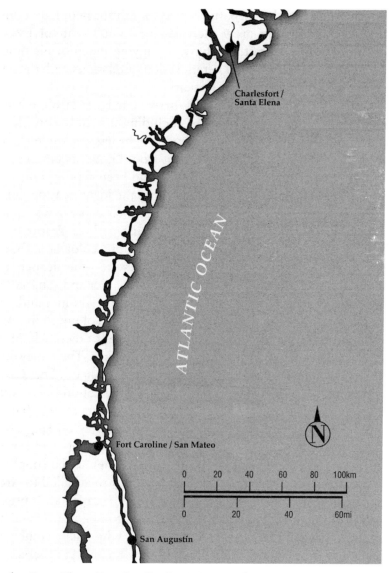

Charlesfort/Santa Elena, Fort Caroline/San Mateo, and San Augustín.

friendship of one by the hatred of another. Saturiwa felt betrayed, and the situation further deteriorated when he returned from a successful raid with prisoners whom Laudonnière confiscated to use in his negotiations with Saturiwa's enemy, the Timucua chief Outina. Laudonnière sought to build an alliance with Outina and even gave him the military aid he had denied Saturiwa. As months passed, Laudonnière's political maneuvering grew increasingly complex, involving more chiefdoms farther from the colony, occupying much of his time and effort with few results except deterioration of relations with the nearest chiefdoms and an increase in violence.

In early September, French ships arrived at Fort Caroline bringing supplies and additional colonists, including a sizable contingent of women and children. The ships also brought less-desirable elements, criminals whom Admiral Coligny sent from France as laborers and a group of unspecified "foreigners" who had been captured during the voyage. The reticence of the sources about the identification indicates the captives were probably Spanish. If so, their capture was a hostile act and a justification for subsequent Spanish actions. Before the supply ships departed for France in November, one colonist accused another of conspiring to murder Laudonnière and other leaders of the colony, although there was no real proof of the plot and some colonists thought the accused was innocent. The man whom Laudonnière thought was the chief conspirator fled from the colony to live among the Indians, and Laudonnière sent seven or eight others whom he no longer trusted back to France with the supply ships. There they and the ships' crews spread news of the deteriorating discipline at Fort Caroline.

After the ships departed, new crises shook Laudonnière and the colony. First, a group of eleven disaffected sailors stole a barque, a ship about thirty-five feet long, and set out to prey on Spanish shipping. Another barque disappeared with two carpenters and was never seen again. The eleven sailed to Cuba, where they seized supplies and took a captive at a village called Savana. They then sailed to Arcos, a small port near Havana, where their prisoner escaped and spread the word of the pirates' activities. The Spanish governor at Havana sent two ships that promptly captured the pirates, who talked volubly when questioned. The Spanish thus learned that French "Lutherans" (the Spanish term for all Protestants at that time) had indeed returned to Florida and established a new colony, which the captives described in detail, including information about the size of the garrison and the colony's defenses.

At Fort Caroline, a second group of sixty-six disgruntled colonists mutinied in early December. They took Laudonnière captive and forced him to sign a document stating they were on a mission to trade for food for the colony, although it was apparent that they too in-

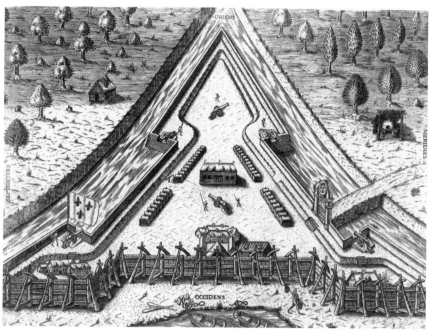

Fort Caroline as seen from the St. Johns River. Theodor de Bry and Jacques Le Moyne de Morgues, *Brevis narratio eorum quae in Florida Americae provincia Gallis acciderunt, secunda in illam navigatione, duce Renato de Laudonniere classis praefecto anno MDLXIIII*, (Frankfurt: T. de Bry, 1591), Plate X.

tended to act as pirates. The mutineers departed on two newly built barques, which they equipped with cannons, shot, and powder. The two ships sailed south, but a storm soon separated them. The sources for the subsequent actions of the two groups consist of Spanish reports, Spanish interrogations of captured mutineers-turned-pirates, and Laudonnière's summary of the accounts of survivors. The pirates were imperfectly aware of Spanish activities, and the Spanish were similarly ignorant of some details of the pirates' actions. Pirates captured by the Spanish sought to minimize their crimes and placate their captors, and survivors who eventually returned to Fort Caroline acted similarly before Laudonnière. There are a number of contradictions, and the accounts cannot be entirely reconciled, but the general course of events is clear.

One barque sailed to the Spanish port of Cagay on Hispaniola where the mutineers captured two prizes, a small ship they ransomed and a larger ship they took, abandoning their own. The group in the second barque touched briefly at La Yaguana, only about thirty miles from Cagay. After Spanish ships chased them away from there, the second barque sailed to Cagay unaware that the earlier raid had thoroughly alerted Spanish forces there. The mutineers landed and surrounded a group of houses when the Spanish counterattacked, killing and capturing several while the rest fled.

The two groups of mutineers met and joined forces on the northern coast of Hispanola, where the first group was refitting its new ship. From there the pirates sailed to Cuba, where they raided the small port of Baracoa, taking supplies and a third small ship. Sailing back to northern Hispaniola, the pirates captured a Spanish ship after a fight, taking about twenty prisoners. They kept that ship, abandoned the second barque from Fort Caroline, and sailed to Spanish Jamaica. There at the harbor of Caguaya they sought to exchange their Spanish prisoners for food. While the Spanish said they were gathering food, they actually gathered their forces and in a sudden attack captured two of the three pirate ships and thirty-two prisoners. The remaining pirates escaped and, lacking any alternative, sailed back to Fort Caroline, where Laudonnière hanged four of the leaders and pardoned the rest.

The royal government in France ordered Ribault and Laudonnière to avoid any offense to the Spanish, but the French colonists repeatedly demonstrated their enthusiasm for piracy against the Spanish. The pirating adventures of the mutineers were small scale and no significant threat to the Spanish Caribbean, which had endured and would endure much worse, but to the Spanish they seemed to portent a much greater threat and compounded the Spanish horror of Huguenot heresy. It took time for the Spanish authorities to interrogate the prisoners, write reports, and send them across the Atlantic, where at the end of March 1565, King Philip II received the report that French heretics and pirates were back in Florida. The king had a plan underway to colonize Florida to prevent any such foreign settlement, and now it had to be redirected to expel the French and secure the peninsula.

The Spanish Reaction

Philip II's plan for Florida relied on Pedro Menéndez de Avilés y Alonso de la Campa. Menéndez was born in Asturias in northern Spain in 1519 to a family of minor gentry. He found success as a privateer, executed royal commissions to hunt pirates, served at sea in the war against France and the continuing rebellion in the Netherlands, and repeatedly led the Indies fleet to the Caribbean and back to Spain. Alarmed at the recent French incursion at Charlesfort and reports of new colonial preparations in France, Philip requested Menéndez to report on the situation of Florida. After recounting the dangers posed by foreign colonies and possible advantages of Spanish colonization, Menéndez proposed the immediate establishment of a colony at Santa Elena, the Spanish name for Port Royal, by an expedition launched directly from Spain. The king was impressed, but the royal treasury was overextended, nearing bankruptcy, and royal forces were engaged on many fronts. The burden of a new royal effort seemed just too much. As an alternative, in March 1565, Philip appointed Menéndez adelantado of Florida, authorizing him to conquer, pacify, settle, and evangelize the province in the name of the king. As adelantado, Menéndez was to rely mainly on his own resources and any funds he could raise from friends and associates, although the king also provided a private grant to aid the endeavor. In recompense for his efforts and expenditures, the king granted the adelantado the right to govern the province, dispense justice, enjoy specific immunities and privileges, carve out an estate for himself, and grant titles and lands to his subordinates. If successful, an adelantado could reap wealth and honors. When Philip received the report that the French had established a new colony in Florida, he quickly modified the arrangement with the adelantado, adding the expulsion of the French to his duties and providing royal ships, arms, men, and money to aid in the effort.

The Spanish expedition required so many ships and men, and so much equipment that all could not be gathered in a single harbor. Menéndez supervised the preparation of the largest contingent in the harbor of Cádiz, while other groups of ships and men were equipped in other Atlantic ports. The Cádiz fleet, consisting of eight ships, including Menéndez's giant galleon, *San Pelayo*, officially set sail on June 27, 1565. All contingents were supposed to rendezvous at the Canary Islands and sail on in one great armada, but the other groups failed to reach the Canaries on time. Menéndez left orders that they were to follow and set sail for Florida with eight ships. One ship turned back leaking badly, and then a hurricane shattered the rest of the fleet: One was blown to Hispaniola and there captured by French pirates, another was wrecked on the coast of Guadaloupe. The surviving ships, all significantly damaged, reached San Juan, Puerto Rico, on August

18, but there Menéndez found that the Spanish Caribbean forces who were supposed to join him were far from ready.

As Menéndez prepared his expedition in Spain, Coligny prepared a fleet in France to reinforce Fort Caroline. Coligny commissioned Ribault, recently returned from England, to lead the effort and, cognizant of the complaints about Laudonnière's leadership, to take command of the colony. The fleet consisted of seven ships, three small and four moderately large, carrying military supplies and additional colonists, many of them soldiers. They departed from France on May 22, 1565, a month before Menéndez left Spain. Adverse winds delayed the French for more than two weeks at the Isle of Wight, but then they crossed the Atlantic without encountering further bad weather.

At San Juan, Menéndez faced a critical decision. He could rest there, have his ships thoroughly repaired, and wait for the reinforcements from Spain and the Caribbean, but if he did so, Ribault's fleet would likely reach Fort Caroline first and reinforce the colony. In that case, the French would be difficult or even impossible to expel. Or Menéndez could proceed with a reduced force and jury-rigged ships, perhaps prevent the juncture of the French forces, and endeavor to defeat the two French forces separately. Menéndez decided to strike immediately and set sail for Florida with four incompletely repaired ships and a fifth ship he had obtained at San Juan, risking a dangerous passage through the largely uncharted Bahamas to save time.

Capture of Fort Caroline

Meanwhile, conditions at Fort Caroline deteriorated. Food became ever scarcer as most of the Timucua left their villages for the annual winter hunt in January and did not return until the end of March. Even after the Indians returned to their villages, it would be months before new crops were ready for harvest. Colonists used threats and violence to extort food from the Timucua's scant reserves, and the once-friendly Timucua became increasingly hostile. Laudonnière expected ships loaded with provisions to arrive in May or June, but they did not appear. In late July, Laudonnière reluctantly decided to abandon the colony and ordered the fort partly dismantled to use its timbers to add space on the colony's small ships to carry settlers back to France.

By early August, plans for departure were nearly complete and the colony had rations for only ten days remaining, when unexpectedly five English ships appeared before Fort Caroline. The fleet was cap-

tained by John Hawkins, a typical English sea rover of the sixteenth century—
merchant, smuggler, slave trader, or
pirate as opportunities dictated.
Hawkins and Laudonnière quickly
reached an accommodation. The
French traded cannons to Hawkins for
a small English ship and enough food
to get the colonists home. By the middle of August, Laudonnière and the
colonists were ready to depart, waiting
only for favorable winds, when Ribault's fleet finally appeared.

After arriving on the Florida coast,
Ribault exhibited no haste in getting to
Fort Caroline, proceeding slowly, stop-
ping to trade and establish relations
with Indians along the coast and finally
sighting the colony on August 28,
1565. Ribault's three small ships were
able to cross the bar at the mouth of the

Engraving of Pedro Menéndez de
Avilés by Francisco de Paula
Marti, 1791, after Titian's portrait painted during Menéndez's
lifetime. (*New York Public Library*)

St. Johns River, while four larger ships anchored outside. Unloading
the ships proceeded slowly and was still underway when, six days later,
Menéndez's five ships sailed into sight. Menéndez realized that the
French ships could outmaneuver his storm-damaged vessels on the
open sea, but he would have an advantage if he could close with the
French ships at anchor. Three of Menéndez's ships were small, but his
giant galleon, *San Pelayo*, was several times larger than the largest
French ship. The *San Pelayo* may not have carried significantly more
cannons than the largest French ship, but it certainly could sustain
much more damage, and in closing its crew could easily board any of
the smaller French ships.

Before Menéndez could attack, a rain squall lasting to nightfall en-
veloped the area. The night was too dark to distinguish friend from
foe, so Menéndez anchored his ships close to the French, intending to
attack at first light. The night was filled with threats, insults, and
shouts of defiance, and shortly before dawn, the four French ships cut
their anchor cables and headed to open sea, where they could outsail
the battered Spanish ships. Menéndez had three small ships that could

cross the bar at the mouth of the St. Johns River, but if they attempted, the French ships in the river could easily bombard them as they maneuvered. Unable to match the undamaged French ships in the open ocean or to attack the smaller ships in the St. Johns River, Menéndez resolved instead to sail south to an inlet he had reconnoitered a few days earlier and had named San Agustín, modern St. Augustine. There he hastily built a rough fortification and began to unload his artillery and supplies, but his major ships could not cross the bar at the mouth of the inlet. If they remained anchored beyond, they would be vulnerable to French attack. When three French ships scouting along the coast sighted the Spanish preparations, Menéndez dispatched his battered large ships south to Hispaniola to avoid the French and seek reinforcements. He was left with only the hastily constructed weak fort equipped with little artillery, limited provisions, and his two smallest ships, which had been able to enter the inlet.

At Fort Caroline, the French debated their next move. Laudonnière later reported that he favored disembarking the French troops, restoring the partly demolished Fort Caroline, and waiting to repel the Spanish in a strong position, but he was overruled by Ribault, who loaded almost all the fighting men on the ships and sailed to attack the hastily prepared Spanish fort at San Agustín. Laudonnière, again ill, remained behind at Fort Caroline with a few soldiers, the sick, disabled, and noncombatant artisans, women, and children.

As Ribault approached San Agustín, he faced a situation similar to that previously confronted by Menéndez at Fort Caroline. Ribault's chief ships could not cross the bar into the tidal river, so he had the choice of either attacking with just his smallest ships or disembarking his fighting force in small boats to make a landing. Either alternative involved risk. The sudden onset of a hurricane nullified whatever decision Ribault may have contemplated. As the hurricane moved offshore from the south to the north, the counterclockwise winds assailed Ribault's ships from the northeast, driving them to the south. The winds that drove Ribault away for the moment also precluded the return of Menéndez's own large ships and any Spanish reinforcements.

Menéndez now determined to risk all on an audacious plan. He would march the roughly thirty-five miles from San Agustín in the midst of the hurricane with five hundred soldiers and a number of Indian allies to attack Fort Caroline. He left behind only a hundred men, his sick, disabled, and noncombatants, too few to mount any meaningful defense if he had miscalculated and the French managed to beat the contrary winds and return to attack San Agustín. Menéndez's forces spent four days covering the distance to Fort Caroline in the midst of the storm, crossing flooded swamps up to their waists in water.

The Spanish arrived before Fort Caroline at night on September 19, 1565, wet to the skin, tired, hungry, their firearms useless, gunpowder and match cord for the arquebuses soaked. The French thought the hurricane rendered them immune from attack and posted a minimal number of sentries in the pouring rain. At dawn the next morning, the Spanish attacked with pikes and swords, rushing through the shallow moat and planting their banners on the walls of the fort. The Spanish cut down the French as they emerged from their sleeping quarters into the rain and half-light. Many of the French died on the spot, others were taken prisoner, and still others, including Laudonnière, fled from the fort into the woods. Menéndez had all but a few of the captured men hanged, including some who had fled and were taken prisoner the next day. The Spanish killed about 140 French at Fort Caroline. Menéndez ordered that women and children were to be spared, and about 50 were taken prisoner and eventually shipped to Spain. Menéndez also spared several drummers and trumpeters who could be useful and two French aristocrats, captured by the tribesmen, who would bring rich ransoms. Nicolas Le Challeux, a carpenter who fled from the fort, later wrote a memoir in which he claimed Menéndez posted a placard with the hanged men: "I do this not as unto Frenchmen, but as unto Lutherans." Neither Menéndez nor other Spanish sources mention such a placard.

Jacques Ribault, the son of Jean Ribault, commanded the three small French ships in the St. Johns River. After a brief and unproductive parley, the Spanish opened fire with cannons on Ribault's ships. One sank, either due to Spanish gunfire or scuttling by the French—sources disagree. Ribault also sank a number of the colonists' small boats to keep the Spanish from using them. A day or several days later—again sources disagree—Jacques Ribault was able to return and rescue about fifty French who had fled to the woods when the fort was taken. Among them were Laudonnière, the artist Jacques le Moyne de Morgues, and the carpenter Le Challeux, all of whom later published memoirs about their experiences. Jacques Ribault set sail for France, carrying the refugees and news of the disaster in Florida.

Menéndez renamed the captured settlement San Mateo and appointed an able officer to remain there with most of the Spanish troops while he marched with thirty-five chosen men back to San Agustín.

Massacres

On September 28, just one day after Menéndez's return to San Agustín, Indians brought word that a large number of Frenchmen were isolated on the sand bar by an inlet, a wide channel separating them from the mainland. Menéndez took about 45 men in the largest boat available to him to confront the French, about 140 survivors of three of Jean Ribault's ships driven on the coast by the hurricane. Isolated on the sand bar, they had little food and water for days and were largely unarmed. The French offered to surrender if Menéndez would spare their lives, but Menéndez rejected the condition, demanding they surrender at his discretion. Facing starvation, the French had no choice but to do so.

At Menéndez's direction, the Spanish troops carried the French across the channel by boat in small groups and then led them, hands tied behind their backs, behind sand dunes, where they put them to the knife. Of the 140, Menéndez let only 16 live, a group of Breton sailors, presumably Catholic, and several carpenters and caulkers whose skills the Spanish needed. Spanish soldiers returning from San Mateo brought Menéndez word that an accidental fire had destroyed the provisions captured there. Menéndez quickly dispatched his small ships to bring supplies and artillery to the fire-ravaged camp, and soon thereafter he received word that a second group of about two hundred Frenchmen led by Jean Ribault had arrived at the inlet where the first group had been encountered. Menéndez responded with about 150 men of his own. Through long negotiations, Menéndez remained firm: the French had to surrender at his discretion. Ribault and about seventy of his men did so; the rest retreated to the south. Menéndez dealt with Ribault and the other men who surrendered as he had dealt with the first group. He spared a few useful individuals and had the rest, including Ribault, slaughtered among the dunes. The site remains known as Matazanas Inlet—Massacres Inlet in English.

About ten days later, Natives brought word that a third group of French castaways had gathered near Cape Canaveral and constructed a ramshackle fort out of the remains of a wrecked ship. Menéndez marched south from San Agustín with about 150 men and sent about

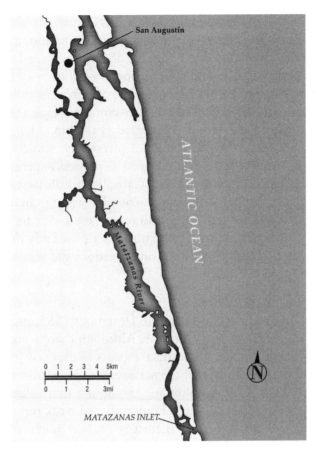

San Augustín to the Matazanas Inlet.

100 more by ship. At their approach, the outnumbered French fled into the woods. Menéndez sent a French prisoner to offer terms: if the French surrendered, their lives would be spared. All but a few accepted the offer and passed into Spanish captivity. The French adventure in Florida was at an end.

The dominant interpretation of Menéndez's actions well into the twentieth century depicted him as a sanctimonious butcher. Recently, historians have sought to explain his actions in pragmatic terms, pointing out that the Spanish would have found it difficult and dangerous to try to control the mass of French prisoners, had no secure housing for them, were short of provisions, and could not have fed the French and themselves. In a letter to King Philip II, Menéndez cited none of these reasons but explained his motivations clearly. He wrote that he came by order of the king to make war with fire and blood against the French who had intruded into Philip II's domain to spread the "odious Lutheran doctrine." Menéndez's position was in no way exceptional or unusual in the sixteenth century, the age of European religious wars. Actions considered atrocities today were commonplace and even considered commendable. Heresy was regarded as a sin much worse than murder, which merely killed a human physically, while heresy condemned a soul to ever-lasting hell. Heresy supposedly spread like a disease, dooming still other souls. For Catholic and Protestant alike, it was holy duty to expurgate heresy. Menéndez was a man of his age, a murderous, intolerant age—not unlike our own. Yet he spared the third group of French captives, who no longer posed any threat to him or his men, so perhaps pragmatic considerations did play a role in his decisions.

Aftermath

Jacques Ribault returned to France in December 1565, bringing news of the French defeat at Fort Caroline. Although there were earlier rumors and speculation, the first official reports of death of Jean Ribault, the destruction of his fleet, and the massacres of his men reached Spain in February 1566. In the diplomatic wrangling that followed, Spain justified Menéndez's actions, and France offered weak remonstrations. The popular reaction in France against Spain was much stronger, particularly in the largely Protestant French Atlantic ports. Exaggerated reports of atrocities attributed to Menéndez and his men played into the Black Legend, the depiction of Spanish culture as inherently vicious, cruel, bigoted, and self-righteous.

After the elimination of the French threat, Menéndez established cordial relations with Ais tribesmen in the Cape Canaveral-Indian River area and built a fort there in which he left two hundred of his own troops and fifty of the French captives. Menéndez then undertook a perilous voyage to the Caribbean in a small ship to raise provisions for his men in Florida. Bureaucratic quarrels and delays and the loss of shipping in storms prolonged Menéndez's stay while conditions deteriorated in Florida. Facing starvation, the garrisons in the Indian River area, at San Agustín, and San Mateo mutinied. When Menéndez was finally able to return, he reasserted control and reinforced Florida with more than two hundred soldiers. He then began to pursue ambitious plans for the development of Florida. He explored the coasts systematically, established additional forts, and built a new settlement, Santa Elena, at Port Royal in close proximity to the deserted French Charlesfort. Impressed by the fine harbor of Port Royal, Menéndez intended to make Santa Elena the capital and chief settlement of his province.

Crises, however, continued to frustrate Menéndez's intentions. Mutineers, led by "heretics," had taken his great galleon *San Pelayo* and sailed to Denmark, where a storm drove the ship onto the coast and destroyed it. Tribesmen attacked San Agustín, burning the fort with great material loss, and the garrison at San Mateo again mutinied when food ran short and promised provisions were late in arriving. Menéndez's subordinates frequently failed to maintain discipline over soldiers, who maltreated Indians, assaulted Indian women, and extorted food. Warfare between the Spanish and Natives became general throughout the settlements and forts in Florida. Mutiny, desertion, illness, starvation, and hostile Indian attacks reduced the Spanish forces in Florida by half in 1565–1566. Menéndez reinforced his bases as best he could, and in October 1565 he departed Florida to lead a campaign against corsairs who were preying on the Spanish in the Caribbean. He hoped prizes captured from the pirates would revive his depleted finances and enable him to better supply Florida.

In May 1567, Menéndez sailed for Spain, where he was greeted as a hero despite some quibbling about bookkeeping and the appropriate use of funds. Philip II appointed Menéndez as governor and captain general of Cuba and captain general of a new royal armada for the West Indies, all in addition to his position in Florida.

Menéndez's officer Juan Pardo led two explorations from Santa Elena into the interior. The first departed in December 1566 and returned in early March the next year. Pardo established Fort San Juan at the Native town of Joara in North Carolina, where he left a garrison. During a second expedition, from September 1567 to March in 1568, Pardo and his soldiers ranged through inland North Carolina into Tennessee, establishing and garrisoning five more small forts and blockhouses among indigenous people who seemed generally docile and friendly. Pardo's explorations and forts were supposed to be the initial phase of Menéndez's dream of establishing a vast personal inland estate, but shortly after Pardo returned, the Indians, probably weary of Spanish demands for food, attacked, burned the forts, and massacred the garrisons. Of 120 men Pardo had left at the forts and blockhouses, only 1 emerged alive. Menéndez's dream of a great inland estate evaporated. Henceforth Spanish occupation of eastern North America would be restricted to the coastal area. Recently, archaeologists have identified the site of Pardo's principal fort at the town of Joara.

In 1567, Dominique de Gourgues, a French adventurer, set out to become the self-appointed avenger of the massacred French in Florida. Born into an aristocratic family, he fought for France in the Italian wars against the Spanish, who captured him in 1557 and reduced him to a galley slave. Turks captured the galley from the Spanish and then the Knights of Malta captured the galley from the Turks, finally freeing Gourgues after several years' servitude. Gourgues then took part in voyages to Africa, Brazil, and the Caribbean and fought against the Huguenots under the Duke of Guise during one of France's intermittent religious wars.

Gourgues was a Catholic, but both French Catholics and Huguenots were outraged by Menéndez's massacres, and Gourgues may well have also entertained a personal grudge against the Spanish. He sold a large portion of his estate to finance a slaving expedition on the African coast, but after only a brief stop in Africa he sailed to the Caribbean, where he first announced his real purpose of upholding national honor by seeking revenge against the Spanish. His modest force consisted of one large ship and two small ones carrying about 150 arquebusiers and 80 sailors.

Gourgues arrived at the Florida coast south of San Agustín and sailed north. Spanish batteries at the mouth of the inlet by San Agustín sighted Gourgues's ships and, assuming they were Spanish, fired a salute. Gourgues returned the salute and continued north to his special target, San Mateo, the former Fort Caroline. He sailed north past San Mateo to the mouth of the St. Marys River, where he unloaded his force and found ready allies in the Timucua, whose relations with the Spanish had deteriorated to open hostility. Just about a month earlier, about four hundred Timucua had attacked San Mateo and overrun one side of the fort before the Spanish repulsed them. Together, Gourgues's forces and several hundred Timucua now marched south to San Mateo.

Both Gourgues's account and Spanish documents concerning the subsequent events survive. They agree in general outline but vary greatly in detail, particularly in regard to the size and scope of the fighting. Gourgues's men and the Timucua first attacked two block-houses that guarded the entrance to the St. Johns River, which they overwhelmed, and then turned their attention to San Mateo itself, which fell to their assault. According to Gourgues, he routed the Spanish forces after fierce fighting and hanged at least thirty Spanish soldiers. According to the Spanish, false reports of the number of French and Timucua coming against them panicked the garrisons that largely deserted before the French arrived. The Spanish also claimed that Gourgues hanged a total of ten men.

French reports claimed that Menéndez posted a placard reading "I do this not as unto Frenchmen, but as unto Lutherans" with the men he hanged at Fort Caroline, and now Gourgues posted a placard with the men he hanged at San Mateo, "Je ne faicts cecy comme a Espaingnolz, ny comme a Marannes, mais comme a traistres volleurs et meurtriers." In 1587, Richard Hakluyt translated the placard as "I doe not this as unto Spaniardes, nor as unto Mariners, but as unto Traiters, Robbers, and Murtherers." This translation has been repeated without question with few exceptions for over four centuries, although it obviously makes no sense. "Marannes" is not the French word for "mariners," and "mariners" makes no sense in the context. "Marannes" was French rendering of the Spanish term "Marannos," the term for Spanish Jews and Moslems who had converted to Christianity under duress. Their conversion was generally suspected to be insincere, and the word took on the additional meaning of "hypocrites," which obviously fits the context better than "mariners." Similarly, during the sixteenth century, "traistres" had a broader meaning that "traitors." Then it included treacherous, evil people in general. Here Gourgues seems to have been thinking of French reports that Menéndez had promised to spare the French but killed them despite his promise. So Gourgues's placard can be better translated as "I do this not to Spanish nor to hypocrites, but to betrayers, robbers, and murderers."

At San Mateo, a Timucua accidentally began a fire that destroyed many of the buildings, and Gourgues had his men and the natives demolish the fortifications. The French got little loot from San Mateo other than half a dozen brass cannons that were originally French. Gourgues had no intention of recolonizing Florida and so soon sailed for France. The Spanish returned and began to rebuild, but the combination of poor agriculture, hunger, and continuing Timucua hostility led them to abandon the settlement in 1569.

In France, Gourgues's attack on San Mateo led to a diplomatic crisis between Spain and France, and Gourgues received a much cooler reception at the royal court than he had anticipated. The Spanish king, Philip II, was so furious that he initially planned a naval expedition to capture Gourgues, and when it became apparent that was not practical, Philip tried to have Gourgues assassinated. Despite official disapproval, Gourgues was a popular hero, and friends protected him while he remained inconspicuous for several years.

Yet another disappointment awaited Menéndez. At his behest, members of the recently established Jesuit order came to Florida to evangelize among the Natives. In 1570, a small group of Jesuits departed from Santa Elena without any accompanying soldiers in a daring attempt to establish a mission in what is now Virginia (see chapter 4). The result was a massacre. The Spanish attempt to establish a settlement in Virginia was not renewed, and soon the English established their hold on the area. Henceforth, not only was Spanish occupation confined to the coastal region, but it was also restricted to the Deep South, the coasts of modern Florida and Georgia.

Despite all, Menéndez continued to work for the development of Florida, but by 1572, it must have become apparent that his greatest ambitions would never be realized. His resources were, even with the aid of the Spanish crown, too little and the challenges too many. He died unexpectedly at age fifty-five while on a trip to Spain in 1574.

Menéndez intended Santa Elena at Port Royal to be the capital of his province, but the colony never prospered, being hampered by poor soil, venial and corrupt administrators, and Native hostility. The Spanish finally abandoned the settlement in 1587. Of his major foundations, only the extemporaneous establishment, St. Augustine, survived.

The fate of French prisoners taken by the Spanish varied. A few seem to have remained as slaves in the Caribbean. The Spanish transported others to Spain, where some disappeared into the cells of the Inquisition or Spanish galleys. Relatives and friends ransomed several wealthy gentlemen, and the Spanish simply released others over the course of several years. A few others managed to escape from custody in Spain, sometimes with French clandestine help.

Admiral Coligny continued to play a significant role in French politics until 1572, when he was murdered at the beginning of the St.

Bartholomew's Day Massacre, during which French Catholics butchered thousands of Huguenots.

René Laudonnière found employment as a naval expert after returning to France. Charles de Bourbon, the archbishop of Rouen and a cardinal of the Catholic Church, employed him as captain of a trading vessel sailing to North America, although Laudonnière persisted in his Huguenot faith. When the rigidly Catholic Duke of Alba attacked Bourbon for engaging Laudonnière, the cardinal replied that Laudonnière had done nothing wrong and he would continue to support and favor him. Laudonnière was captain on a trading voyage to America at the time of the St. Bartholomew's Day massacre. Had he been in France, he would have been singled out for death as a prominent Huguenot. In 1573, Laudonnière was in royal service and bore the title of The Captain of the Western Fleet. He is thought to have died in 1582.

After returning to France, Dominique de Gourgues spent several years evading Spanish revenge. By 1572, the furor over his actions had died down, and he served with the royal French Catholic forces, commanding a ship, during the siege of the Huguenot city of La Rochelle. In 1592, António, prior of Crato, appointed Gourgues commander of his fleet during his last, unsuccessful attempt to oust Philip II and claim the Portuguese crown. Gourgues died during the campaign in 1593.

Philip II ruled Spain until his death in 1598. He gloried in the sobriquet Philip the Prudent, but he was actually an obsessive micromanager who often failed to see the broader implications of his actions. Basic problems that beset Spain throughout his long reign remained unresolved at his death.

In 2016, the salvage company Global Marine Exploration discovered the remains of a sixteenth-century shipwreck near Cape Canaveral. The discoverers first interpreted the wreck as one of Ribault's ships, perhaps his flagship, but shortly afterward they reinterpreted the wreck as an unknown Spanish ship that had been carrying some of the loot from the French colony. Soon, the discovery was the subject of a law case. The French government claimed the wreck was in fact Ribault's ship, originally and still French property, while Global Marine Exploration claimed the ship could not be specifically identified and thus it was entitled to salvage. In 2018, a federal court in Jacksonville ruled the wreck is Jean Ribault's flagship *La Trinite* and the property of France. The attorney representing the French government hailed the ruling as protecting the wreck from private looting, while the salvage company may appeal the decision.

French Sources

Jean Ribault wrote a relatively brief account of his first voyage, first printed in England while he was a prisoner there: *The Whole and True Discoverye of Terra Florida* (London: Rouland Hall, for Thomas Hacket, 1563), of which only two copies survive. There may have been a contemporary English printing in French under the title *Histoire de l'expedition francaise en Floride* (London: [Rouland Hall, for Thomas Hacket?], 1563) but apparently no copy is known to survive. The earliest French edition is Jean Ribault, *Histoire memorable du dernier voyage aux Indes, lieu appele la Floride* (Lyon: n.p., 1566).

Henry Percival Biggar, "Jean Ribaut's Discoverye of Terra Florida," *English Historical Review* 32, no. 126 (April 1917): 253-270, provides a transcription of the original manuscript of the English version of Ribault's account published in 1563. In the footnotes, Biggar points out differences between the manuscript and the printed text. See also Henry Percival Biggar, notes, and Jeannette Thurber Connor, intro., *The Whole & True Discouerye of Terra Florida* (De Land, FL: Publications of the Florida State Historical Society no. 7, 1927), which contains a copy of the original English text and a reprint of Biggar's copy of the English manuscript. A modern, scholarly edition of Ribault's text and that of other French sources is Suzanne Lussagnet, ed. and annot., and Ch.-André Julien, intro., *Les Francais en Floride: textes de Jean Ribault, Rene de Laudonniere, Nicolas Le Challeux et Dominique de Gourgues* (Vendome: Impr. des Presses universitaires de France, 1958).

The most important source for the French in Florida is René Goulaine de Laudonnière, *L'Histoire notable de lat Floride située en les Indes Occidentales, contenant les trois voyages fair en icelle par certains capitaines et pilots françois* (Paris: G. Auvray, 1586), and frequent translations since then. The most readily available translation is Charles E. Bennett, trans., intro., and notes, *Three Voyages* (Tuscaloosa: University of Alabama Press, 2001). Laudonniere's account is generally reliable until the capture of Fort Caroline, although he goes to length to absolve himself of accusations of weak leadership and blame for the Spanish conquest of the colony. He had no firsthand knowledge of subsequent events except his own escape.

An elderly carpenter, Nicolas Le Challeux, took part in the third French expedition to Florida under Ribault. His memoire, Nicolas Le Challeux, *Discours le l'histoire de la Floride, contenant la cruauté des Espagnols contre le subjects du roy en l'an mil cinq cens soixante cinq* (Dieppe: J. Le Sellier, 1566), contains little detail about the colony before the Spanish capture, which he survived by fleeing to the woods along with about fifty others. He accuses the Spanish of great cruelty and is the only source that claims the Spanish killed French women and children at the fort. Spanish sources show that about fifty women and children were taken alive and sent to Spain. A translation of his work is available in Stefan Lorant, ed. and annot., *The New World: The First Pictures of America* (New York: Duell, Sloan & Pearce, 1946).

The artist Jacques Le Moyne de Morgues accompanied Laudonnière to Florida and wrote of events some years later, *Brevis Narrotio eorum quae in Florida Americae provincial Gallis accidenunt, secunda in illam Navigationem duce Renato de Laudonniere classis praefecto anno MDLXIIII* (Frankfurt: Theodore de Bry, 1591). Note the late date of the publication. Le Moyne's work is also available in translation in Lorant, *The New World*. His memory of some details seems inaccurate, but his account generally confirms the accounts of Laudonnière and Le Challeux. He is occasionally critical of Laudonnière but also quotes him extensively with approval. Le Moyne was also acquainted with Le Challeux's publication, to which he refers the reader.

Le Moyne's work also contains forty-two illustrations of great importance. His original paintings were destroyed when the Spanish took Fort Caroline, and he re-created them later from memory, but we do not have even these, but rather Theodore de Bry's engravings copying Le Moyne's work. Moreover, Le Moyne and De Bry employed a number of European artistic conventions, which necessarily distorted North American realities. Like Laudonnière and Le Challeux, Le Moyne had no personal knowledge of events after the capture of Fort Caroline.

The only painting by Le Moyne thought to have survived is almost identical to De Bry and Le Moyne, *Brevis narratio*, plate 8: Athore, son of the Timucua chief Saturiwa, showing Laudonnière in 1564 the column erected by Ribault two years earlier. (Here fig. 3.5). The two images are so similar they raise the question whether De Bry's engravings were truer to Le Moyne's paintings than generally believed or

Athore, son of the Timucua chief Saturiwa, showing Laudonnière in 1564 the column erected by Ribault two years earlier. De Bry and Le Moyne, *Brevis narratio*, Plate VIII.

whether the painting is merely a later copy derived from the engraving. For the account of the discovery of the painting and the argument that it is an original by Le Moyne, see E. T. Hamy, "Sur une miniature de Jacques Le Moyne de Morgues, représentant une scène du voyage de Laudonnière en Flordie (1564)," *Comptes rendus des séances de l'Académie des Inscriptions et Belles-Lettres,* vol. 45, no. 1 (Jan.-Feb. 1901): 8-17, accessed May 8, 2020, https://www.persee.fr/doc/crai _0065-0536_1901_num_45_1_16699?q=Sur+une+miniature+ de+Jacques+Le+Moyne+de+Morgues,+repr%C3%A9sentant+une+sc %C3%A8ne+du+voyage+de+Laudonni%C3%A8re+en+Flordie+(156 4); Paul Hulton, *The Work of Jacques Le Moyne de Morgues: A Huguenot Artist in France and Florida,* 2 vols. (London: British Museum Publications, 1977), and Miles Harvey, *Painter in a Savage Land: The Strange Saga of the First European Artist in North America* (New York: Random House, 2008), express reservations about the reliability of the Le Moyne-De Bry engravings.

Guillaume Rouffin, a fifteen-year-old cabin boy, remained with the Natives near Port Royal when most of the colonists returned to France in 1562 and was subsequently captured by the Spanish. "Report of Manrique de Rojas," in Bennett, *Laudonnière*, 107-124, is a translation of the record of his interrogation. Although he obviously had no access to the highest leadership, he certainly knew what the ordinary colonists believed and discussed, and he told the Spanish that the common colonists looked forward to preying on Spanish treasure ships. He may have tailored his answers to suit what he thought the Spanish wished to hear. He later was a translator for Menéndez and died of natural causes in 1568.

Spanish interrogations of several other French prisoners are of less interest and less reliable. The interrogation of Meleneche is included in Henri Ternaux-Compans, ed., *Recueil de pièces sur la Floride* ([Paris:] A. Bertrand, [1851]). Jean Memyn (or Mennin)'s interrogation contains much false testimony. It is in the papers of the French ambassador to Spain, Raimond de Beccarie de Pavie, Baron Fourquevaux, *Dépêches de M. de Fourquevaux, ambassadeur du Roi Charles IX in Espagne*, 1565–1572, vol. 1 (Paris: E. Leroux, 1896), 131-133. Stefano de Rojomonte's interrogation is in "Noticias de la población que habian heco los Franceses en la Florida, 1564," Ms. Archivo General de Indias, Seville, Patronato, est. 1, caj. 1, leg. 1/19, to. 4, p.1.

John Sparke the Younger accompanied John Hawkins on his voyage of 1564–1565 to the coast of Africa, the Caribbean, and Florida. Richard Hakluyt published his account of the voyage, "The Voyage Made by M. John Hawkins Esquire, and afterward knight, Captaine of the *Iesus of Lubek*, one of her Maiesties shippes, and General of the Saloman, and other two barkes going in his companie, to the coast of *Guinea*, and the *Indies* of Noua Hispania, begun in *An. Dom 1564*," first in R. Hakluyt, ed., *The Principall Navigations, Voiages and Discoueries of the English Nation* (London: George Bishop and Ralph Newberie, deputies to Christopher Barker, 1589), and, more conveniently, in Richard Hakluyt, ed., *The Third and Last Volvme of the Voyages, Navigations, Traffiques, and Discoueries of the English Nation* (London: George Bishop, and Ralfe Newberie, and Robert Barker, 1600), 501-521. The material relevant to Hawkins's visit to the French colony is on pp. 516-520 and contains several interesting observations.

Dominique de Gourgues wrote an account of his expedition, a condensation of which was published as "Le Voyage du Capitaine de

Gourgues dans la Floride" in Martin Basanier, ed., *L'histoire notable de la Floride sitvee es Indes occidentales, contenant les trois voyages faits en icelle par certains capitaines & pilotes francois, descrits par le Capitaine Laudonniere, qui y a commande l'espace d'vn an trois moys: a laquell* (Paris: G. Auvray, 1586). It is often mistakenly stated that this was Gourgues's account, but it is actually a condensation of his "La Repri(n)se de la Floride." Gourgues's full account survives in two manuscripts with only minor variations between them, best published in Philippe Tamizey de Larroque, ed., *La Reprise de La Floride* (Bordeaux: G. Gounouilhou, 1867). In 1587, Richard Hakluyt translated and published *A Notable Historie Containing Foure Voyages made by Certaine French Captaynes unto Florida, wherein the Great Riches and Fruitefulnes of the Countrey, with the Maners of the People, hitherto Concealed, are Brought to Light* (London: Thomas Dawson, 1587), which contains a translation of Basanier's condensation and has often been reprinted.

Spanish Sources

Pedro Menéndez de Avilés's reports to the king are sober, factual, and modest; he attributes his success to the king's planning and divine intervention. His reports are published in M. F. Navarrete, ed., "Correspondencia de Menéndes de Avilés (1565–1568)," *Colección de diareos y relations par la historia de los viajes et decubrimentos* (Madrid: Istituto Histórico de Marina, 1943) and in English translation in Henry E. Ware, trans., "Translation of Seven Letters from Pedro Menendes de Aviles to the King of Spain," *Proceedings of the Massachusetts Historical Society* 8, 2nd series (1892–94): 416-68, accessed May 2, 2020, babel.hathitrust.org/cgi/pt?id=uva.x000315630; view=1up&seq=13. Eugene Lyon, *The Enterprise of Florida: Pedro Menéndez de Avilés and the Spanish Conquest of 1565–1568* (Gainesville: University Press of Florida, repr. 1983), is based on extensive research in the Spanish archives. Lyon's work is fully documented and fundamental to any research on Menéndez and the events in Florida.

Gonzalo Solís de Méras, brother-in-law of Menéndez, was a high-ranking officer who was present during many of the events, but his memoir is self-effacing, and he does not write in the first person. It is difficult or impossible in many instances to determine if he witnessed what he reports or if he relied on what others told him. Despite minor disagreements in details, his narrative agrees with Menéndez's reports. A new and much-to-be-preferred translation based on a more-complete manuscript than previously known is David Arbesú-Fernández, ed., trans., and annot., *Pedro Menéndes de Avilés and the Conquest of Florida: A New Manuscript* (Gainesville: University Press of Florida, 2017).

Friar Francisco López Mendoza Grajales was the chaplain of Menéndez's fleet and later the first parish priest of St. Augustine. His *Memoria del buen suceso y buen viaje, que Fios Nuestra Señor fue servido de dar á la armada que salió de la cuidad de Cáliz para la provincial y cost de la Florida, de la cual fué por general il ilustre señor Pedro Menendez de Avilés, comendador de la órden de Santiago* is more generally referred to simply as *Relacion de la jornada de Pedro Menedez en la Florida*. The original text is most conveniently available in Joaquin F. Pacheco, Francisco de Cárdenas, et al., *Coleccion de Documentos Ineditos relativos al Descubrimento Conquista y Colonizacion de las Posesiones Españolas*, vol. 3 (Madrid: Manuel B. de Quirós, 1865), 441-479. It is available in translation in many sources, none particularly conveniently available in print, but one or more can be found online. The most common are Charles E. Bennett and Edward W. Lawson, trans. and ed., *Statement by Francisco Lopez de Mendoza Grajales* (Washington, DC: n.p., 1901), and B. F. French, *Historical Collections of Louisiana and Florida: including translations of original manuscripts relating to their discovery and settlement, with numerous historical and biographical notes* (New York: A. Mason, 1875), 191-234.

Genaro García, ed., *Dos antiguas relaciones de la Florida* (México: Tip. y lit. de J. Auilar vera y Comp., 1902) contains a copy of Bartolomaeus Barrientos, "Vida y hechos de Pedro Menéndez de Avilés," written in 1568 using some documents no longer extant. Andrés González de Bacia Carballido y Zúñiga, published under the pseudonym don Gabriel de Cardenas z Cano, *Ensayo cronológico, para la historia general de la Florida* (Madrid: n.p., 1723) also uses and reprints some original documents no longer extant.

Charles M. Hudson, *The Juan Pardo Expeditions: Explorations of the Carolinas and Tennessee, 1566–1568. Revised Edition with New Index. With Documents Relating to the Pardo Expeditions Transcribed, Translated, and Annotated by P.E. Hoffman* (Tuscaloosa: University of Alabama Press, 2005) contains the essential primary sources as well as the most important modern account of the Pardo expeditions. For the archaeological discovery of Joara and Pardo's fort in western North Carolina, see Robert A. Beck Jr., David G. Moore, and Christopher B. Rodning, "Identifying Fort San Juan: A Sixteenth-Century Spanish Occupation at the Berry Site, North Carolina," *Southeastern Archaeology* 25 (2006): 1:65–77, and exploringjoara.org and the linked sites, accessed May 2, 2020.

FOUR

Spanish Jesuits *in* Virginia: Ajacán Mission (1570–1572)

Background

In 1565, King Philip II of Spain appointed Pedro Menéndez de Avilés adelantado of Florida to pacify and settle the province. Menéndez was to utilize his private resources in the endeavor, although the king granted a substantial private benefice to aid the effort. Within days of his appointment, word reached the Spanish crown that the French had established a colony in Florida. With additional aid from the Spanish crown, Menéndez quickly eliminated the French interlopers and began his efforts to colonize Florida (chapter 3). As adelantado, he exercised proprietary authority that entailed both privileges and responsibilities, among which was the promotion of religion. In 1566, Menéndez, with the support of the king, persuaded the Jesuits to send their first mission to Spanish America, and during 1567, the king appointed Menéndez governor of Cuba in addition to his other responsibilities.

The first Jesuit vice provincial of Florida, Father Pedro Martinez, arrived in 1566 along with Father Juan Rogel and Brother Francisco Villareal. On the way to the port of Santa Elena (today on Parris Island, South Carolina), Father Martinez and a small group of crew members went ashore for fresh water but found themselves stranded when a storm blew their ship away from the coast. The group soon encountered Natives who killed most of them, including Father Martinez. The few survivors who escaped were eventually rescued. Rogel and Villareal continued their undertaking, initially ministering to the Spanish and attempting to win converts among the Calusa in south-central Florida but with little success. There was some resistance to Christian doctrines, although of greater importance were violent confrontations with Spanish soldiers, which so alienated the Indians of the region that the Jesuits abandoned their efforts there.

A second group of Jesuits arrived in Cuba in 1568: three priests, three brothers, and a number of servants. Jesuit intentions were both educational, to create a college at Havana in Cuba, and evangelical, to establish missions in Florida. The college would teach Indian languages to newly arrived Jesuits and educate the sons of Florida *caciques* (chiefs) and local Spanish inhabitants. It was expected that thoroughly indoctrinated Indians who had been taught at the college would then aid Jesuit evangelical work at missions. The Jesuits closely coordinated their efforts in Cuba and Florida, frequently traveling between the two, and both efforts soon encountered difficulties. The Jesuits had to rely on contributions to establish and maintain the college in Cuba, but sufficient funds were not forthcoming. Some in Havana who might have contributed resented what they saw as Menéndez de Avilés's favoritism of Florida at the expense of Cuba. Others may have felt that the cost of the college was excessive in comparison to the local benefits, and the economy of Havana simply may not have been sufficiently developed at this early date to support the college easily. The Jesuits managed to run a small school for several years, but the planned college was never realized.

After the failure among the Calusa, the Jesuits determined to found missions in the vicinity of Santa Elena. The Guale in this region were organized in chiefdoms, each ruled by a hereditary chief and family, members of which filled various posts in the community. They were also more reliant on agriculture and spent a greater portion of time in settled villages than the Indians of southern Florida. Father Rogel, believing the area offered more potential for missionary activity, began a mission in 1569, but in 1570 the Spanish at Santa Elena ran short of provisions and sent troops to confiscate food from the Indians. Rogel correctly predicted that such confiscation would be violently resisted, and he abandoned the mission before the confrontation.

Planning

In 1570, Governor Pedro Menéndez de Avilés, Jesuit Father Juan Baptista de Segura, and a Hispanicized Indian originally named Paquiquineo met in Havana to plan a new missionary endeavor among Paquiquineo's Algonquian-speaking brethren far to the north. The Spanish rendered the Native name for the intended area variously as Ajacán, Axacan, Axacam, Axaca, Xacan, Jacan, and Iacan, and it included the Chesapeake Bay, known to the Spanish as Bahia de Santa Maria. Menéndez saw that a settlement at Chesapeake Bay would expand the area of Spanish control, deny the area to enemies of Spain, and potentially even develop into an excellent Spanish port. Moreover, there was speculation that the Chesapeake Bay and rivers that fed into it might lead deep into the interior and offer a convenient route to the Pacific Ocean.

Father Segura was born and educated in Spain, where he joined the Jesuit order. He was deeply and sincerely religious, but he may have also had a personal reason to turn to missionary work, an area in which he had no experience before going to Florida in 1568. Although Segura had previously held important posts in Spain, his career had been filled with controversy, and a number of important people, including Menéndez, held reservations about his judgment and abilities. The mission would provide the opportunity for Segura to prove himself.

Before the Virginia expedition, the Native American Paquiquineo was relatively unimportant. Many of the Spanish authors who wrote about his early life did so decades later and apparently had little documentary evidence on which to base their accounts. Their narratives are confused, contradictory, and distorted by later events. All agree he came originally from the southern Chesapeake Bay area, but one author claims that Menéndez received permission from Paquiquineo's father to take him to see Philip II in Spain. Another author claims that when the Spanish took Paquiquineo, his family did not know what had become of him. Most mention Paquiquineo alone, although one tradition claims a second captive was taken with him who eventually died of illness. According to some, the Spanish realized immediately that Paquiquineo was a member of the tribal elite; in other accounts that information seems to have emerged in time. The Spanish either took Paquiquineo to Spain shortly after his capture or after a sojourn of several years in Mexico. There are differing reports about Paquiquineo's apparent age and still more inconsistencies, but it is possible to perceive a basic account among the mass of contradictions, although not all details are certain.

Most likely Antonio Velázquez rather than Menéndez first encountered Paquiquineo. In 1561, Angel de Villafañe attempted to plant a settlement at Santa Elena, but his fleet was scattered by a storm. One of his captains, Antonio Velázquez, sailed later than Villafañe's main fleet, and he too encountered a storm that blew his ship far to the north. On landing in Chesapeake Bay, Velázquez and some Dominicans encountered two Indians, Paquiquineo and another not named, whom they kidnapped to train as translators. When Velázquez attempted to return to the Caribbean, he encountered persistent adverse winds, so he sailed rather to Spain, where he exhibited Paquiquineo to Philip II. Dominicans next brought Paquiquineo to Mexico, where they taught him Spanish and converted him to Christianity. The viceroy of Mexico, Luis de Velasco, stood as godfather at his baptism, and Paquiquineo was renamed Luis de Velasco after him and accorded the honorific title "don," accorded to gentlemen. In Mexico, don Luis/Paquiquineo conversed with Mexican Indians and observed the consequences of Spanish colonialism for Native peoples. In 1566, he was supposed to serve as a translator on a missionary expedition to Ajacán with two Dominicans and thirty Spanish soldiers, but as the expedition sailed north from Florida, it encountered storms, got lost, and returned without having achieved anything. The Dominicans departed for Spain, leaving behind don Luis.

Don Luis may have first suggested to the priest Segura that the missionaries proceed to Ajacán unaccompanied by soldiers, but it was Segura who argued vociferously that just he and few religious colleagues could establish the initial mission unaided. Menéndez wanted to send a substantial number of soldiers along with Segura and the other missionaries to protect them, while Segura argued that the bad behavior of soldiers was the primary cause of the failure of earlier missions. Father Rogel, whose own missions had been disrupted by the misconduct of soldiers, nevertheless agreed with Menéndez that it was too dangerous for Segura and his compatriots to proceed without soldiers. Segura maintained they would be protected by don Luis, comparing their relationship, with obvious spiritual pride, to that of St. Paul and Timothy and St. Francis Xavier and his Japanese convert and companion Paul of Holy Faith. The practical and experienced Brother Juan de la Carrera, who was in charge of the material preparations for the mission, distrusted don Luis and argued that the costly vestments and precious liturgical vessels that Segura planned to take would tempt the Natives and endanger the missionaries, or so Carrera remembered when he wrote an account in 1600. Subsequent events may have colored his reminiscence. The Jesuit superior general, Francisco de Borja y Aragon, granted Segura considerable authority as vice provincial, and because Menéndez was beset with other concerns in Florida that demanded his immediate attention, he finally acceded to Segura's insistence that the missionary effort go forward without soldiers. The ultimate hope was that after peaceful relations were established with the Indians, the initial mission could be supplemented by more settlers, both religious and secular.

Missionary Colony

The ship carrying the missionaries sailed from Santa Elena on August 5, 1570, and arrived in Chesapeake Bay on September 10, 1570. In addition to don Luis, Segura chose eight companions: a fellow priest, Father Luis de Quirós; three Jesuit brothers, Pedro Mingot Linares, Sancho Zaballos, and Gabriel Gómez; three young men seeking admission to the order, Juan Baptista Méndez, Gabriel de Solís, and Cristóbal Redondo; and a boy about thirteen years old, Alonso de Olmos. Segura apparently soon elevated Méndez, Solís, and Redondo to the status of novices, granting them admission to the Jesuit order in recognition of their service in accompanying him. Alonso was to serve as altar boy and servant. None had experience as missionaries in the field among unconverted indigenous people. All hoped and intended to establish a mission that would save souls and begin the process that would transform the area by converting tribes into Christian Spanish colonial towns.

Virginian historians have speculated at great length without achieving consensus about the locations of the Jesuits' initial landing and their settlement that was established a few miles distant. No archeological remains have been found, nor are they likely to be; the remains of the settlement would have been slight, the region has now been heavily overbuilt, and areas have suffered from erosion. In places, riverbanks have retreated over two hundred yards. Most likely, the Jesuits landed in the southwestern area of Chesapeake Bay and established their settlement in the general vicinity of the later Jamestown and Williamsburg.

The ship that brought the missionaries remained for just a few days to unload them and their supplies. The ship's pilot (captain, in modern terms) helped the Jesuits transport the supplies from their initial landing place to the site they chose for their settlement and provided provisions and supplies from his own stores, although his ship was already low on rations. The pilot also had a chapel built for the Jesuits where they could say mass and a modest building in which they could live.

The two priests, Segura and Quirós, had the opportunity to write a generally optimistic letter to Juan de Hinistrosa, the royal treasurer of Cuba and patron of the Jesuits. The Indians had received them well, and don Luis was obedient and respectful and even sent his regards to those in Havana. There were, however, also reasons to be pessimistic. The missionaries had arrived to discover that there had been a famine for six years, many of the Indians had left the area, and although those remaining at first gave the Jesuits food, they soon indicated that they expected something in exchange. The Jesuits requested that the Spanish authorities send a shipload of grain as soon as possible.

Destruction

The ship carried the letter and perhaps others no longer extant to Havana, where the Jesuits and their supporters outfitted a ship to carry supplies to Ajacán, arriving late in spring 1571. The crew observed figures on the shore dressed in Jesuit cassocks signaling them to come ashore, but closer examination revealed they were Indians, not missionaries. Several canoes put out from shore and attacked the ship. The sailors defended themselves with the ship's guns, which had little effect, but when the canoes approached closely the crew dropped heavy ballast stones into them. The Indians retreated, but the ship's crew was able to take two prisoners; while returning to Havana one leaped overboard. The other provided ominous information. He said the missionaries were all dead except the boy Alonso and indicated that don Luis's uncle, an important chief, and other chiefs were responsible.

In 1572, Pedro Menéndez de Avilés, along with Father Rogel and Brothers Carrera and Villareal, sailed to Chesapeake Bay to discover what had happened to the missionaries, recover Alonso, and punish the perpetrators. On arriving, Menéndez dispatched a small ship with Father Rogel, the captured Indian, and thirty soldiers to look for Alonso. The ship proceeded about fifty or sixty miles from where

Menéndez anchored, the last eight or nine miles up a river to the place the Jesuits had initially landed. Indians soon approached the Spanish and after some trading departed. A second group similarly came and went. A third group consisted of a chief and his attendants, one of whom wore a silver paten obviously taken from the dead Jesuits. The Spanish seized the third group, fourteen in number, and moved downstream. Indians along the shore fired arrows at the retreating ship, wounding one soldier, while the Spanish fired arquebuses, wounding or killing several Indians.

At the mouth of the river, Indians in canoes approached Rogel and his companions peacefully to parley. The Spanish demanded the return of Alonso, and the Natives replied that he was with a chief two days' journey from there and dispatched messengers to fetch him. While waiting, Indians approached Rogel's ship in two large canoes, ostensibly bringing oysters to trade. The Spanish watchman detected or thought he detected men hiding in the canoes, and the Spanish prepared for battle, but the canoes retreated and Rogel prevented the Spanish from firing. When Alonso did not appear, Rogel's party set sail with their captives to return to Menéndez's anchorage. As they left, the soldiers, without Rogel's permission or awareness, fired a volley of arquebuses into a group of Indians gathered on shore.

When Rogel and his men returned, they discovered that the chief who held Alonso had sent him directly to Menéndez's ship. Menéndez now declared that he would hang Rogel's captives unless don Luis was turned over to him within five days, and he released one man to bear the message. When don Luis did not surrender himself, Menéndez held a trial, declared eight of the prisoners guilty of taking part in the murder of the Jesuits, and hanged them from the ship's rigging. He released the other five, and the Spanish departed from Chesapeake Bay. Don Luis, now again Paquiquineo, remained with his people.

Menéndez, Rogel, and the others learned the fate of the Jesuits from Alonso, and perhaps some additional details emerged during the interrogation of captives. Paquiquineo had remained with the Jesuits only two days. He spent about five more nights in the village near the Jesuits' settlement and then departed to live with his uncle, an important chief, a day and a half's travel distant. There he reverted to his tribal culture, and although Segura twice sent novices to Paquiquineo asking him to return, he did not. Without Paquiquineo to interpret, the Jesuits could not preach, and the Indians who initially gave food to the Jesuits stopped doing so. Throughout the winter of 1570–71, the Jesuits survived on little and had to barter their meager goods for corn in neighboring villages.

In early February 1571, Segura sent Father Quirós, Brother Solís, and Brother Méndez to Paquiquineo. Segura was ill and could not accompany them. Paquiquineo greeted them cordially, but the Jesuits lectured him publically, telling him to abandon his sinful ways and return to the religious brethren. Paquiquineo indicated he would come to the Jesuits in a few days, but as the three Jesuits were returning home, Paquiquineo and comrades ambushed and killed them. They then proceeded to the Jesuit settlement where they killed everyone except Alonso, buried the bodies, looted the little settlement, and took Alonso back to their village. It was a common practice among some Indians cultures to spare children and adopt them into the tribe.

For Rogel and the other Jesuits, the explanation of Paquiquineo's behavior was simple: he had supposedly fallen under the influence of the devil and his demons. Others offer less-transcendental explanations. Brother Carrera thought that the wealth represented by the church vessels and ecclesiastical robes tempted the Indians. Modern studies explain the massacre in terms of cultural conflict: the Jesuits thought that in Paquiquineo's society, members of the ruling class practiced polygamy, the number of wives reflecting their status, although it is possible the Jesuits misinterpreted Indian matrilineal and matrilocal practices as polygamy.

Father Quirós vigorously and publically reprimanded Paquiquineo for behavior Quirós may not have understood correctly and made demands that would have destroyed Paguiquineo's social position within his culture. The very public scolding was itself deeply offensive and presented Paquiquineo with no alternatives other than retaliation or devastating loss of status. A recent study suggests an even more subtle reason. It is clear the Jesuits did not understand the Native gift-exchange system. The Jesuits expected the indigenous peoples to give them food in appreciation of the blessings of Christianity and civilization. In contrast, Indians understood that their initial gifts of food to the Jesuits established a relationship of obligation. Subsequently, the Jesuits did not present gifts to balance the obligation but rather bargained, offering goods only in exchange for more food. In the eyes of the indigenous people, this was insulting behavior that degraded and cheapened the relationship. Similarly, the Spanish expected Paquiquineo to be grateful for all that they, in their view, had done for him, but Paquiquineo may well have harbored resentment for what he saw as kidnapping and a decade-long imprisonment among the Spanish. It is ironic that Father Segura refused to include soldiers, who would have been likely to alienate the Indians, but the Jesuits' own cultural ignorance and insensitivity proved equally alienating.

Aftermath

Menéndez hoped to return to recover the bodies of the slain Jesuits, but he died in 1574 without having done so. Subsequently the Spanish sent several naval expeditions to Chesapeake Bay to chart the coast and, still later, to investigate English settlements in the area, but they never again established a settlement in the area. The catastrophic end of the Virginia mission in 1571 and its aftermath did much to end the Jesuit efforts on the North American coast. Also important were the failure of the people of Havana to fund the Jesuit college there and the better opportunities for the Jesuit endeavors in Mexico, where they transferred their efforts before the end of 1571. Bartolomé Martínez, a minor official who wrote in 1610 about the ill-fated Virginia mission, includes a bitter comment on the failed Jesuit attempt: "The Governor, if I recall correctly, or some other official of those provinces, used to say—it was a cliché there—that these good Fathers seemed to believe that the sole purpose for which His Holiness and His Majesty and their superiors had sent them was to be martyred and cut to pieces by the savages." In Florida, Franciscans soon replaced the Jesuits. Franciscan mission colonies in north-central Florida and on the Georgia coast were for years more successful, though not without hardships and deaths, until they succumbed to outside forces (chapter 5).

Sources

Primary sources for the Virginia mission are the letter of Fathers Quirós and Segura to Juan de Hinistrosa, written at Ajacán in 1570 at the beginning of their mission, and Father Rogel's letter to Francis Borgia, head of the Jesuit order, written in 1572 describing the just-completed voyage that rescued the boy Alonso and containing the earliest report of the information he provided. David Beers Quinn, trans. and ed., *New American World: A Documentary History of North America in 1612*, vol. 2 (New York: Arno Press, 1979), 557-561, contains translations of both letters.

Subsequent sources are all later and influenced by the vagaries of memory, legendary accretions, hagiographic stereotypes, and hostility toward Paquiquineo, who is often compared to Judas. The first printed account of the Virginia mission appeared in Pedro de Ribadeneyra, *Vida del Padre Francisco de Borja, Tercer General de la Campañía de Jesús* (Madrid: Pedro Madrigal, 1593). The account is short but already incorporated legendary material: three Indians were supposedly struck dead when they attempted to break into a box containing sacred vestments and a crucifix. In 1600, Brother Juan de la Carrera, a companion of Rogel's on the 1572 voyage, wrote an account that also incorporated the tale of the Indians struck dead. Father Juan Rogel wrote an account between 1607 and 1611, but that survives only in a paraphrase of Father Juan Sánchez Vaquero. This account also includes the story of the three Indians struck dead. Bartolomé Martínez, a minor Spanish official, also wrote an account of the Virginia mission. Martínez once lived in Florida, where he knew Alonso de Olmos, the sole survivor of the Ajacán mission. Olmos was a child at the time of the Ajacán mission and was not a witness to Paquiquineo's initial contact or early years with the Spanish, but he was the principal source of the events in Virginia. Olmos grew up to be a soldier and resided for some years at Santa Elena, where he recounted the story of his adventure many times, apparently amplifying it as time passed. For example, Martínez wrote that Olmos reported that the martyred Jesuits were buried by heavenly angels. Martínez also relied on accounts generally circulating at Santa Elena, but street gossip is seldom accurate and never unbiased. Moreover, Martínez wrote his account in 1610, forty years after the events he narrated, while living at Potosi (in modern Bolivia), far from Florida and any documents he might have consulted there. Martínez primarily relied on his memories of accounts of then-distant events, which would explain why his narrative contains many fundamental errors involving geography, dates, names, and events. His account is primarily interesting for the fictional elaborations and distortions that quickly became part of the narrative tradition.

Luis Jerónimo de Oré y Rojas, *Relación de los mártires que avido en las prouincias de la Florida; doze Religiosos de la Compañia de Iesus, que padecieron en el Iacana y cinco de la Orden de nuestro Serafico P.S. Franciso, en la Provincia de Guale. Ponese assi mesmo la discripion de Iacan, donde se an fortificado los Ingeses, y de otras cosas tocates a la conuersion de los Indios* (Madrid[?]: n.p., ca. 1617) is an extremely rare work, with only two original copies known to survive, although it has been reprinted several times—P. Atanasio López, ed., prologue, and notes, *Relación histórica de la Floride, escrita en el siglo XVII*, vol. 1 (Madrid: Impr. de Ramona Velasco, viuda de P. Perez, 1931); and Raquel Chang-Rodríguez, ed., *Relación de los mátires de la Florida de P.F. Luis Jerónimo de Oré (c. 1619)* (Lima: Fondo Editorial de la Pontifica Universidad Católica de Peru, 2014)— and in English translation, Raquel Chang-Rodríguez, ed., N. J. Vogeley, trans., *Account of the Martyrs in the Provinces of la Florida* (Albuquerque: University of New Mexico Press, 2017). Oré's account is long, detailed, and well written, and consequently he has been followed by many modern writers, despite many obvious inaccuracies. For example, Oré claims twelve priests were martyred at Ajacán, rather than nine men, only two of whom were priests, and Oré's dates are wrong by ten years. Similar examples could be cited at length. Oré composed his account about 1617, forty-five years after the events. He reports he had met Juan de Lara, the brother of Alonso de Olmos, whom he calls Alonso de Lara, and a soldier who had been on the expedition of 1572, but otherwise he had no access to witnesses. Oré is the latest writer with any claim of original information, though his work better illustrates the evolution of inaccurate oral traditions about the events.

All these and other less significant works are gathered in Felix Zubillaga, *Monumenta antiquae Floridae, 1566–1572,* Monumenta Historica Societatis Iesu 69, Monumenta Missionum Societatis Iesu 3 (Rome: Monumenta Historica Societatis Iesu, 1946), and more conveniently along with English translations in Clifford Merle Lewis and Albert J. Loomie, *The Spanish Jesuit Mission in Virginia, 1570–1572* (Chapel Hill: University of North Carolina Press, 1953). This is an excellent work, although the authors, both Jesuits, see events entirely from the Jesuit point of view. For a much more nuanced though perhaps excessively speculative view of don Luis de Velasco/Paquiquineo, see Anna Brickhouse, *The Unsettlement of America: Translation, Interpretation, and the Story of Don Luis de Velasco* (Oxford: Oxford University Press, 2015).

In addition to original sources, Saber Gray, "'I Do Not Know How to Fulfill These Demands': Rethinking Jesuit Missionary Efforts in *La Florida*, 1566–1572" (MA thesis, University of South Florida St. Petersberg, 2014) should be particularly noted. Her work effectively describes the mutual dependence of Jesuit endeavors in Cuba and Florida.

FIVE

Spanish Mission Colonies *of* *the* Georgia Coast (1580s–1684)

Background

The first small group of Franciscans arrived in Florida in 1573, shortly after the departure of the Jesuits (chapter 4). They were initially active at Santa Elena, the settlement established by Pedro Menéndez de Avilés at the site of the destroyed French colony of Charlesfort, on Parris Island, South Carolina, where they encountered the same problems the Jesuits had experienced: Spanish soldiery and Menéndez's officials alienated Indians, making any attempt at proselytization virtually impossible. Moreover, by 1575, all was chaos in Florida. Menéndez had died, his heirs were quarreling over the inheritance, the governor and other officials at Santa Elena were corrupt, the colonists were discouraged, and relations between the Indians and Spanish were rapidly moving toward open warfare. When the Franciscans sought to leave the colony, the governor refused permission. Nevertheless, the Franciscans managed to find passage on a privately owned ship, but they were never heard from again, assumed to have been lost at sea.

In 1576, a general revolt swept through Guale, the coastal region of northern Georgia and the area around Santa Elena. The colonists fled by ship to San Agustín, and the Guale Indians burned Santa Elena. Two years later, Spanish soldiers returned to Santa Elena to reestablish the burnt fort, and by 1580 they had brutally suppressed the revolt, and a substantial number of settlers returned to a rebuilt Santa Elena.

The Franciscan Missions

Franciscans came again to Florida in 1577 and 1587. In addition to ministering to the Spanish, they gradually managed to make converts and organize mission communities among the Indians closest to San Agustín. The concentration of previously dispersed villages into larger communities and frequent interaction with the Spanish led to the spread of diseases and the decline in Indian population in the vicinity. After 1606, the Franciscans began to establish missions inland among the Timucua of northern Florida. The missions gradually extended inland across the northern portion of the peninsula throughout Timucua territory and deep into Apalachee. A document of 1655 listed the names of thirty-eight missions in northern Florida. The Franciscans looked on the expanding area of missionary activity as the opportunity to save souls, while secular Spanish authorities saw the opportunity to recruit new sources of Indian labor.

Spanish authorities required missionary settlements to send men to San Agustín annually. There they would labor from March through September in the fields to feed the garrison or work to maintain and improve the fortifications and then return to their communities. This repartimiento system exposed Indians to a variety of European diseases brought to San Agustín by the frequent visits of ships from Europe, the Caribbean, and Mexico. Returning laborers carried diseases with them to the mission settlements, where, as earlier near San Agustín, the concentration of people facilitated their spread and lethality, and the population of the mission colonies declined precipitously. In northern Florida, the number of missions waned as the population declined, and missions moved to new locations as settlement patterns of the surviving population changed.

The Franciscans also planted missionary colonies along the Georgia coast among the Mocama and Guale. The Mocama were part of the Timucuan people who lived throughout northern Florida and along the southern Georgia coast. They had been initially hostile to the Spanish during the 1560s but made peace in the 1570s. The Guale to the north were a separate people who spoke a different language and were frequently at war with the Mocama. In dealing with the Mocama and Guale, the Franciscans resolved to avoid the conflicts created by the interactions of Spanish troops and Indians; they created mission colonies by themselves without the presence of soldiers. Such an attempt by the Jesuits had failed miserably in Virginia, but the Franciscans fared better, though not without setbacks. Franciscans usually sent a single friar to initiate a mission and never more than a few. In addition to establishing and serving at the mission, a friar would often also attend to *visitas*, chapels in villages lacking resident friars.

The Franciscans' first successful mission on the Georgia coast was San Pedro de Mocama, quickly followed by San Juan del Puerto, both established in the 1580s. By 1595, the Franciscans had established five more missions in the villages of the Guale, but in 1597, the missionary effort received a severe setback when the Guale again erupted in revolt. The Guale burnt missions and clerical residences and slaughtered four friars and one brother. One friar, Fray Francisco de Ávila, was wounded, abused, and kept as a slave for ten months before he was rescued. In retribution, the Spanish governor led an expedition that destroyed several Guale villages and drove the Guale inland. Over the course of several years, the Spanish made peace with many of the Guale, and don Domingo, a Guale cacique who led a force of Guale friendly to the Spanish, finally ended the rebellion in 1601. Don Domingo's men killed the paramount chief of the Guale, don Francisco, his heir don Juan, and the entire ruling family.

Most modern accounts of the Guale uprising follow more or less the Spanish accounts written long after the event despite inherently unreliable aspects of their narratives, such as an invented speech supposedly by don Juan and fictional details of the deaths of the friars derived from traditional martyrology. The Spanish accounts portray the events entirely as a rebellion against the friars and their Christian teachings led by don Juan (Juanillo) of Tolomato, heir to the paramount chiefdom of Guale. Recently, J. M. Francis and K. M. Kole have challenged the traditional account, pointing out that don Juan was not even mentioned in contemporary documents until the final battle that crushed the rebellion and that there are elements that do not accord with a simple revolt against the missions, such as the burning of the residences and council houses of certain caciques along with the missions. Antagonism toward the missionaries and Christian doctrines emerge as just one factor in something like a Guale civil war that resulted in the destruction of the traditional hierarchy and a major realignment of power in Guale society. It was convenient for the Guale and the administrators who had to report back to Spain to blame the revolt on the dead don Juan and his supposed hostility toward Christianity. Franciscan missionary activity in Guale resumed, peacefully, in 1604.

Conversion to Christianity was usually a gradual process, beginning with the erection of a cross and teaching reverence for it, proceeding to explanation of the Christian faith and worship, and then catechism instruction leading to baptism. Conversion involved basic changes in aboriginal culture. Missionaries abolished divorce, banned indigenous healing rituals and dances, and discouraged traditional games and amusements, which usually involved gambling. Missionaries also introduced other elements of Spanish civilization, a gradual process over decades. At baptism and sometimes even before, Indians acquired Christian Spanish names. Men cut their long hair to short Spanish style, and men and women gradually altered their dress. Spanish farmers introduced new animals such as horses and oxen, new fruits and vegetables, and agricultural technology such as the plow. Artisans familiarized Indians with innovative weaving techniques and taught skills such as carpentry, masonry, and metal working. Some Spanish men married Native women. Initially the Spanish missionaries learned Native languages, but gradually the Spanish language began to spread, often first among the traditional leadership. Christian teachings, prohibition of intertribal wars, and the establishment of Spanish-controlled militias all combined to supplant old warrior values. Spanish policy generally prohibited giving weapons to Indians, but in the course of the seventeenth century some acquired guns, strengthening the local militias. Eventually a small garrison was placed at the central mission of the two provinces, and soldiers could be sent from San Agustín, but these extraordinary actions were only occasioned by acute crises.

Neither the Spanish administrators nor the Franciscan missionaries attempted to abolish the traditional leaderships of chiefdoms in Mocama and Guale, but rather both sought to bolster their authority while Hispanicizing the leaders and their children. Spanish administrators at San Agustín provided presents, primarily extravagant clothes and iron tools, to friendly and compliant chiefs to enhance their status and bond them closely to the Spanish. Sons of caciques were often brought to San Agustín and even to Havana for education and indoctrination. Over decades, a Native chiefdom insensibly evolved into a typical Spanish colonial community (pueblo). This transformation was completed when secular town government (*cabildo*), the Catholic diocesan church, and a military post (*presidio*)—the three basic elements of Spanish colonial society—superseded the mission status and replaced or incorporated the remnant of the old hereditary tribal leadership. The mission colonies of Mocama and Guale were destroyed during the long evolutionary process before they developed to this ultimate stage of thorough indoctrination.

There is relatively little information about the mission colonies between 1604 and 1661. In 1702, the English attacked San Agustín, and although the fortress held out, the English burned much of the town, including the Franciscan convent and its records. Still, those sources that do survive reveal several trends. By 1655, ten prosperous mission colonies had been established among the Mocama and Guale. As in northern Florida, Spanish authorities required the missionary settlements on the Georgia coast to send laborers to San Agustín, who carried diseases when they returned to their communities, leading to a general decline in population. The gradual indoctrination and conversion of the Indians continued, but at the same time the traditional Native leadership patterns and families continued to remain strong in Mocama and Guale. Particular instances of corruption among Spanish government and church officials stunted to some degree the Spanish indoctrination of the indigenous peoples and the development of the mission communities, such as a corrupt governor who did nothing to stop a cattle rancher who intruded into land reserved for the Indians, and church officials who were slow to remove priests who physically abused Native people.

Slave Raiders

In 1661, a tribe previously unknown to the Spanish descended the Santa Isabel River (modern Altamaha River), attacked, and overwhelmed the mission village of Santo Domingo de Talaje. The Spanish called the tribe Chichimeco after a similarly fierce tribe known to them in the Zacatecas region of Mexico. Survivors of the assault fled to San Joseph de Sapala on the nearby barrier island. The Chichimeco attempted to follow, building makeshift boats from the wood of the mission and the friar's residence, but it soon became apparent that the Chichimeco knew little about the ocean. A current drew the boats out to sea where they foundered, reportedly drowning seventy Chichimeco. On the mainland, the Guale counterattacked the Chichimeco, who began to retreat up the Santa Isabel River. Spanish soldiers, whom the governor at San Agustín sent as soon as news of the attack reached him, followed the retreat and inflicted a few more

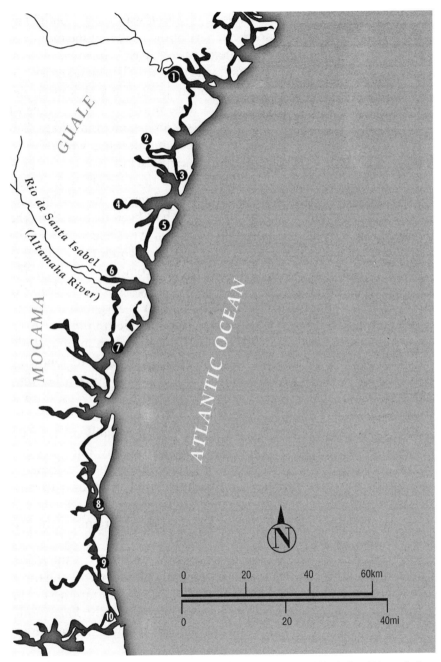

Principal Spanish missions to the Guale and Mocama, ca. 1655. 1. San Diego de Satuache? 2. San Philipe de Alave? 3. Santa Catalina de Guale. 4. Santa Clara de Tupiqui. 5. San Joseph de Sapala. 6. Santo Domingo de Talaje. 7. San Buenaventura de Guadalquini. 8 San Pedro de Mocama. 9. Santa Maria. 10. San Juan del Puerto.

casualties. Santo Domingo de Talaje, however, was never rebuilt. The survivors relocated to the northern part of the island by the mouth of the San Isabel River, on which the most northerly Mocama mission, San Buenaventura de Guadalquini, was located. Their new settlement was called Santo Domingo de Asajo. In 1662, the Chichimeco destroyed a substantial Native town a little north of the province of Guale. In fear, the population of the northernmost mission village, San Diego de Satuache, abandoned their community and withdrew to Santa Catalina de Gaule, located on a barrier island.

The Chichimeco, known as the Westo to the English, were recent immigrants to the southeast. Anthropologists suggest the Chichimeco/ Westo were descendants of the Erie who had been displaced to the south by the Iroquoians. An English colonist who visited one of the Chichimeco villages described it as a palisaded community of bark-covered longhouses decorated with long poles from which scalps hung, all characteristics of the northern Native villages. In their trek to the south, the Chichimeco encountered the English in Virginia.

At first unfriendly, the Chichimeco soon became trading partners, exchanging slaves and deerskins for English guns, ammunition, cloth, and other goods. The Chichimeco ignored Guale in the years following their unsuccessful attack, but rather in alliance with other tribes they extensively raided chiefdoms to the east and north for slaves to trade to the English. The foundation of Charles Town in 1670 brought the English close to Guale and Mocama. The Spanish initially made an ineffective attempt by sea to eliminate the English colony, but otherwise for nearly a decade the English and Spanish colonies did not confront one another directly. Rather, each sought to build alliances with various tribal groups. The Westo reached an accord with the English at Charles Town in 1674, and Charles Town replaced Virginia as the primary market for the Chichimeco slave trade.

The English retained only a relatively small number of the slaves traded from the Westo. Native men were difficult to control and often attempted to escape. The English sold most to plantations in the Caribbean and imported African slaves in their place, who knew nothing of their new surroundings and any refuges to which they might escape.

The slave raids of the Chichimeco and their allies disrupted Native tribal structures over a broad area, leading to flight, migration, and the formation of new coalitions. Refugees fleeing from the Chichimeco slave raids, who were known collectively as the Yamassee, petitioned the Spanish authorities and received permission to enter the Guale and Mocama provinces. The Guale and Mocama had so declined in number that the missionary provinces were underpopulated and land was abundantly available. The refugees increased the number of men available for the annual labor draft and augmented the province's potential for defending against the Chichimeco, and missionaries anticipated that their new access to the Yamassee would result in conversions. The Yamassee migration, begun in the 1660s, persisted well into the 1670s, and throughout this period the threat of the Chichimeco raids remained real and terrifying. During this period, the Mocama abandoned the two smallest of their missionary villages, San Pedro de Mocama and Santa Maria, perhaps simply because the population had fallen so low that the sites were indefensible. Their populations migrated to the larger missions, and the more numerous Yamassee settled at the abandoned sites. About 1670, the Gaule mission San Phelipe de Alve withdrew to an island south of where the Mocama mission San Buenaventura de Guadalquini had long been established. The new settlement was known as San Phelipe de Atuluteca. Before 1675, Santa Clara de Tupiqui also abandoned its mainland position to merge with San Joseph de Sapala on a barrier island.

Great changes took place in 1680. The Chichimeco allied with two other tribes, the Chiluque and Uchise, previously friendly to the Spanish, and attacked Guale. By this time the Chichimeco had mastered the basic use of boats, and they first launched a probing attack on a Yamassee town at the northern end of Guadalquini Island. The mission Santa Catalina de Guadalquini, on the same island, had for some years been the home of a modest garrison and the strongest position in Guale and Mocama. When the garrison hurried to the defense of the Yamassee town, the Chichimeco and their allies withdrew, but shortly thereafter they suddenly attacked Santa Catalina de Guadalquini itself. An estimated three hundred Chichimeco and allies assaulted the town at dawn, killing five of the six sentries. The commanding officer, Captain Francisco de Fuentes, was able to get to the friars' residence along with five Spanish soldiers and forty Christian Guale, including women and children. Although it had long been Spanish policy to deny guns even to friendly Indians, the situation of the coastal missions demanded a more pragmatic approach, and sixteen of the Christian Guale had guns. Fighting from behind the palisade that surrounded the residence, Fuentes and his small force held off the Chichimeco until the late afternoon, when the Chichimeco withdrew, burning the town behind them. The survivors of Santa Catalina de Guadalquini retreated south to San Joseph de Sapala, and when Spanish authorities attempted to get the inhabitants to return to Santa Catalina, they refused, threatening to commit mass suicide rather than return. Santa Catalina remained in ruins.

After the destruction of Santa Catalina, only five mission towns survived of the ten that existed just fifteen years earlier: San Joseph de Sapala, Santo Domingo de Asajo, San Buenaventura de Gaudalquini, San Phelipe de Atuluteca, and San Juan del Puerto. Two, Santo Domingo and San Phelipe, were no longer at their original sites, having relocated far to the south. Refugees from the destroyed mission villages fled mainly to the surviving missions, where they strove to retain their separate village identities and hereditary leadership even while amalgamated into one community. All of the surviving mission villages were then located on the barrier islands; the missions had abandoned the mainland, as had many of the Guale, Mocama, and Yamassee.

During the late 1670s, the relationship between the English and the Chichimeco/Westo deteriorated. The Westo sought to exclude other Native tribes from direct trade with Charles Town in order to benefit from their position as middlemen and to prevent tribes they victimized from acquiring firearms to resist their raids. The Westo even raided tribes friendly to the Carolinians. The proprietary government of the colony, largely composed of men who benefitted from trade with the Westo, were generally satisfied with the situation, but wealthy plantation owners and traders who wished to expand their business came to regard the Westo as a liability. They secretly armed the Savannah, a group of Shawnee who had migrated to the Savannah River area, and, in 1680, the Savannah virtually destroyed the Westo. The surviving Westo became refugees and soon disappeared as a distinct people, last mentioned in the early eighteenth century. That did not end English-sponsored slave raiding. The Savannah and other tribes carried on the destructive trade for the English.

Pirates

The surviving Spanish mission communities retreated to the islands, where it was easier to defend themselves from slave raiders, but a new sort of enemy now appeared against whom the islands offered no protection. At the end of April 1683, pirates commanded by the notorious

Michel de Grammont captured the guard post at Matanzas, south of San Agustín, but before they could reach San Agustín itself, Spanish troops repulsed them with losses. Grammont sailed north, sacking and devastating the mission towns of San Juan del Puerto and San Phelipe de Atuluteca. The pirates so thoroughly looted the towns that they even stole the mission bells. Grammont also seems to have attacked several Yamassee villages. In years past, the Yamassee had also moved in substantial numbers to the barrier islands along the coast of Guale and Mocama, but now they were quick to realize that the island communities were virtually defenseless against seaborne attacks. Within a month the Yamassee fled, reducing the population of the two missionary provinces by half. Many of the Yamassee apparently moved north in an attempt to make an alliance with the English, while others fled far inland.

In 1683, the Spanish government concluded that the remaining Guale and Mocama were too few and too far separated to defend against pirate attacks, so the administrators made plans to move the missionary Indians to the south, where the five remaining mission villages would be reduced to three, all settled close to one another to facilitate defense. One village was to be established in the old abandoned site of Santa Maria, another on the abandoned site of San Pedro de Mocama, and the third at the site of San Juan del Puerto. By early autumn 1684, the resettlement plans were well advanced, but they would never be completed.

In 1684, a fleet of eleven pirate ships massed for an assault on San Agustín, but a storm dispersed them before the attack could take place. Six of the ships regrouped under a captain whose name the Spanish rendered as Thomas Jingle, relying on the testimony of a Flemish witness speaking in English to a Spanish notary. A modern scholar suggests the name may actually have been Hinkley; another suggestion is a pirate who sailed under the name Captain Yankey.

In early October, Captain Jingle's six ships moved north, making various landings in search of provisions and loot. Pirates sacked and burned the missions and the settlements of Santo Domingo de Asajo and San Buenaventura de Gaudalquini, and at least looted San Joseph de Sapala. As word of the depredations spread, the mission Indians, who had been moving their possessions to the south, fled to the mainland. Some joined the Yamassee far inland, while others moved south to the Spanish.

In just twenty-three years, 1661–1684, slave raiders and pirates destroyed the mission colonies of the Georgia coast. The English of Virginia and Charles Town supplied the Westo with guns and bought the slaves they kidnapped. Charles Town also welcomed the pirates, English and French, who preyed on the Spanish missions and provided a ready market for their loot. In 1684, Scots established a colony called Stuarts Town by the site of the abandoned Spanish town of Santa Elena in territory still claimed by Spain, yet another provocation. In 1686, the Spanish launched a retaliatory naval expedition. They managed to burn the Scottish colony and sacked English plantations near Charles Town, but a hurricane disrupted the expedition and no substantial damage was done to Charles Town. The expedition was too little and too late to defend the Spanish mission colonies of the Georgia coast. How differently Georgia might have developed if Spain had risen to the defense of the mission settlements and the English colonials had been less voracious.

Aftermath

The Spanish established three refugee Guale villages in Florida: Santa Maria, Santa Clara de Tupiqui, and San Phelipe, in close proximity on the island where Santa Maria had stood in 1655. San Juan del Puerto remained on the island by the mouth of the Rio de San Juan (modern St. Johns River), and a new village of Santa Cruz y San Buenaventura de Gaudalquini grew up on the mainland near the mouth of the Rio de San Juan. The population of the five villages was small. In the mid-1690s, the inhabitants of Santa Cruz y San Buenaventura de Gaudalquini moved to the less-exposed San Juan del Puerto for protection, and in 1699, Native leaders stated that the three island villages, the remnant of the entire province of Guale, were home to just a hundred men and a number of women and children. In 1702, the English looted and burned the three Guale island villages while on their way to attack San Agustín. The survivors fled to San Juan del Puerto, and within a month the entire remaining population of the missions of Guale and Mocama, about four hundred men, woman, and children, moved to San Agustín, where they settled in villages in the immediate vicinity.

The northern Florida missions in Timucua and Apalachee suffered a similar fate. English-allied tribes sometimes accompanied by English colonists devastated and burned missions, killed some inhabitants, and carried off others as slaves. Survivors and panicked inhabitants of missions not yet attacked abandoned their settlements and fled, some west to the French, some inland, others to San Agustín where they joined the refugees from Guale and Mocama. The last few descendants withdrew with the Spanish to Cuba in 1763, where they merged with the general population.

English-sponsored slave raiding continued throughout the late seventeenth century, ranging as far south as southern Florida and west as far as the Mississippi River valley. These slave raids decimated Native communities, forcing Indians to abandon traditional scattered, open villages to live in compact, palisaded communities. Such settlements were less sanitary and conducive to the ready spread of disease. The concentration of Native communities and the intense interaction and movement of European traders, slave raiders, captives, and refugees set the stage for the immensely destructive Great Southeast Smallpox Epidemic of 1690–1700 and subsequent endemic diseases that killed immense numbers. Entire communities and even entire tribes vanished, and surviving groups suffered losses commonly ranging from 60 to 80 percent and some even higher. So many died that by 1715, the English trade in Native American slaves collapsed. Too few remained in the Southeast to make slave raiding profitable.

Sources

John E. Worth, *The Struggle for the Georgia Coast,* New Edition (Tuscaloosa: University of Alabama Press, 2007) has rendered virtually all previous work on the decline and fall of the coastal missions obsolete. In addition to clear and persuasive narrative from the Spanish perspective, Worth's book includes translation of a wealth of Spanish documents that form the basis of his work and an extensive bibliography of all primary sources. Also of fundamental importance are Worth's *The Timucuan Chiefdoms of Spanish Florida,* 2 vols. (Gainesville: University Press of Florida, 1998), and J. E. Hann and Jerald T. Milanich, *A History of the Timucua Indians and Missions* (Gainesville: University Press of Florida, 1996).

The works of the Franciscan Fray Luis Jerónimo de Oré y Rojas, *Relación de los mártires que avido en las prouincias de la Florida; doze Religiosos de la Compañia de Iesus, que padecieron en el Iacana y cinco de la Orden de nuestro Serafico P.S. Francisco, en la Provincia de Guale. Ponese assi mesmo la discripion de Iacan, donde se an fortificado los Ingeses, y de otras cosas tocates a la conuersion de los In-*

dios (Madrid [?]: n.p., ca. 1617) and Andrés González de Barcía Caballido y Zúñiga, *Ensayo cronológico para la historia general de la Florida* (Madrid: Nicolas Rodriguez Franco, 1723) are the basic sources of the traditional account of the Guale rebellion of 1597 as a revolt against the Franciscan missionaries. Both were written long after the uprising by authors who had no part in the events. Their narrative had been effectively challenged by J. M. Francis and K. M. Kole, *Murder and Martyrdom in Spanish Florida: Don Juan and the Guale Uprising of 1597* (New York: American Museum of Natural History, 2011), who interpret the events as a much more complex power struggle of which the murder of the Franciscans was only one part. Francis and Kole include in their work translations of the significant contemporary documents.

SIX

La Salle's Accidental Colony *in* Spanish Texas (1685–1689)

Background

In 1685, the French attempted to establish a colony at the mouth of the Mississippi River, but they actually landed on the coast of Texas. Disaster followed, and any account of that tragedy must begin with the founder and leader of the colony, René-Robert Cavelier, Sieur de la Salle. La Salle was born in 1643 at Rouen in the Normandy region of France. He joined the Jesuits, taking initial orders in 1660, but he did not submit readily to the obedience and renunciation of autonomy required of a Jesuit. He resigned from the order in 1667 before taking final vows. Under French law, La Salle's entrance into a religious order deprived him of the right of inheritance even though he later abandoned it. La Salle's experiences with the Jesuits permanently estranged him from the order, and he subsequently supported other Catholic orders that competed vigorously for resources and power with the Jesuits.

Shortly before La Salle left the Jesuits in 1666, he migrated to Canada, where he had well-established relatives who helped him get a fresh start. The Seminary of St. Sulpice, rivals of the Jesuits, gave La Salle a grant of land on the frontier near Montréal, which he improved by erecting buildings, attracting settlers, and promoting agriculture, while at the same time trading in furs and learning the Iroquois language. The Iroquoians told La Salle of a great river in the west that flowed far to the south, the Mississippi, a river that La Salle realized might offer the long-sought Northwest Passage, a navigable route to the Pacific and the riches of the Orient. Even if that did not prove to be true, the river could open new lands where furs were abundant, and an expedition there would strengthen French land claims on the North American continent, winning governmental and even royal favor.

La Salle sold his improved land grant and used the funds together with money from fur trading to outfit his first expedition in 1669. For the next twelve years, La Salle repeatedly went on expeditions as far west as Illinois, exploring and attempting to establish bases for profitable fur trade. He frequently had to return to Canada to obtain supplies, raise money, reassure investors, and fend off critics. La Salle even traveled to France on several occasions to gain support for his efforts. Despite La Salle's intense activity, none of his endeavors had produced a substantial profit, and by 1681 he was deeply in debt. Others, Louis Jolliet (also spelled Joliet) and the Jesuit priest Jacques Marquette, reached the Mississippi before La Salle, but they did not travel down the entire length of the river. That was to be La Salle's achievement.

La Salle was a man who attracted friends as diverse as the Shawnee Nika, who became his loyal and constant companion, and Henri de Tonty, his trusted collaborator. Tonty's military career in Europe had been terminated when a wound cost him the loss of a hand, but equipped with an iron substitute, he became a valuable aide to La Salle and an important explorer in his own right. La Salle also made enemies. He consistently supported religious orders in competition with the Jesuits, and his activities threatened the Jesuits' profitable fur trade. He quarreled with government officials who favored the economic development of the Canadian lands already settled and opposed his efforts to expand to the west.

Friends and enemies agreed that La Salle was determined, brave, intelligent, hardworking, visionary, and repeatedly able to charm Indian tribes and French investors to trust and favor him, but he was also frequently aloof, moody, suspicious, given to petty jealousies, loath to accept advice, and plagued by episodes of deep depression. He secured the favor and support of some important men but profoundly alienated others, and as years passed without profits, investors turned hostile. La Salle was at his best in the wilderness with a few companions who found him to be resolute and inspirational, and at his worst when trying to command large groups to whom he appeared cold and dictatorial. He alienated subordinates by his obsessive determination to control every detail, even in matters where he was woefully unqualified.

Late in 1681, La Salle set out to explore the length of the Mississippi. He traveled from Montréal and through the Great Lakes to the future site of Chicago, from which he portaged to waterways that took him to the Illinois River. He and his companions—consisting of French and Indians, including the warriors' wives and children—dragged sleds loaded with equipment and provisions over the frozen river until open water was finally encountered near modern Peoria, where they were able to use their canoes. La Salle chose to travel in the early winter because the tribes had not yet departed from their villages for the winter hunt and he needed to trade with them for food.

At the confluence of the Illinois and Mississippi Rivers, the expedition paused briefly, waiting for the ice on the Mississippi to break up, but after that its progress was rapid. A little north of the current site of Memphis, La Salle established a base, Fort Prudhomme, and left several men there as he proceeded south. Near the mouth of the Arkansas River, La Salle's party encountered the Quapaw and spent a pleasant few days in their village. Proceeding still farther south, the voyage became difficult. They had entered swampy country, the bayous of Louisiana and then the Mississippi Delta. Dry land was rare, alligator became their daily fare, and the river divided into three channels; as it was apparent that they must be near the ocean, La Salle sent parties to explore each. Finally, early in April 1682, La Salle's party reached the mouth of the river and the sea. La Salle remained in the vicinity of the Mississippi's mouth only long enough to erect a cross and inscription claiming the area in the name of Louis XIV, make a few sketch maps, and calculate the latitude. At that time there was still no way for him to calculate the longitude accurately, and La Salle could only make a very approximate estimate, one that haunted him in subsequent years.

Preparations

La Salle returned to Canada and then sailed for France and the royal court to seek permission and support to found a colony on the Mississippi near the mouth of the river. He allied with two rich and powerful clerics, Abbé Eusèbe Renaudot and Abbé Claude Bernou, men who knew whom to approach and how to win the court's favor. La Salle originally envisioned the colony as the key to opening the American interior to French traders and settlers, but his influential friends indicated the French crown was little interested in such a proposal. Influential factions in court opposed further expansion in North America and argued resources ought rather to be used to develop areas already settled. The king and court, however, would be more interested in a colony that could be used to threaten rich Spanish holdings in Mexico. This idea was not entirely new; it had been mentioned in years past, but now it began to assume a much greater role in La Salle's search for support. Abbé Bernou introduced La Salle to Diego de Peñalosa, an embittered Spanish exile who sought support for a scheme to seize the Spanish town at the mouth of the Rio Bravo (Rio Grande) as a base for the French conquest of the silver-rich northern province of Mexico, Nueva Vizcaya (New Biscay). La Salle declined to join his plans to those of Peñalosa, but he adapted Peñalosa's rhetoric to his own cause.

With Renaudot's aid, La Salle submitted several proposals to Jean-Baptiste-Antoine Colbert, Marquis de Seignelay, minister of state. La Salle's plan called for the foundation of a new French colony on good and fertile land some distance north of the mouth of the Mississippi, arguing that the colony would guarantee the French right of possession to the entire watershed of the Mississippi in accordance with recognized international law and would become a center for profitable trade with the Indian tribes of the interior. The very existence of the colony would disconcert Spain, and in case of open war, which seemed imminently probable, La Salle proposed to command an attack of French colonists and as many as fifteen thousand Indians against Nueva Vizcaya. Peñalosa would raid the coast with buccaneers from Saint Dominique (modern Haiti). La Salle anticipated the final conquest would be facilitated by an Indian uprising against the Spanish. This bizarre plan relied on a multitude of assumptions, among which was a profound misunderstanding of the location of the mouth of the Mississippi.

La Salle thought the Mississippi entered the Gulf of Mexico far to the west of its actual position, close to the Spanish settlements in Nueva Vizcaya. Seventeenth-century estimates of longitudes in the Americas in general were wildly inaccurate. For instance, La Salle had to rely on a chart that placed Saint Dominque 150 miles west of its true position. Perhaps La Salle's conclusion that the mouth of the Mississippi lay far to the west was also strengthened by wishful thinking. He needed royal patronage, and that depended on the idea that the colony could threaten Spanish holdings in northern Mexico.

La Salle and his comrades submitted three memoirs to the royal court before they received a royal commission in spring 1684, appointing him commander "in the lands which will be newly subjected under our dominion in North America, from Fort Saint-Louis on the river of Illinois to New Biscay." La Salle immediately set to work to bring together the people and materials for his colonizing venture. His first need was money. Here the king's commission worked wonders, and La Salle was able to raise large loans despite his outstanding debts. He also had at his disposal four ships. The largest was *Le Joly*, a thirty-six-gun ship, which was to act as an escort and transport until La Salle landed and later return to France. *L'Aimable* was a medium-sized cargo ship chartered to carry much of the heavy materials for the colony. The *St. Françoise*, a ketch that La Salle chartered, carried trade goods and provisions. Finally, there was *La Belle*, a small barque carrying just six cannons, a gift of Louis XIV to La Salle.

The proposed colony consisted of about 280 people. Among them were those vital to the initial establishment of the colony, such as sailors, carpenters, blacksmiths, and farmers, but also among the company were merchants, wives, children, clergy, unmarried orphan girls of marriageable age, and refined gentlemen with no skills. All would eventually be required to form a functional colonial community, but the wisdom of bringing nonessential personnel on the initial expedition may be doubted. They constituted a drain on the provisions and resources and contributed little at this early stage of settlement. Also among the colonists were about a hundred soldiers, young recruits with little training, no experience, and few skills. Many had never fired a gun. Clearly, La Salle had no immediate plans to move against Spanish holdings in Nueva Vizcaya. Two particularly able members of the expedition were Nika, La Salle's Shawnee companion, and Henri Joutel, a friend of La Salle's family and a soldier of many years' experience. He would become the chronicler of the expedition. Disastrous components of the company were La Salle's relatives: his quarrelsome and venial brother the Abbè Jean Cavelier, his arrogant and condescending nephew Colin Crevel de Moranger (also spelled Moranget), and a much younger nephew, Colin Cavelier, who was merely useless.

La Salle maintained such strict secrecy about the destination of the expedition that the colonists were recruited without being told where they were going. The king's commission placed La Salle in command of all matters except the actual handling of the ships and crews, but Taneguy Le Gallois Beaujeu (also spelled Beaujeau), captain of *Le Joly* and overall naval commander, resented being kept in ignorance and distrusted the leadership of a man he regarded as an impractical dreamer. Beaujeu, a pragmatic and experienced officer, reasonably argued that he could not prepare for the voyage adequately without knowing where he was going. The commissary issued provisions to *Le Joly* for one hundred people, standard for a crossing to Canada, but La Salle loaded more than twice that number of colonists on the ship. When Beaujeu finally realized they were destined for the Gulf of Mexico, he objected that the provisions were inadequate and the sailing date inappropriate, as it would bring them to the gulf at a time of the autumn and winter storms and hurricanes.

La Salle ignored Beaujeu's objections and suspected the captain of attempting to destroy the expedition, even suggesting he was in league with sinister Jesuit forces. Beaujeu was not the only subject of La Salle's wrath. La Salle argued with a variety of government officials responsible for outfitting the voyage and with the captains of the other ships. La Salle even quarreled with Tonty's younger brother when La Salle reneged on his promise to pay Tonty's back wages to his family. La Salle's behavior during this period was such that modern historians have tended to describe him in clinical terms such as paranoid or bipolar. It is doubtful that such modern terminology does much to illuminate the mental working of a man of the seventeenth century, but certainly La Salle's behavior was the antithesis of the sort of calm, rational planning needed for the occasion; perhaps La Salle was beginning to feel overwhelmed by the scope of the enterprise he had undertaken.

The Expedition

As La Salle ordered the provisions and trade goods for the colony packed aboard the ships, Beaujeu had more objections. The ships were in no way adequate for the mass of material La Salle demanded to be taken. To fit it all in, the areas normally used to shelter people were filled, and the passengers, with the exception of a few of high rank, lived on the open deck during the long crossing of the Atlantic. Even the deck itself was laden with such piles of supplies and trade goods that the colonists barely had room. *Le Joly* was so overloaded that only about 150 miles out of port the ship wallowed into an oncoming wave that broke its bowsprit. La Salle accused Beaujeu of sabotage, although he had to admit that the captain quickly repaired the damage and got underway again. The feud between the two men grew so that they hardly spoke except when arguing with one another and otherwise communicated mainly through subordinates. La Salle's relations were barely better with Captain Claude Aigron of *L'Aimable.*

Beaujeu wished to put into the Azores to refresh his water casks and pick up additional stores for the mass of people living on the deck, but La Salle would not permit it. The winds were favorable, and, as always, he suspected Beaujeu of bad faith. The crew and passengers sided entirely with Beaujeu. Later, when the ship passed the Tropic of Cancer, La Salle refused to let the crew celebrate the traditional "crossing of the line." This ceremony was usually the occasion for the passengers to distribute money and brandy to the crew, who were furious at the loss of one of the few traditional and financially significant benefits of their low-paying profession.

The crossing to the Caribbean isle of Saint-Dominique took a little over eight weeks, and by then fifty of the passengers on *Le Joly* were seriously ill and all had been weakened by reduced rations and water shortage. La Salle himself fell ill during the latter part of the voyage and had a relapse soon after going ashore. *L'Aimable* and *La Belle,* separated from *Le Joly* by a storm, soon arrived, but they brought the news that the *St. Françoise* had been captured by Spanish privateers and with it many supplies destined for trade in Saint-Dominique and for the colony. La Salle recovered slowly, part of the time in a house rented by the Duhaut brothers, Pierre and his younger brother Dominique, merchants from La Salle's hometown of Rouen and major investors in the colonization scheme. La Salle sought to purchase supplies in Saint-Dominique to make up in part for those lost with the *St. Françoise,* but goods were only available at very high prices. Short of cash, La Salle had to seek a substantial loan from the Duhaut brothers.

At Saint-Dominique, several of the colonists died and a few deserted, but several buccaneers joined the expedition, and in November the colonists finally got underway again. As the three ships sailed along the coast of Cuba, La Salle told Beaujeu that the mouth of the Mississippi lay near the western end of the northern shore of the gulf, so the ships sailed north-northwest. They missed the mouth of the Mississippi, sighting the coast a little to the west. It was virtually impossible to compute longitude at sea in the seventeenth century, and La Salle had previously been unable to calculate accurately the location of the mouth of the Mississippi. He knew neither where he nor his goal was. Reports about the direction of the current along the gulf coast were also grossly inaccurate, and wishful thinking influenced La Salle. He had promised Louis XIV a colony close to the rich Spanish possessions. So La Salle sailed west, toward where he imagined the Mississippi to be and farther away from its real location.

The northern coast of the Gulf of Mexico along the modern states of Louisiana and Texas was low and flat. There were abundant shoals, sandbars, off-shore islands, sand dunes, lagoons, swamps, lakes, and marshes. The ocean did not meet the land in a clearly defined border, but rather both formed a zone that was neither sea nor solid. In winter the coast was often cloaked in mist and fog, winds often blew toward the shore, and storms were common. The expedition proceeded slowly along the coast. *Le Joly* became separated from the other two ships in fog and squall but reunited after two weeks. By January 19, 1685, they were at the western end of the northern shore, water was running short, and the coast was beginning to turn increasingly to the south. There they found a long sand bank separating the ocean from what appeared to be a lake formed by water issuing from a river. This seemed to La Salle to be a westerly branch of the Mississippi, conveniently near the rich Spanish holdings and in all probability not too far from the main mouth of the Mississippi. In fact, he was in Matagorda Bay, Texas, four hundred miles west of the Mississippi. Here he decided to found his first settlement, expecting to establish a second in the future on the main course of the Mississippi. In the meantime, the first settlement would provide the threat against Mexico he had promised the king.

The Colony in Texas

La Salle first made camp on Matagorda Island near the entrance to the bay. After carefully sounding the sandbar at the entrance, the ship *La Belle* entered easily. La Salle ordered the captain of *L'Aimable* to follow the channel marked by buoys and sent the pilot who had guided

La Belle into the bay, but the captain of *L'Aimable* dismissed the pilot and attempted to enter the bay unaided. La Salle on shore watched *L'Aimable* approach the sandbar when he was suddenly interrupted by two panicky men who reported that members of the local tribe, the Karankawa, had captured most of a group of men whom La Salle had sent to make a dugout canoe. La Salle hastened to the Karankawa village where he discovered that the Indians had not so much captured the men as escorted them to their village, where they showed curiosity rather than hostility. La Salle easily retrieved his men, but while La Salle was occupied, the captain of *L'Aimable* ran the ship hard aground and it could not be freed. The French were able to salvage some materials, but in a few days the ship broke up and many of the supplies destined for the colony were lost. La Salle was convinced the captain of *L'Aimable* had sabotaged the ship. Other reports suggest the captain was drunk when he attempted to run the ship into the bay, disregarding advice and buoys.

The loss of the supply ship discouraged some colonists who decided to return to France with Captain Beaujeu on *Le Joly*, but about two hundred remained with La Salle. Before Beaujeu departed, he generously offered to go to the French island of Martinique to get supplies for the remaining colonists, but La Salle rejected the suggestion. Whether La Salle's decision was motivated by pride or miscalculation, it was a fateful mistake, and the colonists soon faced food shortages. Beaujeu had now fulfilled his commission to deliver the colonists to the place La Salle designated, and the continued presence of the large ship could only attract the unwanted attention of the Spanish. *Le Joly* sailed for home on March 12, 1685.

Some goods from the wreck of *L'Aimable* washed ashore, and the colonists and the Karankawa salvaged what they could. La Salle hoped to recover some of the goods the Karankawa had found and also to obtain dugout canoes from them. He had always been successful establishing good relations with Indians, but rather than going himself he sent his arrogant and impulsive nephew Moranger with seven other men to the Karankawa village. Moranger's abrupt intrusion alarmed the Karankawa, most of whom fled, and he and the others simply took what the Natives had salvaged and also stole hides and two canoes. Night overtook Moranger and his men before they could return to the French settlement, so they camped without setting an adequate guard. In the middle of the night, the Karankawa showered arrows on the

French camp, killing two and wounding Moranger and one other. This was the beginning of hostilities between the local tribe and the colonists. There were no great battles, but the Karankawa ambushed colonists when they went to hunt or cut firewood, killing one or two at a time. The colonists built a weak, ramshackle fort at the settlement largely out of material from the wreck of *L'Aimable*, including eight cannons that had been salvaged before the ship broke up. The cannon balls for the cannons and much of the gunpowder had been lost with the ship, so the cannons could only be fired with bags of musket balls or rocks. Food was scarce, and the only water readily available was brackish and caused dysentery, which swept through the camp, causing deaths every day.

La Salle departed from the settlement in spring 1685 with about fifty men to explore the bay in search of a branch of the Mississippi River and to find a better and less-exposed site for a permanent settlement, away from the coast where a passing Spanish ship might discover it. The branch of the Mississippi that La Salle sought did not exist, but he chose a new location for the colony, near the head of the bay a few miles up a small river. In early June 1685, the colonists began to move to the new site. This was done in two stages, transferring material first about halfway to a transport camp and then finally to the new settlement, generally called Fort St. Louis, although it may never have been officially named. The colonists used *La Belle* to move much of the heaviest material, such as the eight cannons. No real fort was ever built at Fort St. Louis, and the settlement at its greatest consisted of only five buildings, three of them small, and a work shed. By the time of the move to Fort St. Louis, about a quarter of the colonists had already died.

Exploration and Crumbling Fortunes

In autumn 1685, La Salle and a company of men departed from the settlement for a second time to search for the Mississippi. La Salle stationed another group with *La Belle* anchored in the northern part of Matagorda Bay, and he left Joutel in command at Fort St. Louis with the rest of the colonists. There deaths continued from disease, drowning, rattlesnake bites, bison tramplings, and poisonous plants. Several colonists became separated from their colleagues while hunting or exploring and were never seen again, while others deserted and disappeared into the wilderness. The number of colonists dwindled daily.

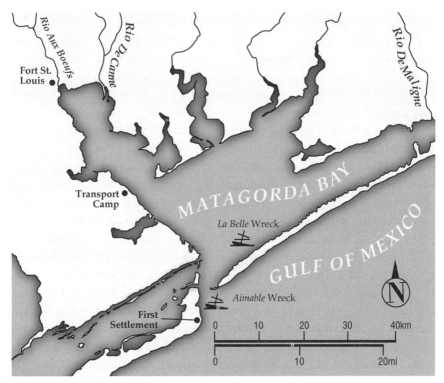

Matagorda Bay, Texas, and the location of Fort St. Louis.

At first La Salle and his companions traveled by dugout canoe. When the men left the canoes to proceed farther on foot, they sank the canoes by filling them with heavy rocks to hide them from the Karanakwa and keep them from drying out and splitting. After leaving the canoes, La Salle led the column, and his nephew Moranger followed at the end to make sure no one deserted or was left behind. One of the men, Pierre Duhaut, the merchant who had aided La Salle at Saint Dominigue and a major investor in the colony, stopped to repair his shoes and pack. Moranger told him to move along, and when Duhaut said he could not until he made repairs, Moranger left him behind. When Duhaut tried to catch up with the column he found himself hopelessly lost, confused by intersecting bison trails. Duhaut soon became convinced that La Salle and Moranger simply abandoned him. Duhaut was in a difficult position; he had only his musket, a little gunpowder, a few musket balls, and little food in his pack. He did not even have a knife with which he might clean and butcher game he might shoot. Duhaut hid from the Karankawa by day and traveled by night, hunting when he could. He found where the men had sunk the dugout canoes and with great difficulty managed to refloat one. Finally, after a month of deprivation and danger, nearly starving, Duhaut arrived back at Fort St. Louis, bearing an enduring grudge against Moranger and La Salle.

While La Salle was away, disaster befell *La Belle* and its crew. The five most able crew members took the ship's small boat ashore to fill water casks, but they did not return, perhaps drowned in a sudden squall or killed by the Karankawa. The people remaining on board were soon out of water, separated from the coast by a considerable distance, and without a small boat. Few seventeenth-century sailors knew how to swim. The crew waited, hoping for the return of the men with filled water casks, but they did not appear. The ship's master appropriated the ship's store of wine and brandy and remained drunk, providing no leadership. Several of the crew weakened and died of thirst. The others tried to sail the ship to the settlement, but a strong wind drove the ship across the bay, where it grounded near the long peninsula that separated the bay from the open ocean. The men built a raft so they could float to shore, but rough water broke up the raft and two drowned. When the seas calmed, the seven remaining men built a second, better raft. They got to shore and were able to salvage some goods from the ship, although they remained on the long peninsula far from Fort St. Louis. They stayed on the peninsula for three months, hunting, fishing, and gathering oysters. As their supply of food began to run out, they had the good fortune to find a dugout canoe that had drifted across the bay, and they used it to return to Fort St. Louis. *La Belle* was the colony's last link to the outer world. As long as it existed, the colonists could have sent a message to one of the French islands in the Caribbean requesting supplies or evacuation, but without a ship they could only hope La Salle would find the Mississippi. From there he could travel to Canada and then France and send supplies.

La Salle's expedition traveled to the northeast, where he managed to establish friendly relations with distant tribes but failed to find the Mississippi. He finally returned to the settlement at Matagorda Bay in March 1686 with just six or seven men. About a half dozen more soon appeared after having looked for *La Belle* in vain. The others had fallen victim to a variety of dangers or simply disappeared, including Dominique Duhaut, Pierre Duhaut's younger brother. Several deserted, preferring to take their chances in the wilderness and among friendly tribes.

In April 1686, La Salle again departed to seek the Mississippi. He went farther than on his previous expedition and met new tribes with whom he established friendly relations, but again he failed to find the Mississippi. He returned in October with just eight of the twenty who had initially accompanied him. The other men died, deserted, or just disappeared.

The Death of La Salle

La Salle now realized that the Mississippi River was nowhere near his settlement but rather must lay far to the east, and he set out again to find it in January 1687. This expedition consisted of only seventeen men, the healthiest at the colony, among whom were Henri Joutel and Pierre Duhaut. They traveled first north and then northeast. By mid-March, despite aid from friendly tribes, the men were fatigued and provisions nearly exhausted. La Salle sent a group to retrieve food he had cached the previous year, but it had spoiled. One of the group, La Salle's Shawnee companion Nika, managed to kill two bison. The men camped and set about smoking the meat to preserve it; they also boiled the marrow bones and perishable parts of the kill to make a nourishing broth, traditionally the hunters' portion. The men sent back to the main camp to inform La Salle, who sent his nephew Moranger. He approached the hunters with typical arrogance, announcing that all the meat would be confiscated including the hunters' portion, and that he would decide who got to eat and what they got to eat.

Moranger's haughty presumption was too much for the long-suffering men. That night, five plotted revenge. Pierre Duhaut also nursed resentment over the loss of his brother and his own abandonment in the wilderness. Liotot, the expedition surgeon, had also lost a brother and had devotedly nursed La Salle when he was ill and Moranger when he was wounded, but Liotot felt he had been treated with disdain rather than gratitude. Hiems (also spelled Heins), a German buccaneer, and Tessier, the often-drunken ex-master of *La Belle*, joined the conspiracy, as did Jean L'Archevêque, Duhaut's young servant. That night they slaughtered Moranger, Nika, and La Salle's personal servant Saget. Realizing they had no chance of clemency, they resolved to kill La Salle too. When Moranger did not return, La Salle went to find him; as he approached the hunters' camp, L'Archevêque hailed La

Salle. When La Salle asked where Moranger was, L'Archevêque replied that he had wandered off, and before La Salle could say anything else, Duhaut shot from ambush, killing La Salle.

L'Archevêque carried the news of the murders to La Salle's camp, where the Abbè Jean Cavelier, Colin Cavelier, and Henri Joutel feared they also would be killed. The murderers assured them that there would be no more killings, but tensions remained high as the murderers assumed leadership of the expedition. Shortly afterward in an Indian village, the men encountered two deserters from La Salle's expedition the previous year, Grollet and Ruter, who joined the expedition. Duhaut increasingly attempted to take complete control, acting with the same arrogance that had characterized Moranger. The murderers began quarreling, and Hiems shot and killed Duhaut, and Ruter shot Liotot. Hiems and Joutel then agreed to divide the supplies and each go his own way along with those who wished to join him. There are contradictory reports about the fate of those who remained with Hiems, but it seems that new arguments broke out, leading to killings and perhaps desertions until only one remained, perhaps Ruter, who returned to his life with the Indians.

Joutel's group of seven continued to the northeast, but one man drowned while crossing a river. L'Archevêque and another young man, Pierre Meunier, claimed illness and stayed in another village, but Joutel wrote they really stayed behind because they enjoyed the attentions of young Indian women. Joutel, the Abbè Cavelier, the young Colin Cavelier, and two others eventually reached the Mississippi River in summer 1687. The abbè claimed that the Indians' affection for La Salle was so great they would abandon them if his death were known. Joutel and the others followed his advice as they traveled up the Mississippi and Illinois Rivers and then on to Canada and France, finally arriving in October 1688. It is more likely that the abbè was eager to keep La Salle's death secret so he could take control of La Salle's estate in France before creditors could act. Despite appeals, the royal government sent no relief force to the colony.

The Spanish Reaction

The Spanish first learned of the French venture in mid-1685 through men who had deserted from La Salle's expedition at Saint-Dominique. Some of the deserters had turned pirate, were captured by the Spanish, and gave statements before they were executed. The Spanish colonial authorities were greatly alarmed and quickly sent the information to the royal court, which was equally apprehensive. Over the next few years, more reports and rumors about the French colony came to the attention of the Spanish. Some were unreliable, even contradictory, and would prove grossly exaggerated, such as the claim that the French colony had 1,500 inhabitants, a large stone fortress mounting many artillery pieces, well-established farms, port facilities, wide-ranging trade, and alliances with strong tribes. Although such reports were obviously untrustworthy, the potential danger posed by the French colony was so great that no report could be disregarded.

The Spanish launched naval explorations from various ports around the Caribbean and six land expeditions from Mexico, all seeking the French colony. Although the Spanish had long claimed the entire gulf coast, finding the French colony proved difficult. There was not a single permanent Spanish settlement on the coast north of Tampico, and the coast itself was poorly known and difficult to explore. The Spanish knew La Salle sought to colonize where the Mississippi River flowed into the sea, and everyone, including La Salle, assumed that the Mississippi, like other major American rivers, entered the sea at the head of a large bay rather than at the end of a long, peninsula-like delta. The French colony was sought in the shallow gulf coast bays among navigation hazards such as barrier islands and sandbars. Large ships could not enter such waters; small ships and galleys were vulnerable to storms and found it difficult to carry sufficient provisions for extended searches.

The Spanish also faced other concerns that they could not ignore and that divided their attentions and resources. English and French buccaneers sailed the Caribbean, sometimes combining into large fleets stronger than the opposing Spanish forces. In 1683, they sacked the major port of Veracruz, and two years later a pirate fleet captured Campeche and held it for nearly two months before withdrawing. Buccaneers even crossed the Isthmus of Darien (modern Panama) and pillaged Spanish holdings on the Pacific coast. Pirates often found refuge in the French Saint-Dominique and operated with the cooperation and connivance of French colonial officials. Inland Spanish frontier settlements in northern Mexico frequently suffered from raids by hostile tribes, and the Spanish forces available to protect the settlements were weak. A French colony near northern Mexico could potentially compound these problems, offering a safe port to pirates and privateers and persuading tribes to act in concert against the Spanish to over-whelm the feeble frontier garrisons.

Although none of the Spanish naval explorations found the colony, two came close. In 1687, a Spanish naval recognizance arrived at Matagorda Bay, where it found evidence of the wreck of *L'Aimable* and *La Belle* half sunk and going to ruin where it had run aground, but the Spanish failed to find the colony. Later another Spanish recognizance visited the bay, by which time *La Belle* had disappeared except for some wreckage cast up on the beach. Again, the Spanish failed to find the colony inconspicuously hidden several miles up a small river.

Spanish expeditions by land faced difficult travel in a largely barren region inhabited by Indians. Exhausted and running short of provisions, expeditions repeatedly turned back. One Spanish expedition found a Frenchman, apparently a deserter from the colony, living with Indians, but he had broken down mentally and gave only rambling, contradictory, and improbable accounts of the colony. Finally, in 1689, a Spanish expedition headed by a tough, experienced frontiersman, Alonso de León González, located the French colony. La Salle had left about twenty-six people at Fort St. Louis, but González found only death and destruction. The buildings still stood, but they had been ransacked and their contents destroyed. The Spanish found three skeletons, one of which still had an arrow in its back. Later the Spanish learned that L'Archevêque and Grollet had returned to the colony shortly before De Lèon arrived. They had found no one alive and buried fourteen skeletons before they departed. The Karankawa spared only the children, whom the Spanish eventually rescued.

Before De Lèon departed, he carefully buried the eight cannons he found at the colony in anticipation of the Spanish using them when they returned to establish their own *presidio* there. He duly recorded their location, but by the time the Spanish did return some years later, the report was buried in bureaucratic files and the location of the cannons forgotten. They were found in 1995 beautifully preserved. That same year, archaeologists discovered the remains of *La Belle*. An exemplary excavation recovered a significant portion of the hull, bronze cannons, crates of trade goods and supplies, and even the skeletal remains of two crew members who had presumably died of thirst before the wreck of the ship.

By any standards, La Salle's colony was a disaster. The settlement was founded at the wrong place, far from the Mississippi River at the head of a shallow, useless bay on the edge of a barren hinterland. The Karankawa, initially friendly, were foolishly provoked to war. La Salle's autocratic leadership was inept, fatal to the colony and himself.

Aftermath

Of the nearly two hundred French colonists who remained in Texas when *Le Joly* returned to France, only fifteen survived to come out of the wilderness: eight found by the Spanish (five of whom were children of Lucien and Isabelle Talon), Joutel's group of five, and L'Archevêque and Grollet, who tired of their life among the Indians and surrendered to the Spanish. The viceroy of Mexico took the Talon children into his own household, and subsequently they enjoyed adventurous lives in Spain, France, Portugal, and North America. A Spanish expedition brought L'Archevêque and Grollet to Mexico, and the colonial authorities sent them to Spain, where they sat in prison for several years. The Spanish then sent them back to Mexico and enlisted them in the army. Later they settled near Albuquerque and Santa Fe in modern New Mexico, where descendants live today; the Spanish versions of their family names, Archibeque and Gurulé, may still be found. Grollet married in 1699, and the baptism of his son is recorded in 1703. L'Archevêque became a prosperous trader. He was killed by Indians in 1720 while accompanying a Spanish expedition in Nebraska.

Henri Joutel returned to Rouen, where he became a member of the city guard. When the French again determined to plant a colony on the northern shore of the Gulf of Mexico, the minister of the marine invited Joutel to join the expedition. Joutel declined and remained in France. The minister borrowed Joutel's journal of the La Salle expedition, which he forwarded to Pierre Le Moyne d'Iberville, leader of the new colonizing effort. The journal was returned to Joutel five years later, but some pages had been lost. Joutel seems to have lived peacefully in Rouen until his death about 1725.

Subsequent to his return to France, Abbè Jean Cavelier wrote an account of the colonial expedition but otherwise paid little attention to the fate of the colonists abandoned in Texas. He prospered and died a wealthy man in 1722.

La Salle's failure had lasting effects for Spain and France. The attempt to establish the French colony turned Spanish attention to the gulf coast, ignored since after the attempt to establish a colony at Pensacola in 1559 (chapter 2). After many postponements, in 1698, the slow-acting Spanish again set up a colony in Pensacola, the best harbor on the gulf, barely in time to prevent the French from occupying the site. Pensacola's hinterland, however, was sandy, swampy, and unproductive. The settlement was not self-sustaining and had a well-deserved reputation as unhealthy; the colony survived, but remained weak. The Spanish government was unwilling to commit resources to develop Pensacola substantially; Spain had occupied the bay merely to keep other powers from having it.

The French never forgot La Salle's dream. When they again turned their attention to the gulf coast and found Pensacola Bay occupied by the Spanish, they established settlements at Dauphine Island, Mobile, and Biloxi before founding New Orleans near the mouth of the Mississippi. The French culture and language that endures in Louisiana even today is in some measure a heritage of La Salle.

Sources

Henri Joutel's journal is the best and fullest account of La Salle's colony: *Journal Historique du Dernier Voyage que feu M. de La Salle fit dans le Golfe de Mexique, pour Trouver L'embouchere, & Le Cours de La Rivere de Missicipi, nommee a present La Rivere de Saint Louis, qui traverse la Louisiane: ou l'on voit l'histoire tragique de sa mort, & Plusiers coses Curieuses du noveau monde*, ed. Michel de Michel (Paris: Chez Estienne Robinot, 1713). Although a friend of La Salle's and respectful of social hierarchy, he was capable of independent judgment and at least mildly critical of La Salle and the Abbè Cavelier. The editor of the first printed edition, Jean Michel, "improved" the text without Joutel's agreement by severely cutting large sections and altering and elaborating other portions, often to make them more dramatic. This was a common practice in the seventeenth century. The nineteenth-century editor Pierre Margry produced a better version of Joutel's journal by consulting original manuscripts: *Mémoires et documents pour servir l'histoire des origines françaises des pays d'outre mer: Découvertes et établissments des Français dans l'ouest et dans le sud de l'Amérique Septentriolnale*, 6 vols. (Paris: [D. Jouaust], 1876–1886). The recent translation by Johanna S. Warren improves Margry's readings in a number of instances: *The La Salle Expedition to Texas: The Journal of Henri Joutel 1684–1687*, intro. and ed. William C. Foster (Austin: Texas Historical Association, 1998).

The Abbè Jean Cavelier wrote two self-serving, often-unreliable accounts of the colonization venture. The shorter is a report to the French minister of the marine, Jean-Baptiste Antoine Colbert, Marquis de Seignelay. A translation is included in John Gilmary Shea, *Early Voyages Up and Down the Mississippi*, 2 vols. (New York: John Shea, 1881). The longer account is translated in Jean Delanglez, *The Journal of Jean Cavelier, the Account of a Survivor of La Salle's Texas Expedition* (Chicago: Institute of Jesuit History, 1938).

Father Anastasius Douay, who took part in the colonization attempt and accompanied Joutel on the final expedition, also wrote an account, but he took no notes during the events and had to rely entirely on his memory. The result is often unreliable, made more so by his editor, Chrétien Le Clerq, who radically elaborated Douay's account. An English translation is available in John Gilmary Shea, ed. and trans., *First Establishment of the Faith in New France*, 2 vols. (New York: John Shea, 1881).

The engineer Jean-Baptiste Minet went with La Salle but decided not to stay and returned to France with Beaujeu. His journal is important for the early part of the venture: "Journal of our voyage to the Gulf of Mexico," in Robert S. Weddle, Mary Christine Morkovsky, and Patricia Kay Galloway, eds., *La Salle, the Mississippi and the Gulf: Three Primary Documents* (College Station: Texas A & M University Press, 1987).

The Spanish interrogation of one of the rescued members of the expedition, Pierre Meunier, is significant. Meunier was only about fourteen when La Salle's expedition sailed from France and a commoner, far removed from the colony's leaders. His knowledge of events was limited, and his statement is much shorter than Joutel's extended narrative, but it is forthright and an important source for the colony. There is a translation in Warren, *La Salle Expedition*. Abundant records survive of the Spanish searches for La Salle's colony. Detailed information about the records are in Robert S. Weddle, *Wilderness Manhunt: The Spanish Search for La Salle* (Austin: University of Texas Press, 1973).

PART TWO

First French Attempts in Canada

Cartier *and* Roberval *in* Canada: Ste.-Croix, Charlesbourg-Royal, *and* France-Roy (1541–1543)

Background

During the first half of the seventeenth century, France fought a series of ultimately unsuccessful wars against the Holy Roman Empire and Spain for dominance in Italy, and during the second half of the century, French Catholics and French Protestants (Huguenots) fought one another in recurring religious wars within the country. These events limited the ability of the French monarchy to explore and colonize in the New World, but humble fishermen played a role in opening North America for the French. Basque whalers may have first discovered the rich fishing grounds of the Grand Banks of Newfoundland, and they were joined by Breton fishermen there certainly by 1504. There are claims that Basques and Bretons may have sighted and landed on Newfoundland and even the mainland of North America before Columbus, but documentation is lacking. Fishing boats from other areas of France, Portugal, Spain, and England soon flocked to the Grand Banks in pursuit of cod to satisfy the growing European population's demand for protein. Some salted their fish while at sea, and others dried their catch on the coasts of Newfoundland and the mainland. Inevitably, fishermen met Indians, with whom they traded European goods for furs. Initially there was little demand for furs in France, but as a market developed in the course of the sixteenth century, French ships began sailing to North America specifically to trade with Indians for furs. The concerns of fishermen and fur traders were pragmatic and immediate. To the extent that knowledge of their discoveries spread, it was mainly by word of mouth. They were not part of the intellectual world of cosmographers, cartographers, and explorers.

In 1523, the Italian explorer Giovanni da Verrazzano led the first official French exploratory expedition to North America, jointly funded by merchants and the French king Francis I. Verrazzano explored the coast from the Carolinas to New York searching for a Northwest Passage to the Orient. Although he failed in that endeavor, his discoveries excited French interest in North America and formed the basis of later French claims. Evidence is less than decisive, but Verrazzano may have led a trading expedition to Brazil in 1527 and another expedition to North America in 1528, apparently exploring to the south of his earlier effort, but little is known about that voyage or the fate of the explorer.

Cartier's First Voyage of Exploration

In 1534, Jacques Cartier, a mariner from St.-Malo in Brittany, led a new French expedition searching for the Northwest Passage. Cartier was born in 1491, and by 1519 he had attained the respectable post of master pilot of the Port of St.-Malo. In that year he also made an advantageous marriage to Marie Catherine des Granches, daughter of the constable of St.-Malo. In the accounts of his voyages, Cartier often makes references to Brazil, and later in life he served as a translator of Portuguese, indications that he took part in the Brazil trade. He may have also visited the Newfoundland fishing grounds before this first exploration voyage.

Cartier's voyage of 1534–1535, financed by Francis I and merchants of St.-Malo, consisted of two ships of about sixty tons each and a crew of sixty-one. They explored in the vicinity of Newfoundland, the Gulf of Saint-Laurent (St. Lawrence), and the adjacent North American coast, encountering Native Americans of several tribes. On the Gaspé Peninsula, near the mouth of the Saint-Laurent River, Cartier became the first European to encounter the Iroquoians. Held there by adverse winds, Cartier and his company remained for ten days in Chaleur Bay, during which time he met members of the tribe who came there to fish. At this time Iroquoians lived along the Saint-Laurent River, but Cartier did not discover that river during this first voyage. Initially, the relations between the two groups were unreservedly friendly. The Iroquoians greeted the French with joy and feasting, and the French presented gifts of knives, glass beads, and trinkets much prized by the Iroquoians.

Shortly before departing, Cartier had his men erect a thirty-foot-high cross on shore. Donnacona, chief of the local Iroquoians, accompanied by his brother and two sons, approached the French ship by canoe. They apparently complained about Cartier's presumption in erecting the cross without permission, or at least the French thought that was Donnacona's meaning. The two groups had no language in common. When Donnacona's canoe came alongside the French ship, Cartier had the Iroquoians seized. Cartier regaled Donnacona with assurances of friendship and provided his party with a feast before revealing his true desire, to take two of the chief's sons, Domagaya and Taignoagny, to France with him. As a captive, Donnacona was in no position to refuse as Cartier sailed for France with his sons, who were to be trained as translators.

Cartier's Second Voyage of Exploration

Despite Cartier's failure to find the fabled Northwest Passage, Francis I financed a second, larger expedition in 1535 consisting of three ships of about 110 tons, 60 tons, and 40 tons, crewed by 110 men. This second voyage, like the first, was planned as purely exploratory. During the time between the voyages, Cartier learned much from the two captives. The Iroquoians told him of the Saint-Laurent River, called the *Rivière du Canada* by Cartier and other early explorers. Cartier hoped its course, flowing from the southwest to the northeast, would provide a way to approach the western ocean and the Orient. Chief Donnacona, residing at the village of Stadacona, dominated the lower course of the river. His small chiefdom was called Canada, the name that would, of course, in time be applied to the vast nation stretching across the continent. The site of Stadacona, though not known precisely, is certainly subsumed in the modern city of Québec and its suburbs. Farther upriver to the southwest was the chiefdom of Hochelaga, at modern Montréal, to which Donnacona and his people were subject. To the north lay the chiefdom of Saguenay, the source of copper. All of these Cartier intended to explore.

Cartier sailed from St.-Malo on May 19, 1535. The crossing was stormy, and Cartier explored along the coasts before sailing to the Saint-Laurent River, where he met Donnacona late in the season, on September 8. As the season advanced, Cartier and his men built a winter camp that he named Ste.-Croix near Stadacona at the head of a large island in the Saint-Laurent that Cartier named the *Isle d'Orléans*. Donnacona was, of course, delighted to see his sons and greeted the French enthusiastically, but soon Cartier perceived a cooling of relations. The French expected Domagaya and Taignoagny to be grateful for their introduction to European civilization and true religion and to represent French interests fully and devotedly. Cartier and his compatriots seem to have been oblivious to the possibility that the two Iroquoians might have harbored resentment about their kidnapping or that the two felt that their primary attachment and loyalty was to their fellow Iroquoians rather than to the French.

Soon Taignoagny revealed another source of tension. Donnacona did not want Cartier and the French to go upstream to Hochelaga. The sources offer no explanation of Donnacona's opposition to the trip, but perhaps he feared he would lose his potentially important position as the intermediary between the French and rest of the Iroquoians if Cartier entered into direct relations with Hochelaga. Donnacona and his sons tried a number of tactics to discourage Cartier's plans. Taignoagny and Domagaya had initially agreed to accompany Cartier to Hochelaga, but now they refused. When that failed to discourage Cartier, the brothers argued that the river was not worth exploring. When that also proved unsuccessful, they tried to bribe Cartier with a present of two young boys and a young girl, and finally the Iroquoians performed a farcical charade in which three men dressed as "devils" sailed by the French in a canoe. Then Domagaya and Taignoagny came to Cartier claiming that the Iroquoian god Cudouagny had sent those spirits to warn the French that if they went to Hochelaga they would all perish from the cold. Cartier told them their god was a fool and Jesus would protect them. Cartier interpreted the Iroquoians' reluctance to cooperate fully as due to treacherous, treasonous, and malicious intentions, with no apparent awareness that French actions may have provoked apprehension among the Iroquoians.

When Cartier and fifty men departed for Hochelaga, neither Domagaya nor Taignoagny accompanied them, so the French had no means of communication other than the little Iroquoian they had learned. At Hochelaga, more than a thousand Iroquoians by Cartier's estimate greeted the French enthusiastically and presented them an abundance of food, while the French reciprocated with trade goods. The Iroquoians welcomed the French into their village, which was encircled by a strong palisaded fortification of the type that would become familiar to later French explorers. The Iroquoians expected Cartier to be a healer of some sort, and he did what little he could, laying on hands, giving simple massages, and praying. Cartier and his men did not remain long at Hochelaga, but before departing they traveled a short distance to a high ground they named Mont Royale from which they could see the course of the Saint-Laurent and rapids that blocked their further progress.

Cartier returned to Ste.-Croix after an absence of only a week, where the men who had remained behind had fortified the camp, erected a palisade of vertical logs, and mounted artillery brought ashore from the ships. Cartier had the fort further strengthened, surrounding it with substantial ditches, a drawbridge, and a strong gate. Watches were posted day and night. Trade went on between the French and Iroquoians, but it was apparent that each had developed similar wariness of the other; superficial protestations of friendship disguised deep, abiding suspicions. The French were conscious that they were outnumbered strangers in a strange land, and the Iroquoians feared French firearms and may have been concerned about French territorial ambitions.

In the middle of November, the Saint-Laurent froze, imprisoning the French ships until spring. Despite continuing trade and the absence of any overt acts of hostility, Cartier's fear of the Iroquoians continued to grow, amounting to obsession. In December, scurvy broke out at Stadacona. According to Cartier, more than fifty Iroquoians died and the illness spread among the French until only three or four remained healthy. Cartier thought the Iroquoians might attack if they learned the French were weak, so he went to extreme measures to conceal the condition of his men. The situation was relieved when he learned from Domagaya that a drink made from leaves and bark of the white cedar cured the malady. The French recovered, but not before 25 of the original company of 110 died. During the winter, Donnacona seems to have played on French imaginations with strange tales of fabulous peoples and exaggerated accounts of the wealth of Saguenay. Originally described simply as a source of copper, Saguenay now became, at least in French imaginations, a marvelous land richly endowed with gold and rubies. It is doubtful that Donnacona understood the difference between copper and gold. The Iroquoians in this period seem to have had only one word for metal, which they applied without distinction to copper, gold, iron, and lead.

In the spring, an Iroquoian named Agona challenged Donnacona's leadership. Taignoagny proposed that Cartier carry Agona off to France, but Cartier decided it would be to his advantage rather to depose Donnacona along with this family and chief supporters while earning Agona's friendship and gratitude. Cartier craftily informed Taignoagny that he would be willing to maroon Agona on an island near Newfoundland, but the king forbade him to take anyone to France except two or three boys to train as translators. Thus falsely assured of their own immunity, Donnacona, with his two sons and two chief supporters, entered the French fort, where Cartier had them immediately seized and brought aboard the ships. Cartier assured Donnacona and the others that they would be well treated and returned home after an interview with the king. When the weather permitted, Cartier and all the French sailed away, abandoning the fort at Ste.-Croix that was never meant to be more than a winter camp and one ship. Too few French had survived the winter to crew it. Cartier brought ten Iroquoians to France, including Donnacona's group of five and children who had been presented to Cartier. All arrived safely, but none ever returned to North America.

Cartier's Third Voyage and Roberval's Voyage

Cartier returned to France in July 1536, where Donnacona told Francis I tales about the rich land of Saguenay and Cartier assured the king of wealth just waiting to be found. The king, however, was engaged in yet another war against Charles V, Holy Roman emperor and king of Spain. Only after the truce of 1538 could the French monarch turn his attention to establishing a colony from which the imagined riches could be exploited. Francis I appointed Cartier as the chief pilot of the ships and in charge of further exploration, but he named the chevalier (knight) Jean-François de La Roque, sieur de Roberval-en-Valois, generally referred to simply as Roberval, as the king's lieutenant (i.e., representative of the royal interests) and governor of the colony. Roberval was a hereditary member of the aristocracy and so thought to be a more appropriate figure to head the colony than the navigator Cartier,

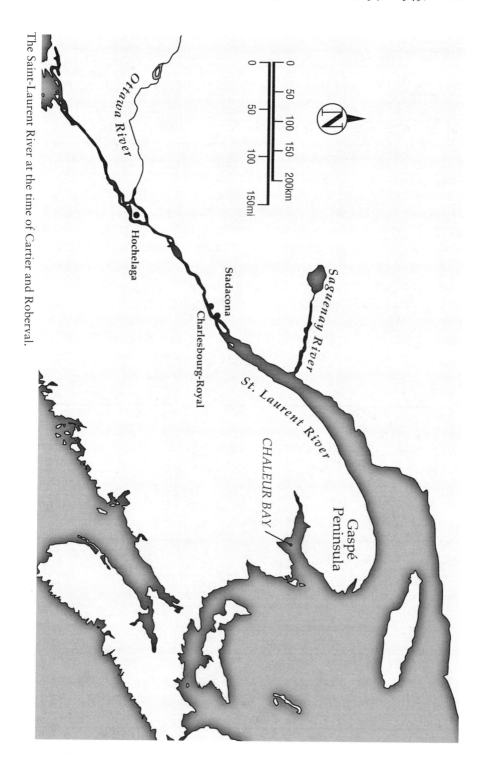

The Saint-Laurent River at the time of Cartier and Roberval.

who had achieved the lesser rank of esquire. Roberval seems to have thoroughly trusted Cartier, more so than Cartier deserved.

Although Roberval was an aristocrat of distinguished lineage, he was a somewhat odd choice as the colonial leader. One of the stated purposes of the colony was to propagate the Catholic faith, but Roberval was a Protestant. It is possible that he returned to the Catholic Church to gain favor of the king and the commission to lead the colonial venture, but the sources are silent in this regard, and he certainly followed the Huguenot faith later in life. The public commitment to Catholic proselytism seems to have been mainly designed to disarm Spanish objections to the establishment of the French colony, and it actually was a minor concern of the colonists. The king provided 45,000 livres to fund the expedition, and Roberval was expected to make a substantial contribution as well, but he was already deeply in debt. He may have hoped to recoup his fortune in Canada, but initially he had to plunge even further into debt, and if the colonial venture failed, he faced ruin.

The expedition took until 1541 to prepare. Five ships that gathered at St.-Malo were to carry four hundred colonists, supplies, equipment, and domestic animals such as cattle, goats, and pigs. By that time, all of the Iroquoians who had come to France with Cartier had died, presumably of European diseases, except one ten-year-old girl. Her ultimate fate is unknown. In May, the ships were ready to sail except for the artillery and munitions for the colony, which had not yet been received at St.-Malo. Cartier sailed with the five ships, while Roberval remained behind ostensibly to gather the armaments, but rather than following Cartier, Roberval spent the summer as a pirate preying on English shipping to relieve his cash shortage. The English ambassador complained to Francis I, who paid apparently earnest attention to the grievance but did nothing to punish Roberval.

The late spring and summer proved exceptionally stormy. Cartier's ships took three months to reach North America, a voyage that normally took about one month. The ships ran so short of water they had to give the surviving animals cider and other unspecified "beverages" to drink, probably beer. Cartier finally arrived at the site of his old winter camp, Ste.-Croix, on August 23, far too late for the colonists to plant crops. The French were greeted cordially by the Iroquoians. Cartier told Chief Agona that Donnacona had died but then lied, claiming that the others were all well, had married in France, and were living the life of wealthy aristocrats and did not want to return.

Rather than plant the colony at the old site of Ste.-Croix, Cartier continued about nine or ten miles upriver to Cap-Rouge, a high bluff of reddish rock where the small Cap-Rouge River enters the Saint-Laurent River. This was a good location to build a defensible settlement and an adequate anchorage for his ships. Cartier formally named the colony Charlesbourg-Royal after Charles II of Orléans, the third son of Francis I. After the colonists landed along with their supplies, equipment, and armaments, Cartier sent two of the five ships back to France to inform the king of the progress and that Roberval had not yet arrived.

Jean-François de la Roque, sieur de Roberval-en-Valois. Before 1537, atelier of Jean Coulet. Le musée Condé, inventory no. MN 195.

Cartier had the colony built on two levels. The upper level was constructed on a promontory of the Cap-Rouge bluff about forty yards above the river as a defensive position and an administrative center. It consisted of a wooden palisade in which stood a strong tower and several other buildings. The lower fortress, located about five hundred yards to the northwest on the Cap-Rouge River, was also surrounded by a palisade and contained a defensive tower and other buildings. The promontory shielded the lower settlement from winds on the Saint-Laurent, so it could serve as a protected anchorage and port for ships as well as housing for many of the colonists.

While the colonists constructed the fortifications and buildings, Cartier set out with two boats for Hochelaga to survey the rapids that barred further explorations. At the first substantial rapid, Cartier left one of the boats and its crew. A second rapid defeated their efforts to pass by boat so they continued by foot along a well-worn portage path. They encountered two Iroquois settlements, where they were hospitably greeted, but Cartier remained highly apprehensive. Although he was convinced that they were close to Saguenay, further progress would have required an expedition by land that Cartier was not equipped to undertake at that time.

Events at Cap-Rouge also may have curbed Cartier's enthusiasm for travel to Saguenay. There the French found shining, clear crystals that they concluded were diamonds, a large deposit of sand glinting with gold, and nearby outcroppings of a black stone cut through with mineral veins showing bits of silver and gold. Cartier returned to Charlesbourg-Royal amid growing apprehension of the Iroquoians who seemed to be massing at Stadacona and were no longer bringing fish to the colony. The Iroquoians may have been engaged in nothing more than preparing for the annual winter hunt after the end of autumn fishing season.

Almost all of what we know of Cartier's third voyage and the establishment of the first French colony in Canada comes from a single narrative account that suddenly breaks off at this point. A bare summary of what happened at Charlesbourg-Royal during winter 1541–1542 can be gleaned from the narrative of Roberval's expedition in 1542 and from Spanish interrogation of French and Spanish cod fishermen who heard reports in the vicinity of Newfoundland. During the winter, relations between the French and Iroquoians deteriorated to open hostility, but it is unlikely that the Iroquoians attacked the colony directly. More likely, the Iroquoians ambushed individuals or groups who ventured beyond the fortifications. Sources indicate they killed a group of carpenters, probably while they were felling trees for construction. Firewood gatherers, hunters, and those harvesting white cedar bark and foliage to treat scurvy were similarly vulnerable. Harsh weather and poor food exacerbated the situation, and by spring thirty-five colonists had died or been killed. Cartier abandoned Charlesbourg-Royal in June 1542. Eagerness to take credit for the discovery of diamonds and gold likely also affected his decision.

Roberval's Expedition and the Stranding of Marguerite de Roberval

Roberval sailed from France in spring 1542 with three ships and two hundred colonists. During the voyage, an incident occurred of little importance to the history of the colony but significant to European literary history and of enduring interest. On board Roberval's ship was an unmarried relative, Marguerite de Roberval, who during the voyage fell in love and had an affair with a fellow passenger. Roberval, morally outraged and personally humiliated, marooned the couple on an island, one of a group of islands known today as the Harrington Islands, then called the Isles de la Demoiselle by Roberval's pilot, Jean Fonteneau, also known as Jean Alfonse de Saintonge. Roberval left

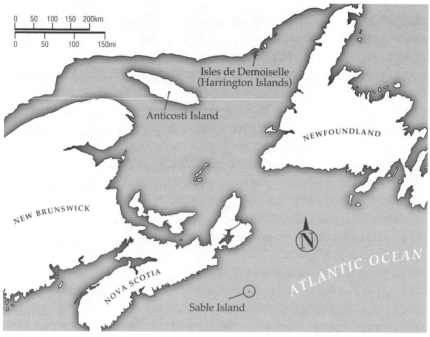

Newfoundland, Sable Island, and the Gulf of St. Lawrence, with the Isles de la Demoiselle, the place of Marguerite de Roberval's exile.

the marooned couple with some supplies, arquebuses, and ammunition. Marguerite de Roberval may have borne a child, but she was left
alone when her lover and the child died. She survived by hunting and
gathering until she was rescued by a passing ship and brought back to
France. The basic story was quickly subject to elaboration, and even
the earliest sources disagree greatly about basic facts, yet the basis of
the story seems true, and Marguerite de Roberval has emerged as a
modern feminist hero.

Three accounts of her island exile were published before 1600. The
earliest appears in the *Heptameron* of Marguerite d'Angouleme, commonly referred to as Marguerite de Navarre, the sister of King Francis
I of France and wife of King Henri II d'Albret of Navarre. The title
Heptameron derives from the Greek for "seven days" and was applied
to the work after the death of the author. She followed the structure
of Boccaccio's *Decameron* in the *Heptameron*, intending to include
one hundred tales recounted by a group of noble men and women over
the course of ten days. But de Navarre died in 1549 having completed

only the stories for the first six and the beginning the seventh day, hence the later title. The *Heptameron* has been published in many editions, and early editors felt free to alter the arrangement of the tales and edit the text. The first defective edition, Pierre Boaistuau, ed., *Histoires des amans fortunez: dédiées à très illustre princesse Madame Marguerite de Bourbon, duchesse de Nivernois* (Paris: Par G. Giles, 1558), includes the story of the exiles as the fifty-eighth, but the subsequent Claude Gruget, ed., *L'Heptameron des Nouvelles de tresil lustre et tresexcellente Princesse Marguerite de Valois, Royne de Navarre, remis en son vray ordre, confus au paravant en sa premiere impression* (Paris: B. Prevost pour G. Robinot, 1559) includes the tale as the sixty-seventh. This is followed by most modern editions.

When de Navarre wrote, Roberval, a favorite of her brother Francis I, and Marguerite de Roberval were both alive. De Navarre was no mere gossip and had no desire to embarrass the Robervals. She wrote to depict a strong, faithful woman who faced and overcame tremendous trials. Consequently, while she depicted the events as taking place during Roberval's colonial expedition, she disguised the couple as anonymous members of the artisan class. The disguise is transparent. During the sixteenth century, it was rare for an author to depict members of the working classes. Literature was for and about the aristocracy.

In the queen of Navarre's version, the couple were married before the colonial expedition began. The husband was involved in a conspiracy against Captain Roberval, who condemned him to death. The wife successfully entreated Roberval to spare her husband's life and rather maroon the two on an island. Roberval set the couple ashore with some supplies, most important of which was the wife's New Testament. The couple suffered through trials, the husband died, but the wife—supported by pious study of the Bible, prayer, and contemplation—endured. Finally, by God's will, sailors spotted smoke from the widow's fire, rescued her, and brought her to France.

The second account was published by François de Belleforest, a prolific translator and author, once a member of the court of Marguerite de Navarre. Belleforest wrote in many genres, including history, literary criticism, poetry, moral philosophy, cosmography, and, most successfully, *histoires tragiques*, short stories generally with a tragic ending pointing out some moral lesson. Although Belleforest published abundantly, his contemporaries criticized him as a tedious writer, ill organized, repetitious, and digressive, and modern commentators agree. His version of the story of Marguerite de Roberval appears in the fifth volume of *Discours Memorables de Plusieurs Histoires Tragiques, le succez, & euenemet desquelles est pour la plus part recueilly des choses aduenuës de nostre temps, & le reste des histoires anciennes* (Paris: I. Hulpeau, 1570). The sole extant copy is in the National Library of Scotland, but the second edition (Paris: I. Hulpeau, 1572) survives in greater numbers, and the account has frequently been reprinted.

Belleforest began his account by stating that he knows but withholds the name of a gentleman who, accompanied by his sister, led a voyage to the New World "in the time of Cartier." During the voyage a young gentleman particularly accomplished on the lute courted the sister. The two exchanged vows privately and considered themselves married. When it became apparent that she was pregnant, the indignant captain marooned the couple on the Isle des Espirits. The woman gave birth to a boy who died. The husband also died, but the woman survived to be rescued by a passing merchant vessel. The sailors informed her that her brother the captain was also dead. The woman returned to France, treasuring her husband's lute in his memory.

Despite his pretense of reticence, it would have been apparent to any reader in the seventeenth century that the unnamed captain was Roberval, and it would probably have been equally apparent that Belleforest had added specious details to improve the story. Marguerite de Roberval and Jean-François de La Roque de Roberval were relatives, but their exact relationship is not known. They were, however, certainly not brother and sister. Also, at the time of Marguerite's rescue and for years afterward, Roberval was alive and active.

André Thevet, a cosmographer and the author of a number of works on geography, wrote a third version. He recounted the story of Marguerite de Roberval in several works: *Les singularitez de la France antarctique, autrement nommée Amerique, & de plusiers terres & isles decouvertes de nostre temps* (Anvers: De l'imprimerie de Christophle Plantin a la lcorne d'or, 1558); *La cosmographie universelle d'André Thevet, cosmographe du roy: illustrée de diverses figures des chose plus remarquables veues par l'auteur, & incogneuës de noz anciens & modernes* (Paris: Chez Guillaume Chandiere, 1575); and "Grand insulaire et pilotage," 1586–1587, unpublished except for extracts. Clearly referring to Belleforest yet without actually naming him, Thevet claimed Belleforest had plagiarized the story of Marguerite de Roberval's that he had told years earlier and then elaborated it with lies, follies, and fables. Although it is apparent that Belleforest and Thevet had no use for one another, they were similar as authors. Contemporaries also criticized Thevet as tedious, ill organized, repetitious, and digressive, and additionally ponderous, verbose, and grammatically defective. He also habitually introduced fictional elaborations into his writing. Yet Thevet's account cannot be dismissed out of hand. He repeatedly claims he was a friend of Roberval's who related details to him and that he heard Marguerite de Roberval's own account of the affair.

Thevet was the first to name Marguerite de Roberval, whom he indicates in his *cosmographie* was a close relative of Roberval's; in "Grand insulaire" he calls Roberval her uncle. Thevet introduces an older female servant into the story who first helped disguise the couple's affair and then shared their exile. The servant is a frequent figure in stories of illicit romance during the early modern period and here most likely a typical invention of Thevet's. Thevet repeatedly contradicts himself about the location of the island of exile, and he introduces supernatural spirits who harass the couple as a major factor in his account. They were not mentioned at all in the *Heptameron* and played only a minor role in Belleforest's account. According to Thevet, Marguerite de Roberval was rescued by Breton fishermen, contradicting the accounts of Marguerite of Navarre and Belleforest. Thevet's account is superficially plausibile when considered in isolation, but when his account is compared to those of Marguerite of Navarre and Belleforest, it becomes apparent that Thevet heavily and unnecessarily larded his account with romantic fictions. The bare facts of Marguerite de Roberval's exile and survival are sufficient to stand by themselves, deserving of respect and admiration.

Roberval paused briefly at Newfoundland, where he encountered Cartier, who had just abandoned the colony. Roberval ordered Cartier to follow him back to Charlesbourg-Royal, but Cartier, apparently eager to gain credit for his discoveries, defied orders and set sail at night for France. Roberval and his company proceeded to the colony, which he renamed France-Roy. There he disembarked the colonists, who comprised a very mixed lot, ranging from aristocratic men and women to convicts, including murderers, thieves, and counterfeiters who escaped hanging when their sentences were commuted to exile in the colony. Roberval dispatched two ships back to France to return in the spring with food and word about Cartier's gold ore and diamonds.

Roberval clearly intended that the colony would endure. He had the colonists improve the defenses and construct additional buildings, but soon the colony faced a threat against which fortification was useless. The store of provisions brought from France was inadequate to support the colony through the winter. The Iroquoians brought fish to trade for knives and trinkets during the autumn, but that source of food disappeared as the winter set in and the river froze. Roberval put the colonists on short rations. The diet was inadequate in quantity and quality, and during the winter, illness, possibly scurvy, struck the colony. Roberval and his colonists must not have known the remedy for scurvy that the Iroquoians had revealed to Cartier. About fifty colonists, a quarter of the population, died.

Roberval has been called harsh in regard to both the stranding of Marguerite de Roberval and subsequent events at France-Roy. André Thevet, who described himself as a friend, wrote that Roberval was cruel to his men, hanging six, exiling others to an island for theft, and whipping others for theft and assault. Thevet, however, could seldom resist improving a story by exaggeration. The primary account of Roberval's voyage presents a less drastic account of his actions, claiming he hanged one man for theft, kept another (said by Thevet to have been hanged) in irons, and whipped others for theft and assault. The anonymous author praises Roberval for good justice that enabled the colonists to live in quiet. Considering that a significant number of Roberval's colonists had been recruited from French jails and included murderers and thieves, Roberval must have had to exercise a firm hand to maintain control. He could also be merciful. Aussillon de Sauveterre, commander of one of Roberval's three ships, killed a disobedient sailor. Roberval pardoned him and issued a letter of remission dated September 9, 1542, the oldest known official document issued in Canada. By sixteenth-century standards, Roberval's actions seem moderate.

The winter ice began to break up at France-Roy in April 1543, and on June 5, Roberval left the colony to travel to Saguenay by going up the Ottawa River. He initially expected to arrive there within a few weeks, but on June 14, several men returned to France-Roy from the expedition bearing news that one of the boats had been lost in rapids and eight men drowned. On June 19, still more men from the expedition returned to the colony, this time carrying 120 pounds of corn. At this point, the narrative account, our chief source of Roberval's colonizing effort, breaks off abruptly, but other sources allow some understanding of subsequent events.

Roberval seems not to have reached Saguenay, but perhaps he learned enough to realize there was no gold, no store of rubies, just some copper, insufficient to pay the cost of colonization much less make his fortune. Ships arrived from France bringing word that the diamonds gathered by colonists were just quartz crystals, the gold was actually just iron pyrite, and glints of silver and gold in the hard rock ore were only mica—all worthless. One can imagine the disappointment, compounding the memories of the hard and deadly winter. Moreover, France was once again at war. There would be little or no support for the colony in the foreseeable future. Roberval loaded the surviving colonists aboard his ships and sailed for France, ending the first French attempt to colonize Canada.

In 2005, the archaeologist Yves Chretien surveyed a promontory by the confluence of the Cap Rouge and St. Lawrence Rivers preliminary to the construction of a proposed public view point, planned as part of the celebration of the four-hundredth anniversary of the foundation of Québec in 1608. Chretien was, of course, aware that the site of the colony of Cartier and Roberval lay somewhere in the vicinity, but attempts to locate the site over half a century had yielded no positive results. Chretien dug a small test square to see if there were any indication of remains on the site. There he found a fragment of colorful ceramic, obviously from a vessel of high quality and quite old. Study revealed it was a piece of an Istoriato plate, made in Faenza, Italy, between 1540 and 1550. Further investigation revealed that Chretien had discovered the site of Charlesbourg-Royal. Subsequent archaeological excavation revealed details of the upper fortification at the edge of the promontory at the Cap Rouge River.

Aftermath

Even if all other factors contributing to the failure of Charlesbourg-Royal/France-Roy had been overcome—cold, disease, famine, and conflict with the Iroquoians—the colony would not have survived. It was not economically viable: It failed to discover resources that could bring profit in the immediate future, and there was no support in France to maintain the colony until it might have been able to stand on its own at some time. The fur trade had not yet developed sufficiently to support the colony, and the Iroquoians had no other exportable goods to trade. The need to find a viable economic basis for the colony elevated Saguenay in the French imagination from a source of copper to a land of gold and gems, which drove the attempts of Cartier and Roberval to reach that chiefdom. But like so many other storied sources of wealth, Saguenay proved to be exaggerated and beyond reach. Then, when the diamonds and gold from Charlesbourg-Royal turned out to be illusions, the colony lost its last reason for existence and with it died the dreams of Cartier and Roberval. *"Faux comme un diamant du Canada"* ("false as a Canadian diamond") became a proverb, and two generations passed before France again sought to colonize the St.-Laurent River valley.

Cartier returned to St.-Malo, where he pursued trade and where he died in 1557. Roberval never recovered financially and spent the rest of his life fending off creditors. In 1560, while he and other worshippers were leaving a Huguenot meeting, they were attacked by Catholic fanatics, and in the subsequent melee, Roberval was killed. After returning to France, Marguerite de Roberval became a teacher to daughters of the gentry. There is some indication that she lived to old age, perhaps as late as 1608.

Sources

CARTIER AND ROBERVAL

The chief sources for Cartier's three voyages and colonization effort are three narrative accounts, each reporting one voyage, and a separate account of similar character that describes Roberval's voyage. No author's name is attached to any of the narratives, but it is apparent that the narratives of Cartier's first two voyages are based in large part on his ship logs. The text of the first voyage preserves specific compass bearings, warnings of hazards to navigation, and even references Cartier in the first person. There has been much debate about the identity of the writers who worked these and other materials into the four accounts. Some have argued that Cartier lacked the literary sophistication to compose such narratives, but in reality nothing is known of Cartier's literary capacity. The first two narratives may be entirely his work. Others suggest Cartier's nephew Jacques Noël, himself active in the early Canadian trade, may have been the author, but in regard to the narrative of the third voyage which is incomplete, Noël wrote, "I can write nothing else unto you of anything that I can recover of the writings of Captaine Jacques Cartier my uncle diseased, although I have made search in all places that I could possibly in this Towne." That, at least, seems to indicate that Noël considered the narratives to be the work of his uncle and that he apparently was not the author.

Still others suggest Jehan Poullet, a companion of Cartier's, was the author. His name is absent from manuscript versions of the second voyage but was interpolated into the printed version several times. Poullet may have had some editorial role in the printed version, but there is no indication that he had any influence on the basic composition of the extant manuscripts. It was even once suggested that Rabelais composed the narratives. Rabelais certainly knew of Cartier's voyages and incorporated some elements in his imaginative fictions, but the idea that he created or edited the narratives has been thoroughly discredited. The questions of author and editorship remain unresolved. M. Bideaux, *Jacques Cartier Relations* (Montréal: Les Presses de l'Université de Montréal, 1986) reviews at length the evidence concerning the authorship and editing.

The publishing history and problems surrounding each of the four narratives are even more perplexing than the question of authorship. The account of the first voyage was first published in Italian, "Prima Relatione de Jacques Cartier della Terra Nuoua detta la nuoua Francia, trouata nell'anno. M.D. XXXIIII," in Giovanni Battista Ramusio, *Terzo volume delle Navigationi et Viaggi* (Venice: Stamperia de' Givnti, 1565), and then an in English translation, J. Florio, trans., *A Shorte and Briefe Narration of the Two Nauigaions and Discoueries to the Northwest Parts called Newe Frauvnce* (London: H. Bynneman, 1580). This has been recently reprinted as J. Cartier, *Navigations to Newe Fraunce*, trans. J. Florio (Ann Arbor: University Microfilms, 1966). A French version appeared only in 1598, *Discours du voyage fait par le capitaine Jaques Cartier aux Terres-neufues de Canadas, Norembergue, Hochelage, Labrador, & pays adiacens, dite nouuelle France, avec particulieres moeurs, langage, & ceremonies des habitans d'icelle* (Rouen: l'imprimerie de Raphaël du Petit Val, 1598). In 1867, researchers published a French manuscript of the first voyage, then recently discovered in the Bibliothèque Impériale, Paris: Henri Michelant and Alfred Ramé, eds., *Relation Originale du Voyage de Jacques Cartier au Canada en 1534*. Documents inédits sur Jacques Cartier et le Canada (nouvelle série) (Paris: Librairie Tross, 1867). The manuscript is probably not the original but a nearly contemporary copy from the first half of the sixteenth century, and modern editions rely on this manuscript rather than the early printed versions. Several good modern translations into English are readily available: James Phinney Baxter, *A Memoir of Jacques Cartier Sieur de Limoilou* (New York: Dodd, Mead, 1906); Henry Percival Biggar, *The Voyages of Jacques Cartier* (Ottawa: F. A. Acland Printer, 1924), and in a new reprint omitting many notes and the French text, Ramsey Cook, ed. and intro., *The Voyages of Jacques Cartier* (Toronto: University of Toronto Press, 1993).

The account of the second voyage was actually published before that of the first, *Brief Récit, & succincte narration de la nauigation faicte es ysles de Canada, Hochelage & Saguenay & autres, auec particulieres meurs, langaige, & cerimonies des habitans d'icelles: fort delectable â veoi* (Paris: Ponce Roffet & Anthoine Le Clerc, 1545). In 1556 it was translated into Italian and in 1580 into English. Three manuscripts of the second voyage survive, exhibiting only minor differences among them, but they demonstrate that the publisher of the 1545 printed edition altered the text, changed wording, and even omitted several substantial sections. Publishers during the sixteenth through eighteenth centuries seldom felt obliged to respect the integrity of a text but rather commonly modified manuscripts to better entertain readers and increase sales. The second narrative begins with a long dedication to the king of France, written in a substantially different style than the body of the narrative.

The account of Cartier's third voyage and the foundation of Charlesbourg-Royal presents new problems. The author claims to have sailed on Cartier's ship during the expedition, which of course does not exclude Cartier himself, but the third narrative lacks excerpts from the logbooks, unlike the first two, and seems a more literary product. Peculiarly, the second and third narratives, unlike the first, seem to avoid mention of Cartier's name, referring to him simply as the captain. The conclusion of the third narrative is missing and was so in the French original. Jacques Noël, Cartier's nephew, wrote that he could not find the rest of the account. The extant portion of the third narrative survives only in an English translation, and it is impossible to tell what sort of editorial revisions may have been made to the lost French original. The English version was published by Richard Hakluyt in 1600 along with English-language translations of the other narratives,

"The third voyage of discovery made by Captaine Jaques Carier, 1540, unto the Countreys of Canada, Hochelaga, and Saguenay," 232-237, in Richard Hakluyt, ed., *The Third and Last Volume of the Voyages Navigations, Traffiques and Discoueries of the English Nation* (London: George Bishop, Ralfe Newberie, and Robert Baker, 1600). The narrative breaks off at the beginning of winter 1542 when troubles with the Iroquoians were becoming serious and when we are most curious about the reasons Cartier evacuated the colony the next spring.

The fourth narrative is also preserved in Hakluyt's *Third and Last Volume*, 240-242, and like the third narrative it is incomplete, breaking off in summer 1543 while Roberval was attempting to reach Saguenay and before he had decided to abandon the colony. The author of the fourth narrative is unknown, but it is apparent that Cartier did not write it. The author refers to events in the second person plural "we" where Cartier was not present, and the narrative is critical of Cartier's behavior and motivation. When Cartier defied Roberval's orders to return to Charlesbourg-Royal with him and secretly set sail for France, the narrative describes him as "mooved as it seemeth with ambition."

The four main narratives are supplemented by other material. Jean Fonteneau, better known as Jean Alfonse, was the pilot for Roberval's expedition, and his *routier* (ship's log) of the voyage was printed in English translation in Hakluyt, *Third and Last Volume*, 237-240. A superior edition of the routier is contained in a French manuscript of Fonteneau's cosmographie: Georges Musset, ed. and annot., *La Cosmographie avec l'espère du soleil et du nord par Jean Fonteneau dit Alfonse de Saintonge, Captaine-pilote de François Ier* (Paris: E. Leroux, 1904), and Biggar, *Voyages*, 278-303, further improves Musset's French text.

Henry Percival Biggar, *A Collection of Documents Relating to Jacques Cartier and the Sieur de Roberval* (Ottawa: Public Archives of Canada, 1930), contains 293 items. Many are not directly relevant to the colonial efforts of Cartier and Roberval, but documents such as those recording Cartier's frequent role as a godfather reveal much about his status within the community of St.-Malo, and Roberval's sale of properties expose his financial difficulties. Particularly interesting are the Spanish and Portuguese diplomatic protests and reports about the French explorations and colony, even mentioning the dispatch of spies to secure information. Biggar provides English translations of the Spanish documents but not of the French. Cook, *Voyages of Jacques Cartier*, includes translations of some of the more important French documents in his abbreviated edition of Biggar's *Voyages*. W. F. Ganong, *Crucial Maps in the Early Cartography and Place-Nomenclature of the Atlantic Coast of Canada*, T. E. Layng, intro., commentary, and map notes (Toronto: University of Toronto Press, 1964) is of enduring value.

R. Galbraith provides an excellent and succinct account of Yves Chretien's discovery of the site of Charlesbourg-Royal, "The Accidental Discovery of North America's Oldest French Settlement," accessed May 3, 2020, www.robertgalbraith.com/the-accidental-discovery-of-north-americas-oldest-french-settlement/. *Recent Archaeology of the Early Modern Period in Québec City*, special issue of *Post-Medieval Archaeology* 43, pt. 1 (2009) contains important articles interpreting the archaeological investigations made subsequent to Chretien's discovery: Marcel Moussette, "A Universe Under Strain: Amerindian Nations in North-Eastern North America in the 16th Century," 30-47; Richard Fiset and Gilles Samson, "Charlesbourg-Royal and France-Roy (1541–43): France's First Colonization Attempt in North America," 48-70; Hélène Côté, "The Archaeological Collection from the Cartier-Roberval Site (1541–43): A Remarkable Testimony to French Colonization Efforts in the Americas," 71-86; and Julie-Anne Bouchard-Perron and Allison Bain, "From Myth to Reality: Archaeobotany at the Cartier-Roberval Upper Fort Site," 87-105.

MARGUERITE DE ROBERVAL

In addition to the early sources mentioned above, Arthur Phillips Stabler, *The Legend of Marguerite de Roberval* ([Pullman]: Washington State University Press, 1972), is of basic importance to unraveling the traditions about the island exile of Marguerite de Roberval. Marguerite de Roberval is confirmed to be a real person in an act of "faith and homage" of 1536 ("faith and homage" was a ceremony of medieval origin acknowledging mutual rights and obligations among the nobility). It is published by Robert La Rogue de Roquebrune, "Marguerite de la Roque et l'ille de la Demoiselle au Canada," *Nova Francia* 6 (mai-juin, 1931): 131-143, and Robert La Rogue de Roquebrune, "Un Rival de Jacques Cartier: Roberval," *Revue des questions historiques* 121 (Sept. 1934): 9-14.

Jean Fonteneau, generally called Jean Alfonse de Saintonge, was Roberval's chief pilot. His routier of the voyage includes the location of the Isles de la Demoiselle, generally acknowledged to refer to Marguerite de Roberval's exile. The French text of the relevant portion of the routier is published in Biggar, *Voyages*, 278-303, and an English translation of the relevant section in Harrison F. Lewis, "Notes on Some Details of the Explorations by Jacques Cartier in the Gulf of St. Lawrence," *Transactions of the Royal Society of Canada*, sec. 2, 3rd ser., vol. 27 (1934): 143-144. Hakluyt, *Third and Last Volvme*, 237-240, published a variant of the routier that omits the reference to the Isles de la Demoiselle. Jean Alfonse's routier definitely establishes Marguerite de Roberval's place of exile as one of the Harrington Islands. The Isles de la Demoiselle also appear on a Mercator chart of 1569 in the correct location, conveniently reprinted in Stabler, *Legend*, 26.

EIGHT

The Marquis de La Roche de Mesgouez's Colony: Sable Island (1598–1603)

Background

The failure of Cartier and Roberval in the St.-Laurent River valley did not end French interest in Canada, but a number of attempts to organize new colonial efforts collapsed while still in the planning stage, the result of a basic conflict over the exploitation of resources. Canada offered no immediate bonanzas such as the Spanish found in Mexico and Peru. A Canadian colony would require economic support for a substantial time before it could become self-supporting, and a trade monopoly was the only practical way to provide such support. Any trade monopoly, however, was vigorously opposed by those engaged in free commerce, cod fishing, fur trading, and whaling. Cod was of fundamental importance to the European diet and economy, and every year large numbers of ships from France and other Atlantic nations traveled to the Grand Banks and Newfoundland to fish. Some fishermen also engaged in the fur trade, and as the market for furs grew during the latter sixteenth and early seventeenth centuries, Europeans sailed to Canada exclusively to trade for furs and hides. Whaling also became significant as whales grew scarce in European coastal waters.

Both would-be colonizers seeking trade monopolies and free traders had influence in the court, and throughout the sixteenth century and beyond, the two forces battled for their respective interests. To a very real degree, the dispute was never settled during the French regime in North America. Well into the eighteenth century, those who wanted to strengthen the primary agricultural areas of French Canada sought to limit and control free traders who trapped and traded for furs on scattered posts and Indian villages far beyond the St.-Laurent valley.

The marquis Troilus de la Roche de Mesgouez, generally referred to simply as La Roche, was the next to found a northern French colony. La Roche found early preferment as a courtier and rose to become a royal counselor and governor of Morlaix in Brittany, where he observed the great profits made from cod fishing and the growing trade in furs and hides. He was convinced of the great potential that Canada held for a successful colonizer but soon found himself beset by a host of problems, including the hostility of the free traders. In 1577 and 1578, King Henri III granted him commissions to establish settlements in North America, along with the grandiose title of viceroy in New France. Along with other entrepreneurs, he outfitted a ship and a small pinnace with the intention of exploring preliminary to establishing a colony, but the effort came to nothing. The English, suspicious of La Roche because of a previous association with an Irish rebel, captured his ship, ending the expedition soon after it got underway. La Roche tried again during 1583 in association with ship owners of St.-Malo and St.-Jean de Luz, but the expedition failed again when the chief ship foundered.

In 1589, La Roche joined with other Catholics and Huguenots in support of Henri IV against the Catholic League, but he was captured and imprisoned until 1596. On release, he again took up the effort to found a colony. In 1597, the king granted him authorization to send an exploratory expedition to America. The expedition reported favorably about the prospects for colonization, including a positive evaluation of Sable Island, nearly a hundred miles off the coast of Canada, although they spent little time there. In January 1598, Henri IV appointed La Roche lieutenant general of Canada, Labrador, Newfoundland, and Norumbega (a vague term referring variously to a semimythical city, a river, and an ill-defined territory in northern New England), along with a monopoly of the fur trade in these areas. It was, of course, one matter to have a royal grant of monopoly but quite another to enforce it against roving traders of various nationalities.

La Roche determined to found a colony on Sable Island (see map, page 125), a seemingly unlikely site, but the colony survived for several years before perishing in strange and peculiar circumstances. Sable Island lies on the edge of the continental shelf, ninety-nine miles from the nearest point on the mainland to the northwest. The island, in the midst of rich fishing grounds and major shipping routes, is a long, narrow arc, about twenty-six miles long but only a little over a mile wide at the greatest and tapering toward the extreme ends. The modern name Sable Island is derived from the French l'île de Sable, literally Isle of Sand. The island consists entirely of sand dunes, the largest as much as eighty-five feet high. There are no native trees, but the sand is anchored in large part by grasses and low-growing bushes watered by a lens of fresh water, renewed by frequent rains, that sits on heavier, underlying salt water. There are several freshwater ponds, and more freshwater can be found by digging shallow holes.

Dangerous shoals surround the island, stretching as far as seventeen miles, always shifting. Nearby the cold Labrador and Belle Isle currents meet the warm Gulf Stream, often producing dense fogs. Rain is frequent, storms and hurricanes tracking up the coast of North America regularly pass over the island, and gales can last for weeks. The Portuguese were the first who certainly encountered the island, perhaps as early as 1502, and they left distinctive red-haired Iberian cattle there as a food source for future explorers. In 1583, Humphrey Gilbert's largest ship, the *Delight*, wrecked on the shoals with the loss of about a hundred lives, the first of about 350 shipwrecks that are recorded on the island and the surrounding shallows.

La Roche initially hoped to found a colony much larger than the modest establishment he eventually created and may have initially intended to plant the colony on the coast of Newfoundland or Nova Scotia. The Parliament of Normandy authorized him to carry 250 colonists to Canada, and the king granted him the commission to raise a company of soldiers for service there, but La Roche's resources were less substantial than his ambitions, and the colony he established consisted of just fifty men. The necessity to scale back his original plans may have led him to choose Sable Island as the site for a colony rather than the mainland.

Sable Island seemed to offer some advantages. The Gulf Stream kept the island relatively warmer than the coast, and it is less rugged. There were no potentially hostile indigenous people and no dangerous predators. The colonists could fish and hunt seals for hides and oil and walrus (now locally extinct) for their ivory, oil, and thick hides in much demand to be made into strong rope prized by mariners. A description of the island written about thirty-five years later noted the presence of many beautiful black foxes, now also extinct. La Roche's colonists trapped them for their fur. The colonists were to subsist on meat from seals and the red cattle and on vegetables they grew on the island. They had to rely on driftwood for heat and cooking.

It was not easy to find colonists to live on a sand spit in the North Atlantic. La Roche's commission granted him the authority to recruit men who could not refuse: strong beggars and sturdy tramps rounded up by the police, and convicts, including serious criminals condemned to death or the galleys. A Commandant Querbonyer was to lead the colony, assisted by a Captain Coussez as *garde magasin* (in charge of the storehouse). These officers were presumably attracted by high wages, the best accommodations, and better rations. They may have commanded a small number of regular soldiers, no more than ten, but the sources are unclear. If so, the common soldiers must have soon found themselves working side by side with the convicts in order to survive.

Colonization

La Roche embarked his compulsory colonists on two ships that took them to Sable Island, where they built living quarters and a storehouse, which La Roche stocked with food, clothing, furniture, tools, and arms. La Roche also did his best to promote a favorable image of the colony in France. He renamed the island the Île de Bourbon in honor of the governor of Normandy, Henri de Bourbon, duke of Montpensier, and he grandiosely titled a shallow tidal drainage from a salt lake the Boncœur River. La Roche then sailed away to fish for cod and trade for furs, after which he intended to return to Sable Island, but a fierce storm drove the two ships back across the Atlantic to France.

La Roche may have hoped that the Sable Island colony could develop into an entrepot for fur traders, fishermen, and whalers where they could exchange their goods for letters of credit redeemable in France. They could then resume their work rather than having to return to France as soon as their small ships were filled. La Roche's storekeeper would, of course, pay less for goods than they would fetch in France, but the ability of fishermen and traders to fill their ships two or three times and sell them at Sable Island before returning to France could more than compensate. Such trade would also ensure a fine profit for La Roche when his large ships brought the goods back to France for sale. Any such hope, however, was in vain. Fur traders, fishermen, and whalers saw no advantage to trading at Sable Island. They had no reason to support a monopoly to which they were opposed, Sable Island was often dangerous to approach, and merchants learned to send out large storage vessels to hold the goods gathered by the small ships.

La Roche had colonial ambitions beyond Sable Island, and he may have also thought Sable Island could provide a base to establish a second colony on the Acadian mainland, serve as a port from which ships could patrol the Grand Banks, and enforce his monopoly. If so, these were also unrealistic expectations. La Roche had neither sufficient funds to establish an additional settlement nor a fleet of patrol ships, and Sable Island had no harbor. Foreigners simply ignored La Roche's claim of monopoly, and even French traders easily disregarded La Roche's entitlements by landing goods surreptitiously or selling them in other countries.

In 1599, Henri IV granted La Roche a subsidy that helped maintain the colony, one écu for every barrel of goods landed in Normandy. Over the next couple of years, La Roche received 12,000 écus, a substantial sum, and he sent ships annually to Sable Island in each of the three years following the establishment of the colony, 1599 through 1601, to resupply the colonists with wine and clothing and to collect the skins and oil the colonists produced.

La Roche's relations with the king were not always so supportive. In 1599, Henri IV granted Pierre Chauvin de Tonnetuit a trade monopoly in Canada, the coast of Acadia, and other regions of New France, which would have deprived La Roche of a large portion of his grant. Henri IV may have felt that La Roche had accomplished disappointingly little, and the king was eager to reward Chauvin, who had been an ardent and valiant supporter during recent wars. La Roche protested, and the king modified Chauvin's grant, terming him La Roche's lieutenant and defining his sphere of operations as the Gulf of St.-Laurent to Tadoussac, at the confluence of the St.-Laurent and Saguenay Rivers, where Chauvin soon sought to establish a settlement. Despite Chauvin's official position as La Roche's lieutenant, the two had nothing to do with one another and operated independently.

In 1602, La Roche did not send the annual supply ship to Sable Island. That year there was a royal inquiry into the administration of the colony in response to criticisms probably carried to France with the return of the 1601 supply ship. In 1603, a ship sailed to Sable Island carrying supplies and a royal commissioner ordered to examine the resources and administration of the island and to bring back Querbonyer, Coussez, and three other individuals. The ship arrived to find just eleven of the fifty colonists alive, who told tales of revolt and murder.

Destruction

La Roche is our chief source for the events that occurred on the island during winter 1602–1603. His account is not richly detailed and leaves many questions unanswered, but it provides a basic sketch of events. For four years the colonists survived on Sable Island by their own labor and toiled for La Roche's gain, supported by only a single annual shipment described as nothing more than clothing and wine. By winter 1602, it became apparent that even that annual shipment was not coming. The bitterness of the unwilling colonists must have grown during the cold and storms until it finally erupted in mutiny and deadly violence against the privileged officers. The violence seems to have occurred not all at once but in several stages. Mutineers first killed Commandant Quesbonyer, and then after some time they murdered Captain Coussez. According to La Roche, the mutineers then turned on one another, killing six or seven more. By the time the supply ship arrived in 1603, only eleven of the colonists remained alive. La Roche's report accounts for only seventeen or eighteen of the original fifty colonists, and if this is accurate, the other thirty-two or thirty-three must have perished otherwise, which suggests the conditions that led to the revolt.

The supply ship returned to France carrying the eleven survivors, who appeared before the king to answer for the events on Sable Island. They must have provided an extraordinarily sympathetic and self-serving account of their experiences. The king pardoned all and gave each a purse of fifty écus, a considerable sum for a poor man, probably more than many had ever possessed before. La Roche was indignant, maintaining they were murderers and ought to have been hanged.

The failure of the Sable Island colony was almost a foregone conclusion. La Roche based the decision to colonize Sable Island on the inadequate and overly optimistic report of the 1597 expedition that spent only a brief time on the island. In reality, the resources of the island were limited, the climate challenging, and dangers of navigation near the island daunting. The prospect of colonizing a small island in the North Atlantic was unattractive, and La Roche had to force vagabonds and convicts, hardened men, to staff the settlement. Officers commanded the convicts but ultimately could not control them or even defend themselves. With that semblance of authority gone, the convicts turned on one another until only a remnant survived.

Aftermath

Chauvin fared little better than La Roche. In 1600, Chauvin sailed to the St.-Laurent River with a group of colonists whom he intended to settle at Tadoussac at the confluence of the St.-Laurent and Saguenay Rivers. The site was well suited for a trading post but an unsuitable choice for a colony. The soil was poor and rocky, the terrain rugged, and the site windy and cold. By autumn, almost all the colonists decided to return to France, and Chauvin left just sixteen men to overwinter. By spring only five remained alive and then only because the Indians provided for them. Tadoussac survived but only as a seasonal trading post. In 1604, La Roche wrote a letter to the king complaining about the loss of his monopoly, disparaging Chauvin's effort, and indicating a continuous interest in Sable Island, but La Roche lacked resources to initiate a new effort. La Roche survived until early 1606, long enough to gloat over Chauvin's death in 1603 and to complain about the privileges the king accorded to Pierre du Gua de Monts, the next to try to establish a French colony in North America.

Sources

The sources for the history of La Roche's Sable Island colony are few and scattered. Most documents date from the beginning of La Roche's efforts in 1598. The royal decree granting La Roche his monopoly was published in France shortly after the decree was promulgated, *Edict du roy: contenant le pouvoir & commission donnee par Sa Majesté, au Marquis de Cottenmeal & de la Roche, pour la conqueste des terres de Canadas, Labredor, Isles de Sable, Norembergue & pays adjacens avec l'arrest de la court sur la verification dudit edict du deuxiéme mars, 1598* (Rouen: Raphaël du Petit Val, [1598?]), and is available at eco.canadiana.ca/view/oocihm.63278/3?r^2=0&s^2=1 (accessed May 3, 2020).

The Houghton Library at Harvard University holds the royal order of 1598 granting La Roche immunity from lawsuits while in the king's service during the expedition to Canada: MS Fr 324, Houghton Library, Harvard University.

W. I. Morse, *Acadiensia Nova (1598–1770): New and Unpublished Documents and Other Data Relating to Acadia*, vol. 2 (London: Bernard Quaritch, 1935), 17-39, contains transcriptions and translations of three documents from 1598: the governor of Normandy, Henri de Bourbon's authorization of La Roche to raise a company of soldiers to take to Canada, the Parlement de Normandie's authorization of the chief of police of Rouen to gather 250 strong beggars and tramps for La Roche to transport to Canada, and the police chief's report about rounding up beggars and tramps.

Ultimately, La Roche did not raise the company of troops nor transport 250 people to Canada. His resources were not sufficient to realize these early plans. Some of the 50 people La Roche sent to Sable Island were almost surely among these 250, but also included in that number were men convicted of far more serious crimes than begging. Morse, *Acadiensia Nova*, 26, argues that Sable Island was not a penal labor colony but rather "a military establishment for watching the sea-lanes to the continent with forces to seize all ships or French boats fishing without permits," but Morse greatly exaggerates the capacities of the colony and ignores that the colony lacked port facilities and sailing ships, without which no such role was possible.

Morse also includes a translation of a portion of La Roche's letter of 1604 to the king cataloging his services to the crown, his effort on Sable Island, his account of the end of the colony, and his complaints about Chauvin and De Monts. The copyist titled the letter "Escrit envoyé par le Marquis Troille du Mesgouez de la Roche escouez en Bretagne au Roy Henri IV environ l'année 1596 ou 1597 (ou plutôt 1598 ou 1599) lors de la Paix aves le duc de Mercœr sur le subject principalement de la traverse et contestation qui luy estait faite dans l'isle de Bourbon a vingt lieues de distance du Cap Breton vers la Nouvelle-France et la Florida en l'Amérique, dans la Baye le long de la rivière vers Cadessart, dont la possession luy avait esté donnée par Henri III et IV." The manuscript is held in the Bibliothèque de l'Institut (de France), Collection Godefroy, vol. 291, fol. 149.

David Beers Quinn, *New American World: A Documentary History of North America to 1612*, vol. 4: *Newfoundland from Fishery to*

Colony. Northwest Passage Searches (New York: Arno Press, 1979) contains the same documents from 1598 that are contained in Morse, *Acadiensia Nova,* and a record of the Parlement of Normandy indicating that La Roche failed to get a particularly egregious criminal reprieved for transport to Canada, as well as the portion of La Roche's autobiographical letter dealing with Sable Island.

Until relatively recently, the events on Sable Island after the initial establishment of the colony were seriously misrepresented. Samuel de Champlain, never slow to criticize the efforts of others, wrote that after La Roche landed colonists, he abandoned them, and they remained on Sable Island in misery for years before a remnant were rescued. Other writers of the seventeenth and eighteenth centuries echoed the accusation that La Roche had simply abandoned the colonists, and it was not until the late nineteenth and twentieth centuries that historians discovered documents that revealed La Roche had sent out supply ships for all but one year of the colony's existence: Charles and Paul Bréard, *Documents relatifs à la marine normande et à ses armements aux XVIᵉ et XVIIᵉ siècles* (Rouen: A. Lestringant, 1889), particularly 51-59; Gustav Lanctot, "L'etablissement du Marquis de la Roche à l'Ile de Sable," *Report of the Annual Meeting of the Canadian Historical* Association 12, no. 1 (1933): 33-42; and Joseph Le Ber, "Un document inédit sur l'ile de Sable et le marquis de La Roche," *Revue d'historie de l'Amérique française* 2, no. 2 (Sept. 1948): 199-213, publishes the commission for the supply expedition of 1603.

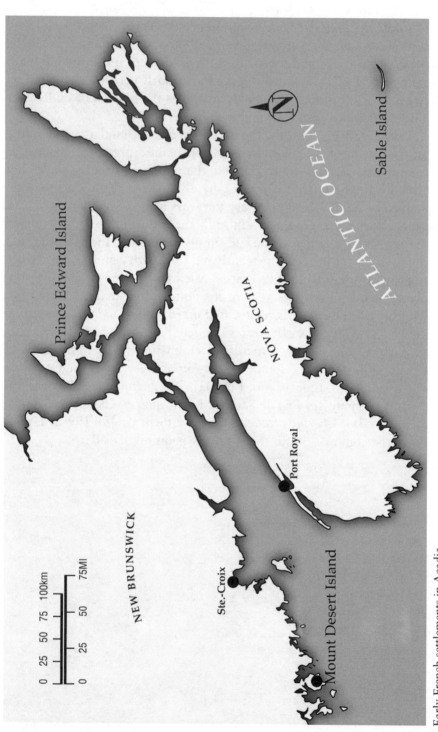

Early French settlements in Acadia.

NINE

The French Venture *in* Arcadia: Ste.-Croix, Port Royal, *and* St.-Sauveur (1604–1614)

Exploration

The French King Henri IV, losing faith in both La Roche's attempts at Sable Island and Chauvin's at Tadoussac (chapter 8), turned to a man of distinguished accomplishments, François Aymar de Cleremont de Chaste, Knight of Malta, Grand Prior of Auvergne, Governor of Dieppe and Arques la Bataille, Commander of Limoges, French Ambassador and Ambassador Extraordinary to England, Vice Admiral of France, Commander of the French and Portuguese naval forces supporting António, Prior of Crato's unsuccessful attempt to free Portugal from Spanish control, Gentleman of the King's Chamber, and a principal creditor of the king. In 1602, the king granted De Chaste the trade monopoly in New France to support anticipated colonies. De Chaste attempted to form a trade company with the merchants of St.-Malo and Rouen to share in the venture, but while merchants of Rouen agreed, those of St.-Malo remained resolutely opposed to any monopoly and the expenses of colonization. Nevertheless, De Chaste was able to launch an expedition of two ships in spring 1603 commanded by François Gravé du Pont, generally referred to either as Gravé or du Pont. Also onboard was Samuel de Champlain, whom De

Chaste had invited to accompany the expedition in an unofficial capacity. Both Gravé and Champlain were destined to play great roles in the future of Canada, but no such fate awaited De Chaste, who died two months after the expedition sailed.

The expedition launched by De Chaste explored the St.-Laurent and a number of its tributary rivers, where they found conditions much different than Cartier had experienced about sixty years previously. The Iroquoians were gone from the valley, and their settled communities were overgrown ruins, while their less-sedentary enemies, such as the Etchemin and Montagnais, today called the Innu, now freely roamed the area. The difficulties posed by intertribal warfare and the navigation of rivers barred by fierce rapids turned French attention away from the St.-Laurent temporarily and toward the coast of Acadia, the coastal regions of the modern Canadian provinces of Nova Scotia, New Brunswick, Prince Edward Island, a portion of eastern Québec, and in the United States the coast of Maine at least as far south as the Kennebec River. This area seemed to offer less-challenging conditions and good prospects for fur trade.

After the death of De Chaste, Henri IV turned to Pierre du Gua, sieur de Monts, generally referred to as either Dugua or De Monts. He, like La Roche and Chauvin, was a member of the minor gentry, and he had distinguished himself fighting in the king's service during the French religious wars. He had also taken part in several trading voyages to Canada, including Chauvin's expedition to Tadoussac. King Henri granted De Monts the rank of vice admiral and appointed him lieutenant general in "Acadia, Canada, and other places in New France." The king's commission included a ten-year monopoly of the fur trade and the obligations to establish colonies, to bring sixty settlers from France each year, and to convert the Indians to Christianity.

De Monts successfully convinced some merchants from the port cities of Rouen, St.-Malo, St. Jean de Luz, and La Rochelle to join him in a company to share in the exploitation of the monopoly and, almost incidentally as far as the merchants were concerned, to found a colony in Acadia. De Chaste had previously sought to involve merchants with indifferent results, but De Monts proved more successful by dangling the prospect of great profits. By convincing merchants to invest, De Monts raised substantial funds to finance the colony and effectively stifled the voices that argued for free trade. In 1604, De Monts sailed with three ships to trade for furs and two to establish a colony. The

ships carried ample supplies and personnel, including several aristocrats, skilled artisans of many sorts, soldiers, and conscripted
vagabonds. Samuel de Champlain joined the expedition as cartographer at De Monts's invitation. The colonists included Catholics and
Huguenots, including two priests and a minister, but no women. The
colonists generally seem to have worked together with a minimum of
religious acrimony, but during the voyage the relations between the
minister and a priest deteriorated to a fistfight.

Arriving on the eastern coast of Nova Scotia, De Monts and company explored to the south and then rounded the end of the peninsula
and sailed north into the Baie Française, the modern Bay of Fundy, exploring first the eastern side. The area now called the Annapolis Basin
impressed all favorably for the large, safe harbor and the agricultural
potential of the region. One of the gentlemen accompanying the expedition, Jean de Biencourt, Seigneur de Poutrincourt et de Saint Just,
referred to as Poutrincourt, was so impressed with the area that he requested that Du Monts grant it to him as a seigneurial holding. Du
Monts made the grant, which included fur-trading privileges and fishing rights. The explorers proceeded to investigate the northern reaches
of the bay and then sailed down the western side, where they came to
a large river they named the Rivière St. Jean because they discovered
it on the feast day of St. John the Baptist.

Ste.-Croix Island (1604–1605)

Moving farther south, in June they came to an anchorage, today's Pas-
samaquoddy Bay, into which flowed a river they called the Rivière des
Etchemins after the local Etchemin tribe, also known as the Pas-
samaquoddy. Today it is called the Ste.-Croix River. In its lower course
the river is tidal, brackish, and about a mile wide, and there Du Monts
and his party found a small island near midstream where they resolved
to make a temporary settlement. They named the isle Ste.-Croix, today
known locally as Dochet Island. The site offered some advantages: it
provided a protected anchorage, and there was good soil on the mainland nearby. The climate initially seemed mild, there was enough time
to prepare the island before winter, and it could be readily defended,
in contrast to any place on the adjacent mainland. The island, however,
was too small for a permanent settlement. The expedition hoped to
find a more advantageous location for a permanent settlement in the
spring, but the island would serve until then.

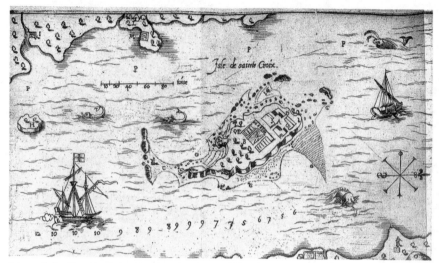

Map of the Ste.-Croix settlement by Samuel de Champlain. *Les voyages du sieur de Champlain.* Paris: Chez Iean Berjon, 1613, p. 34.

The men fell to work clearing the island and building cabins. Many of the buildings erected on the island were made of sawn boards, some from lumber brought from France. A few log cabins were also constructed on the mainland. On the island, the men also constructed a Catholic chapel, storehouse, blacksmith shop, well, oven, kitchen, mess hall, and positions for cannons, more to defend against possible attack by the English or Spanish than the peaceful local Etchemin. Although it was late in the season, the men sowed gardens on the island and the adjacent mainland, where they also planted rye. The soil on the island was sandy, and the gardens there did not prosper, but the men were heartened to see the plants on the mainland did well during the long northern summer days. Relations with the Etchemin in the area were cordial, and they were eager to trade.

On the last day of August, De Monts sent Gravé du Pont and Poutrincourt back to France with the ships to arrange supply ships to return in the spring. De Monts, Champlain, and seventy-seven other men remained behind to overwinter on the island. On September 2, Champlain set out in a small boat with twelve sailors and two Indian guides to explore to the south. Others had sailed along that coast, but it was still poorly known. Champlain carefully examined about 150 miles of the coastline and sailed 50 miles up the Penobscot Estuary and River without finding a site he considered satisfactory for a colony.

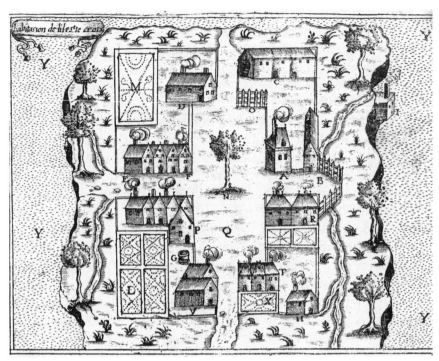

Schematic plan of the northern portion of the Ste.-Croix settlement by Samuel de Champlain. *Les voyages*, p. 38.

About the time Champlain returned, on October 3, snow began to fall and winter set in. It was soon apparent that the settlers had an inadequate appreciation of the severity of the climate. Snow blanketed the area, remaining over three feet deep at the end of April, and the poorly insulated cabins proved cold and drafty. The little wood that grew on the small island had been cut for construction except for a narrow fringe at the north end of the island, left in the vain hope that it would break the cold winds that blew down the river valley. The French had to harvest firewood on the mainland and laboriously transport it to the island. The river water was too brackish to use, and the well the men dug on the island was inadequate so they also had to fetch water from the mainland. Ice flows made movement across the river difficult, dangerous, and sometimes impossible.

The winter forced the men to subsist mainly on salted meat, and soon scurvy, little understood in the early seventeenth century, appeared among them. The colonists recognized that the disease was somehow connected with diet, but they knew of no way to prevent or alleviate it. The leadership of the colony, better nourished than the common workmen, suffered less. Cartier found a remedy in the St.-Laurent valley in 1536 (chapter 8), but that remedy was apparently unknown to the Etchemin of Acadia and De Monts's men. Thirty-five colonists died during the long, bitter winter, and twenty more men were near death when spring came at last and the Etchemin returned from their winter hunt bringing fresh meat to trade to the French. The ill revived, though some long suffered from the effects of scurvy.

Thoroughly disillusioned with Ste.-Croix Island, De Monts decided to explore to the south in hope of finding a better site for his colony. He reconnoitered again the territory Champlain had previously examined and continued much farther south, rounding the end of Cape Cod before turning back without having found anyplace that seemed ideal for a colony. Returning to Ste.-Croix, De Monts and the colonists anticipated the arrival of supply ships from France in April, but when they had still not appeared by the middle of May, De Monts began to prepare two boats to go in search of cod-fishing vessels to carry the men back to France. Before he could leave, however, Gravé du Pont arrived in mid-June with supplies and about forty men.

Port Royal, First Occupation (1605–1607)

De Monts decided to transfer the colonial effort across the Bay of Fundy at least until a better location could be found. The colonists disassembled most of the buildings at Ste.-Croix and in several trips transferred them to the new site, named Port Royal, where they had to clear forest, reassemble buildings, construct some anew, and unload the supplies shipped from France. In September, De Monts returned to France to defend his monopoly and arrange new support for the colony, and along with him went all but three of the survivors of the dreadful winter at Ste.-Croix Island. Champlain was one of the three who remained. Gravé became the new leader of the colony.

The colonists entered their second winter on the coast of Acadia determined not to suffer the ills of the previous year. They had more and better supplies from France, and the local Mi'qmak (Souriquois) band traded fresh meat to them during the autumn and early winter. Membertou, chief of the local Mi'qmak, proved a trustworthy friend to the colonists and provided them valuable aid. Still, about a dozen of the French died during the winter, probably of scurvy. Among the dead were a quarrelsome Catholic priest and his foe, an equally contentious Huguenot minister. They expired at about the same time, and the colonists, with morbidly ironic humor rare in the age of religious wars, buried both in a single grave to see if they could find the peace together there that had eluded them in life. In the spring, Gravé attempted another reconnaissance to the south, but the small boat he had prepared for the journey encountered a contrary wind at the mouth of the Port Royal harbor and was wrecked on the rocks.

Meantime in France, De Monts enlisted Jean de Biencourt de Poutrincourt, who had earlier received a grant of land at Port Royal, to lead the upcoming expedition and assume command at Port Royal. Along with Poutrincourt and at his invitation came Mark Lescarbot, a disgruntled French lawyer and sometime poet. He would become a principal chronicler of events over the next year. An accident to the supply ship before leaving La Rochelle harbor and unfavorable combinations of wind and tide delayed departure until mid-May. After further delay by storms and unfavorable winds, the ship finally arrived at Port Royal at the end of July, by which time Gravé du Pont, like De Monts the year before, was ready to abandon the colony and had gone in search of cod fishermen who could transport the men back to France. Poutrincourt's arrival saved the colony at least for the moment.

After about a month, Gravé and a number of others returned to France, and Poutrincourt set out along with Champlain to explore to the south. Although it was already late in the season, Poutrincourt spent considerable unproductive time and effort reexamining the coast that Champlain and De Monts had previously surveyed before advancing into new territory. The expedition finally rounded the tip of Cape Cod before turning back, supplies and time nearly exhausted, and again without finding a place considered suitable for colonization, mainly because of the large and aggressive Indian population. About a decade later, from 1616 to 1619, an epidemic ravaged the New England tribes, largely depopulating the coastal region. The Pilgrims, arriving in 1620, saw the great mortality of the Native peoples as God's plan for their benefit, making it convenient for them to colonize the area.

While exploring, Poutrincourt left Lescarbot in command at Port Royal, and he and those remaining with him reconnoitered the area, planted crops, and improved the housing. On Poutrincourt's return, Lescarbot greeted him with a theatrical spectacle written for the occasion entitled *Théâtre de Neptune*, enacted on boats near the shoreline. In the spectacle, Neptune himself greets Poutrincourt, followed by six attendant Tritons who praise Poutrincourt and promise him future success. Finally, four men in the character of Indians approach in a canoe offering subservience, gifts, and praise. Lescarbot's verse is not among the great monuments of French literature, but the production is nonetheless impressive given the place and circumstances and an able reflection of the much greater spectacles enacted throughout Europe to greet visiting nobility and mark special occasions. Predictably, in recent years the work has been fashionably denounced as culturally misappropriating and genocidal.

Winter proved much milder than the terrible season at Ste.-Croix Island or even the previous year at Port Royal, and provisions were usually abundant. At the suggestion of Champlain, Poutrincourt established a dining club, the Order of Good Cheer, although membership consisted of only about fourteen of the high-ranking colonists. Early in the winter and during the spring, colonists hunted, fished, and traded with the Mi'qmak for fresh meat and fish, but during the depths of winter the Mi'qmak were sometimes absent for weeks, away on their seasonal hunt, and fresh meat was not widely available. Provisions and wine brought from France were distributed to all the colonists, but again the lack of fresh food led to the appearance of scurvy, although it was less widespread than in previous years. Lescarbot records that four men, whom he describes as downcast or slothful, died in February and March, not realizing that depression and lethargy were symptoms of scurvy rather than causes. Champlain wrote that seven died during the winter, perhaps including deaths from other causes.

With the coming of spring the colonists planted crops and gardens and built a watermill to grind grain, but a heavy blow fell in May. A small vessel from France brought news that during the previous year, Dutch traders had secured most of the Indians' peltry in the St.-Laurent valley, and a number of French traders and even some of the members of De Monts's trading company also took furs privately with no regard to the company's monopoly. The trading company had consequently suffered heavy losses and disbanded, cutting off funding for the colony. Furthermore, the advocates of free trade had persuaded the King's Council to revoke De Monts's monopoly. Once again it was apparent that a royal grant of monopoly was meaningless without effective power to enforce the claim on distant shores and consistent royal commitment. Lescarbot maintained, probably overoptimistically, that the colony would have been self-sustaining in a year, but it certainly was not yet, and Poutrincourt and the colonists reluctantly abandoned Port Royal and returned to France.

The initial settlement at Port Royal was overcome not by weather, foreign enemies, nor hostile Native Americans but rather by inadequate, precarious financing and the political influence of commercial rivals. After the withdrawal from Port Royal, De Monts reckoned that the venture cost him over 10,000 livres, and he was ready to abandon any connection to Nouvelle-France. Champlain, however, convinced De Monts to support a return to the St.-Laurent valley, where in 1608 they founded a fur trade post at a narrows of the St.-Laurent River. Despite hardship and death, the post survived to become the first permanent French settlement in North America: Québec.

Within a few months of the French departure from Port Royal, the English established two colonies in North America. One, in Virginia, survived. The other, by the mouth of the Sagadahoc (Kennebec) River a little south of the French efforts in Acadia, failed (chapter 13).

Port Royal, Second Occupation (1611–1614)

Poutrincourt was yet determined to return to Port Royal, where he firmly believed he could make the colony a success, but his financial resources were strained, and there were few potential sources of aid. There was no prospect that the king would fund the colonization effort, but in 1607, Henri IV approved Poutrincourt's efforts to revive the colony and ordered that Jesuit missionaries should accompany the expedition to proselytize among the Indians. Poutrincourt was genuinely eager to convert the Indians, but he was not enthusiastic about Jesuit missionaries. We do not know the exact cause of his antipathy, but the order had already earned a reputation in some circles as manipulative, domineering, and excessively concerned with financial matters. In 1608, Poutrincourt wrote to Pope Paul V, gaining spiritual support for his return to Port Royal. Perhaps he hoped that papal approval would lead to financial support in France, but it produced no windfall. Personal matters, continuing financial difficulties, and disagreements about the inclusion of the Jesuits delayed Poutrincourt's departure for Port Royal until 1610, when he sailed in one ship along with his son, Charles de Biencourt, and a small contingent of colonists but no Jesuits. Poutrincourt claimed he could not accommodate two Jesuits until he constructed an appropriate residence for them, but he brought a secular priest, the Abbé Jessé Fléché, on the voyage.

The colonists were relieved on arrival to find the settlement intact except for a little deterioration of the roofs due to weather. Membertou and his Mi'qmak band had not disturbed the buildings or their contents at all and now greeted the French enthusiastically. While the colonists set to work repairing the settlement and planting crops, the priest Fléché provided religious instruction to Membertou and his family. The chief had previously received a little religious indoctrination, and now, just three weeks after the colonists arrived, Fléché baptized him and twenty members of his family. Undoubtedly, this conversion was made with such haste so that news of it could be carried by Biencourt, who sailed for France in early July, a little over a month after the initial landing. Poutrincourt's colonial venture needed support from France urgently, and he hoped that the mass baptism would win the backing among churchmen and at the court.

Biencourt's arrival in France produced no wellspring of support. His efforts to obtain a monopoly of the fur trade to support the colony were rejected by the court, destroying efforts to gain a cash advance from French hatmakers who utilized beaver fur to make felt, and the mass conversion of Membertou's family was criticized as so rushed that they could not have yet understood and absorbed the essential elements of Christianity. King Henri IV had been assassinated after the colonists had sailed for Port Royal, and the royal government was now in the hands of the Queen Mother and regent of Louis XIII, Marie de Médicis. With the regent's approval, the young king granted Biencourt the high-sounding title of "Vice Admiral in the Sea of the Setting Sun" with the right to approve passports for sailings to and from Acadia for which he was entitled to a fee, but the entitlement provided little income.

Marie de Médicis favored the Jesuits, as did her wealthy and influential first lady in waiting, Antoinette de Pons-Ribérac, comtesse de La Roche-Guyon and marquise de Guercheville, generally known as simply Madam de Guercheville. The two pressured Biencourt to take two Jesuits, Pierre Biard and Énemond Massé, who were supposed to have taken part in the original voyage with Poutrincourt but had been left behind. In his desperation for financing, Biencourt conspired with two Huguenot ship outfitters to extract money from the court and the Jesuits. The Huguenots had agreed to invest in the ship in anticipation

View of the Port Royal settlement by Samuel de Champlain. *Les voyages*, p. 99.

of a share of the profits from the voyage, but now, expressing horror that the ship would transport Jesuits, they refused to finish outfitting it, although they offered to transport members of any other Catholic order. Contemporary rumor associated the Jesuits with the assassination of Henri IV, so the Huguenots were able to mask their hostility to the Jesuits as patriotic zeal rather than religious bigotry. In reality, it was neither. Even with the investment of the two merchants, Biencourt did not have the resources to fund the voyage. Madam de Guercheville contributed 4,000 livres to buy the Huguenots' interest so the voyage might go forward and the Jesuits travel to Port Royal. That sum was far more than the merchants had actually invested, and after receiving the profitable payment, they quietly lent Biencourt 1,225 livres.

The Queen Mother granted the Jesuits 1,500 livres to cover expenses, and they received additional contributions from others. Biencourt then entered into complex contractual agreements with the Jesuits by which they paid substantially for their transport to Acadia and made Biencourt unsecured, interest-free loans sufficient to complete financing the voyage. The Jesuits effectively provided three-quarters of the capital for the voyage but were guaranteed only half the profits, if any. The complicated financial negotiations delayed Biencourt's departure along with the Jesuits until the end of January 1611.

The voyage proved long, requiring four months, by the end of which the crew and passengers of the small ship had consumed much of the provisions they were supposed to be bringing to Port Royal. Biencourt finally arrived in late May to find the colony had survived the winter, but at the usual cost of hardships. On arrival of the supply ship, Poutrincourt immediately departed to trade for the furs that Indians had gathered over the winter, but to his disappointment other French traders had come before him and already secured almost all the peltry. This was a major financial blow to the woefully underfinanced colony. Poutrincourt then sailed for France, hoping to find backing for the colony and arrange for a new shipment of supplies. He took Fléché with him on the return trip and left his son Biencourt in charge of the colony.

Poutrincourt arrived in France heavily in debt and with no immediate prospects of finding support. He approached Madame de Guercheville, who had contributed to the last voyage, and out of regard for the Jesuits, she remained willing to support the Port Royal colony, with certain reservations. She would share in any profits from the voyage, and she placed her investment not with Poutrincourt but rather with a representative of the Jesuits, Brother Gilbert Du Thet, who was supposed to deal directly with the ship's outfitter. Guercheville also directly approached De Monts, whose trade monopoly had been revoked but whose grant of land was still valid, and, with the king's approval, she gained title to all of Acadia except Port Royal.

Poutrincourt remained in France but was able to dispatch a small supply ship at the end of November 1611. It arrived safely in the last days of January 1612. Food was in short supply at Port Royal, but otherwise the colony had come through the worst of winter without disaster. The colony, however, was the scene of growing distrust and confrontations between Biencourt and the Jesuits, ranging from where the deceased Chief Membertou should be buried to how Biencourt conducted the fur trade. These disagreements blossomed into open hostility after the arrival of the supply ship. Brother Du Thet, who had come on the voyage, accused Poutrincourt's agent of financial irregularities, and the agent accused Du Thet of treasonous utterances about the assassination of Henri IV. Accusations flew back and forth until in March 1612, the Jesuits resolved to return to France with the supply ship. Biencourt, who had initially not wanted the Jesuits in the colony, now did his best to prevent their departure. If the Jesuits abandoned Port Royal and their negative reports about Biencourt and the management of funds reached Madame de Guercheville, she would surely refuse any further support of the colony and possibly institute a lawsuit. The struggle between Biencourt and the Jesuits lasted from March to June 1612 before a compromise was achieved: Fathers Biard and Massé remained at Port Royal while Brother Du Thet went to France, probably as a passenger on a cod-fishing ship, to defend himself against accusations and arrange a new supply shipment to the colony.

Winter 1612–1613 and spring 1613 were times of hunger, terminated by disappointment when two ships, the *Jonas* of about one hundred tons and a tiny pinnace of twelve tons, finally arrived from France in May 1613. They bore news that Madame de Guercheville would no longer fund the colony and that the Jesuits would withdraw from Port Royal to take part in a new colony elsewhere.

St.-Sauveur

The site chosen for the new colony, to be called St.-Sauveur, was south of Port Royal on Mount Desert Island at what is now Fernald Point near the entrance to Somes Sound. The personnel of the new colony, under the command of Madame de Guercheville's agent, René Le Cocq de La Saussaye, consisted of four Jesuits—Fathers Biard and Massé who had been at Port Royal; Father Jacques Quintin, newly arrived from France; and Brother Gilbert Du Thet—and about eighty laborers and artisans. Once the essential structures of the colony were completed, all were to return to France except thirty men who would overwinter at the new site. La Saussaye, aware that the colonists would face a pressing need for food during the winter, set the men to work clearing land and planting crops. He ignored the advice of those who wanted to give priority to fortifying the colony and unloading the supply ship.

In the meantime, the English colony at Jamestown, founded in 1607, dispatched Captain Samuel Argall in the ship *Treasurer*, best described as a fishing vessel equipped for war with fourteen cannons and a crew of sixty. The English were aware that the French had settled to the north and sent Argall to patrol an area claimed by both nations. Fogbound, Argall anchored his ship in a bay by chance close to the French colony. An Indian encountered the English there and, mistaking them for French, guided them to the colony, where the French ship *Jonas* and the pinnace sat at anchor with furled sails and largely unmanned. When the English appeared, Brother Du Thet and a few others scrambled aboard the *Jonas*, but they could offer no effective resistance. Du Thet fired a cannon, but the only result was to attract return fire. Du Thet was shot through the body, and Argall's men brought him ashore, where he died the next day. La Saussaye and others who had remained on land retreated to the woods, and Argall seized the settlement and looted La Saussaye's belongings, including his commissions and royal letters that would have enabled him to show that he had a legitimate reason to be in territory claimed by the French crown. Without supplies or means to resist, La Saussaye and the others had no alternative but to surrender. Argall now had to deal with his prisoners. He gave La Saussaye a shallop, a small boat about thirty feet long, into which he crowded all but fourteen of the French, including Father Massé. La Saussaye was fortunate to soon encounter French fishing and trading vessels along the coast, on which he and the others returned to France. Argall took Fathers Biard and Quentin, the captain of the *Jonas*, and eleven others to Virginia.

In Virginia, the ruling council ordered Argall to take his ship and the two captured French ships, the *Jonas* and the pinnace, to attack and destroy all French establishments in the territory claimed by England. Argall forced Fathers Biard and Quentin and several of the other French prisoners to take part in the expedition. He first returned to St.-Sauveur, where he destroyed the little settlement and cut down the Catholic cross the Jesuits had erected and immediately replaced it with a virtually identical Anglican cross bearing the name of the king of England. Argall next sailed to St.-Croix Island, where he burned the remaining buildings and then crossed the bay to attack Port Royal. The blow there was totally unexpected and fell when most of the men were working in the fields. Argall's men looted the settlement, carried off some livestock, butchered the rest, and then burned down all of the buildings except the mill and a couple of barns that were not visible from the main settlement, but they took no prisoners, merely ordering the French to leave the area. As they sailed for Virginia, Argall's little fleet was struck by a fierce storm and the ships separated. The pinnace was never seen again; the *Jonas* was driven far to the east and finally landed in England. Only Argall's ship, the *Treasurer*, returned to Virginia.

The second French occupation of Port Royal was probably doomed from its beginnings. Poutrincourt's own ability to finance the colony was simply inadequate, and the only other feasible source of finance, Madame de Guercheville, was alienated by the feud between Charles de Biencourt and the Jesuits, which led her to divert her resources to the foundation of St.-Sauveur. It is commonplace to blame the destruction of the French colony on La Saussaye's command to plant crops rather than fortify the colony, but his decision was rational, although unfortunate. The appearance of a hostile English ship equipped for war was a relatively remote possibility, but the coming of winter a certainty, and without adequate provisions, winter at St.-Sauveur might have been worse than the disastrous season at St.-Croix. Argall attacked St.-Sauveur before it was really established and took Port Royal by surprise, but it is unlikely that either could have offered more than token resistance even in the most favorable circumstances. St.-Sauveur might have survived if the English had not intervened, but Argall's burning of Port Royal probably only slightly hastened the end of the colony there.

Aftermath

Argall's raid was the effective end of the second occupation of Port Royal. Although crippled by debt, Poutrincourt entered into a partnership with fur traders to organize another voyage to Port Royal in 1614. After viewing the ruins of the burnt colony, he signed over the title to Port Royal to his son and brought most of the starving colonists back to France. A few remained along with Charles de Biencourt, but henceforth Port Royal was just a small trading post. After 1618, fur trade in the area declined greatly, and Biencourt came to live increasingly with the local Mi'qmak. There he died in 1623 or 1624, a strange fate for a man who once bore the title of vice admiral of France.

Poutrincourt did not long survive his last voyage to Acadia. He was killed in uncertain circumstances during the attempt to recapture the town of Méry-sur-Seine in Champagne in December 1615.

Despite the losses in Acadia, Champlain encouraged Pierre Du Gua de Monts's belief in the potential of Canada, and De Monts supported Champlain's return to the St.-Laurent valley, the development of Québec, and exploration. De Monts was active in Canada until he was about sixty years old, and a shareholder in a trading company even after that. He deserves high honors as one of the founders of Nouvelle-France. He died in France in 1628.

Mark Lescarbot returned to France at the end of the first occupation of Port Royal. He wrote on many themes, but his most important work is *Histoire de la Nouvelle-France*. Some ill feeling grew between Lescarbot and Champlain. Champlain may have resented that Lescarbot published first and felt that Lescarbot underrated his role and overstated his own. Lescarbot died in France in 1642.

Samuel de Champlain led a complex and adventurous life, during which he traveled across the Atlantic over twenty times, lived among the Indian tribes, explored lands previously unknown to Europeans, and gained renown as geographer, cartographer, diplomat, and author. His foundation at Québec became the first permanent French settlement in North America, and he is rightly regarded as the Father of Nouvelle-France. His work *Les voyages dv sievr de Champlain Xaintongeois*, published in 1613, is of fundamental importance to understanding events in Acadia. Champlain died in 1635.

Charles de Biencourt accused Father Pierre Biard of leading the English to Port Royal, while Biard put the blame on an Indian. After returning to France, Biard wrote a lengthy account of the events in Acadia. He occasionally reaches conclusions about events without full knowledge of the circumstances, and the enduring enmity between Biard and Biencourt is evident in his writings. He died in 1622. Father Énemond Massé returned to Nouvelle-France as a missionary in 1625 and died there in 1646.

Madame de Guercheville sought in vain to get compensation from England for Argall's attack on St.-Sauveur, as negotiations floundered amid conflicting territorial claims. She received only the return of the ship *Jonas*. Guercheville maintained her title to Acadia until 1627, although after the destruction of St.-Sauveur she no longer invested money or sponsored missionaries. She died in 1632.

In 1614, Samuel Argall returned to England, where an inquiry found his actions in Acadia legal and proper. Argall went on to become deputy governor of Virginia, a member of the Council of New England, and admiral for New England. He was knighted in 1624 and served as admiral of a fleet of twenty-eight vessels operating off the coast of France in 1625. He died in early 1626.

During the Anglo-French War of 1627–1629, England managed to secure for a short time control over nearly all of French North America. James I of England (James VI of Scotland) granted Acadia, then to be called Nova Scotia, to Sir William Alexander, who led seventy

Scots to colonize Port Royal near the previous French settlement. The settlement, however, was returned to the French by treaty in 1632. The English and French repeatedly fought over the town until the English conquered it permanently in 1710, renaming it Annapolis Royal in honor of the English Queen Ann. Later, the French tried unsuccessfully to retake the town.

Sources

Mark Lescarbot's *Histoire de la Nouvelle-France* is one of the basic sources for the French venture in Acadia to the end of the first occupation of Port Royal. The first edition was published in Paris by I. Milot in 1609, followed by a second augmented edition by the same publisher in 1611 and 1612, and a third augmented edition also published in Paris but by Adrian Perier in 1613. The early chapters that narrate the French ventures in Brazil and Florida are derived from earlier published works, but his account of events in Acadia and his time there are of great worth and enduring interest. Lescarbot believed sincerely that colonization in Canada and Acadia was in the best interest of king and country, that the advocates of free trade put self-interest ahead of both, and that the revocation of De Monts's monopoly that ended the first occupation of Port Royal was an unmitigated disaster. Lescarbot's views led him to minimize the difficulties faced by the colony and to maximize the positives. W. L. Grant, *The History of New France*, intro. Henry Percival Biggar (Toronto: Champlain Society, 1911) is a readily available translation of Lescarbot's work. Particularly interesting are Grant's notes indicating changes made in the second and third editions.

Jerry Wasserman, ed. and intro., *Spectacle of Empire: Marc Lescarbot's Theatre of Neptune in New France* (Vancouver: Talonbooks, 2006) places the *Théâtre de Neptune* in its social context in the early seventeenth and early twenty-first centuries and presents the original French text, two English translations, and an enlightening parallel, Ben Jonson's *The Masque of Blackness* (1605), with theatrical design by Inigo Jones.

Lescarbot also wrote *La Conversion des Savvages qui ont esté baptizes en la Novvelle France, cette annee 1610* (Paris: Jean Millot, [1610]) in defense of Abbé Fléché's baptisms of Membertou and his family at Port Royal, criticized by the Jesuits and others as premature and canonically improper. It is conveniently published in Reuben Gold

Thwaites, *The Jesuit Relations and Allied Documents*, vol. 1 (Cleveland: Burrows Brothers, 1896), 53-113.

Samuel de Champlain, *Les voyages dv sievr de Champlain Xaintongeois, capitaine ordinaire pour le Roy, en la marine: Divisez en devx livres. ou, Iovrnal tres-fidele des observations faites és descouuertures de la Nouuelle France: tant en la descriptiõ des terres, costes, riuieres, ports, haures, leurs hauteurs, & plusieurs declinaisons de la guide-aymant; qu'en la créace des peuples, leur superstition facon de viure & de querroyer: enrichi de quantité de figures* (Paris: Chez Iean Berjon, 1613) stands beside Lescarbot's work as a chief source for the unsuccessful French efforts in Acadia, but it is only one of a number of his works detailing his career. Champlain's accounts lacked Lescarbot's classical and literary allusions, and he sometimes undervalued the achievements of others, but he was at the center of events that he recounted frankly. His later actions at Québec assured his position as the Father of Nouvelle-France. The standard edition of Champlain's work is Henry Percival Biggar et al., eds., *The Works of Samuel de Champlain*, 7 vols. (Toronto: Champlain Society, 1922–1936), which has been reprinted several times.

Father Pierre Biard's primary narrative of the last phases of the French in Acadia, *Relation de la Novvelle France, de ses terres, natvrel dv Pais & de ses Habitants* (Lyon: Lovys Mvgvet, 1616) is republished along with an English translation in Thwaites, *Jesuit Relations*, vol. 3 (Cleveland: Burrows Brothers, 1897), 23-301, and vol. 4 (Cleveland: Burrows Brothers, 1897), 7-167. Biard's work includes valuable though not entirely original ethnographic information about the indigenous peoples he encountered. Much of the work is a justification of his actions and those of other Jesuits in reaction to an anonymous pamphlet, thought by some to be by Lescarbot, *Factum du procez entre Messire Iean de Biencourt cheualier sieur de Poutrincourt, baron de S. Iust, appellant d'vne part, et Pierre Biart, Euemond Massé & consorts, soy disans prestres de la societé de Iesus, intimez* (Paris[?]: n.p., [1614]). Several letters by Biard and other minor documents are also in Thwaites, *Jesuit Relations*, vols. 1-2.

William Inglis Morse, Esther Lowrey Houghton, and Mrs. Walter Edwards Houghton Jr., *Pierre Du Gua, sieur de Monts; records: colonial and "Saintongeois"* (London: B. Quaritch, 1939) provides a valuable collection of documents relevant to the important initiator of the Acadia endeavor and the cofounder of Québec. De Monts has also been the subject of several recent studies: Jean Liebel, *Pierre Dugua, sieur de Mons, fondateur de Québec* (Paris: Le Croît vif, 1999); Jean-Yves Grenon, *Pierre Dugua de Mons: fondateur de l'Acadie (1604–1607) et cofondateur de Québec (1608–1613): conférence prononcée dans le cadre des conférences de l'Association des Amis des Archives départementales de la Charente-Maritime* (Charenti-Maritime: Archives départementales, conseil général de la Charente-Maritime, 2001); Guy Binot, *Pierre Dugua de Mons: gentilhomme royannais, premier colonisateur du Canada, lieutenant général de la Nouvelle-France de 1603 à 1612* ([Vaux-sur-Mer, France:] Bonne anse, 2004).

Henry Percival Biggar, *The Early Trading Companies of New France* (Toronto: Warwick Bros. & Rutter, 1901) is over a century old and outmoded in some details, but it remains a valuable overview, particularly in regard to financial matters. É.-H. Gosselin, *Documents authentiques et inédits pour servir à l'histoire de la marine normande et du commerce rouennais pendant les XVIᵉ, et XVIIᵉ siècles* (Rouen: H. Boissel, 1876) is even older but remains a basic collection of source documents bearing on shipping and commerce. Marcel Trudel, *The Beginnings of New France 1524–1663*, trans. Patricia Claxton (Toronto: McClelland and Stewart, 1973) provides an excellent overview, treated in greater depth in Marcel Trudel, *Le comptoir, 1604–1627. Histoire de la Nouvelle-France*, vol. 2 (Montréal: Fides, 1966).

No account of the early activities of the Jesuits in Acadia can fail to mention the abundant works of Lucien Campeau, SJ, most prominently *Monumenta Novae Franciae : a patribus ejusdem societatis edita / 1 La première mission d'Acadie : 1602–1616* (Québec: Presses de l'Université Laval, 1967); *La première mission d'Acadie, 1602–1616* (Québec: Presses de l'Université Laval, 1967); *The Beginning of Acadia, 1602–1616* (Bridgetown, NS: Gontran Trottier, 1999); *The Beginning of Acadia 1602–1616, Book 2, The Souriquois* (Bridgetown, NS: Gontran Trottier, 1999); *The Beginning of Acadia 1602–1616, Book 3, The Mission* (Bridgetown, NS: Gontran Trottier, 1999), and, with William Lonc and George Topp, *Early Jesuit Missions in Canada* (Halifax, NS: W. Lonc, 2001); *Jesuit Mission to the Souriquois in Acadia, 1611–1613* ([Halifax, NS]: W. Lonc, 2004). Predictably, Campeau is sympathetic to the Jesuit view of matters.

Leading scholars in their areas of specialty have contributed the biographies in the *Dictionary of Canadian Biography/Dictionnaire bi-*

ographique du Canada, http://www.biographi.ca/en/welcome.html. These biographies are always thoughtful and provide the reader with useful bibliography.

PART THREE

English Endeavors

TEN

The English Arctic Endeavor: Meta Incognita (1576–1578)

Background

Martin Frobisher, one of the most famous mariners of Queen Elizabeth's time, made the first attempt to establish an English colony in North America. He was in many ways typical of the adventurers of the sixteenth century, whatever their nationality: brave and adventurous, but also brutal and unreliable.

Born in a small town in northern England about 1535, Frobisher was orphaned about the age of fourteen and went to live at Portsmouth with an uncle who invested in shipping. From there, in 1553, at about age eighteen, Frobisher first went to sea on a trading venture to western Africa, a dangerous voyage. Tropical diseases little known to Europeans could sweep through a ship, the coasts were poorly charted, and the Portuguese who claimed the entire area were prepared to enforce their ban on foreign trade with violence. The Englishmen found a source of abundant pepper, a cargo of great value, but before they could load the ships and depart, most of the crew was struck down by fever. Two of the three ships had to be abandoned, and only 40 men lived to return to England out of the 160 who had sailed from Portsmouth.

In 1554, Frobisher again signed on to one of a small group of ships heading to the coast of Africa. The commander of this expedition was John Lok, whose brother would later play an important role in Frobisher's life. On the African coast, the English bartered for pepper, and a Native chief demanded an English hostage to ensure their peaceful intention. Frobisher volunteered, but the arrangement went wrong. The chief turned Frobisher over to the Portuguese, who fired on the English ships. Lok sailed away, abandoning Frobisher but returning to England with a valuable cargo of pepper, ivory, gold, and slaves.

Frobisher's captivity was unusually mild. He was held for about nine months, during which time the Portuguese treated him civilly and allowed him much freedom. The details of his return to England are not known. He may have been ransomed by a subsequent English trading expedition or perhaps sent to Lisbon and released there. In any event, the Portuguese kindness did not deter Frobisher from involvement during 1559 in an abortive plot to seize Mina, the main Portuguese trading station on the African coast.

By 1563, Frobisher was involved in piracy, raiding Spanish and French cargoes of wine and smuggling the stolen goods into England. He was apprehended and spent a short time in prison. A few years later he was again in prison, although the reason is not known.

In 1568, Frobisher accepted a commission from the Protestant Huguenots to act as a privateer against their enemies, the royal Catholic forces of France and their Catholic allies. During the next year, Frobisher accepted a second similar commission from the Dutch Protestants. In practice, however, he proved ecumenical, pirating from any party he could overpower, including English ships. Complaints led to another imprisonment, but he was soon freed again, the result of bribery and Queen Elizabeth's need for privateers to bolster England's modest sea power.

Shortly after Frobisher's release from prison on charges of piracy, Elizabeth's Privy Council placed him in command of four ships fitted out at government expense with orders to suppress pirates. He was, however, soon ordered instead to take his squadron to Ireland, there to aid English forces active against rebels. Although mainly occupied with transporting supplies, Frobisher also used the opportunity to capture several foreign vessels.

It was about this time, the late 1560s or early 1570s, that Frobisher seems to have become interested in the possibility of a Northwest Pas-

sage to China and India, an idea much discussed at the time. Theorists believed the
earth was necessarily symmetrical in distribution and form of land masses, so there
had to be northern passages analogous to
the Straits of Magellan and the passage
around the southern tip of Africa. In 1553,
English mariners first attempted to find a
Northeast Passage through the Arctic Sea
north of Russia, and two years later the English Crown granted the Muscovy Company
a monopoly to seek such a passage. The
company failed to find the passage but did
establish profitable commerce with Russia.
The company's monopoly included any potential passages to the northeast or northwest, and Frobisher and anyone else who
wished to attempt to find a Northwest Passage had to come to terms
with the company or have royal support to override its claims.

Martin Frobisher, from
Henry Holland, *Herwolo-
gia Anglica* (Arnhemiensis,
1620).

   Frobisher's initial step was to gain the support of William Cecil,
Lord Burghley, Elizabeth's lord treasurer, who wrote to the Muscovy
Company endorsing a proposal that Frobisher be allowed to seek the
Northwest Passage. Despite this support, the company initially rejected
the proposal, so Frobisher sought backing from additional influential
courtiers. Early in 1575, members of Elizabeth's Privy Council wrote
again to the Muscovy Company, instructing it to either approve Frobisher's plan or mount its own expedition to find the Northwest Passage. The company gave Frobisher permission to proceed.

   Among the directors of the company was Michael Lok, brother of
John Lok, who had been the captain of the expedition when Frobisher
was captured in Africa. Michael Lok was born about 1522 into a
wealthy merchant family, and by 1575, he had spent considerable time
in Flanders, France, Spain, and Portugal, and traveled even more
broadly. He had captained trading expeditions into the eastern Mediterranean, earned a reputation for his knowledge of languages, geography,
and commerce, and he was alive to the possibilities of a Northwest Passage. Intrigued by Frobisher's proposal, he resigned from the Muscovy
Company to become Frobisher's chief agent and partner. Frobisher
would sail the seas; Lok would run the business end of the enterprise.

First Exploration

Michael Lok invited investors to back Frobisher's expedition, but at first few responded. Frobisher's reputation for reckless and piratical behavior did little to encourage trust, but Lok was able to soothe suspicions to some degree by hiring a purser to watch over money and goods, and two master navigators. In addition to wealthy merchants, many of the notables of Elizabeth's court now invested money in the venture, including the poet Philip Sidney, the scholar John Dee, Elizabeth's spymaster Francis Walsingham, the powerful Earl of Warwick, and his brother, the Earl of Leicester, the queen's favorite. Despite the prominence of some of the investors, the amount raised was disappointingly small, and the expedition had to be reduced in size from the initial plan of three ships of a hundred tons each to two smaller ships of thirty tons and a tiny pinnace of perhaps seven tons. Even the two chief ships, the *Gabriel* and *Michael,* were hardly vessels in which one would gladly challenge the North Atlantic, just about fifty feet in length and fifteen feet in beam. The crews of the two larger ships were seventeen or eighteen men each, and just four manned the pinnace.

Frobisher's little fleet sailed early in June 1576, but the pinnace collided with another ship even before leaving the Thames, and the ships had to halt for repairs. When they finally departed, Frobisher sailed up the eastern coast of England and Scotland, where he encountered strong storms and repeatedly had to seek shelter in harbors. After two and a half weeks, the ships reached just the southern Shetland Islands, where they had to pause for repairs and refresh the water barrels.

Leaving the Shetlands, the ships encountered a fierce gale that blew for a week. The pinnace disappeared in the midst of the storm, and neither it nor the crew were ever seen again. After five weeks, on July 11, Frobisher sighted land bordered by ice. This he identified in accord with what passed for contemporary geographic knowledge as the coast of the island of Frisland. In fact, he had sighted the southern coast of Greenland, but Greenland was thought to lie far to the north and west. The isle of Frisland was actually a fantasy, originating apparently in the misidentification and incorrect location on early maps of the Faroes Islands and Greenland.

Amid the fogs and ice floes near Greenland, Frobisher's two remaining ships became separated. The *Michael* returned to England, where the officers reported that the Northwest Passage was blocked with ice

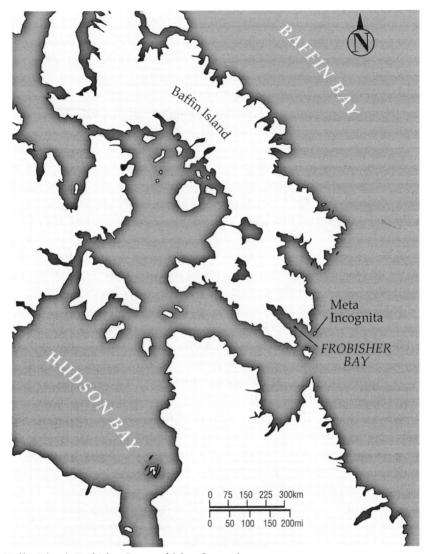

Baffin Island, Frobisher Bay, and Meta Incognita.

and the *Gabriel* had been lost with all hands. In fact, the *Gabriel* was still afloat and Frobisher still pursuing his quest.

A few days after becoming separated from the *Michael*, the *Gabriel* encountered the worst storm yet. The ship survived, but much of the cargo was lost, and at the height of the storm Frobisher had to cut down the mizzenmast to reduce the strain on the hull. Still, he persisted. By July 21, he had sailed into the Davis Strait between the west coast of Greenland and Baffin Island. He sighted ice-shrouded land that day at what he calculated to be a little above 62 degrees north. For the rest of July and early August, he slowly worked his way north amid icebergs and along the edge of the ice pack extending out from the shore as far as several miles. On August 10, a shift in the wind moved the ice pack, and Frobisher at last had a chance to send some of the crew to land on a small island. Nothing of immediately apparent significance was found, but one of the sailors brought back a black rock about the size of a large brick and curiously heavy. Nothing was made of the find at the time; at first the stone was mistakenly believed to be coal. All were, however, excited by what appeared ahead: an opening in the coast tending toward the northeast. This, surely, thought Frobisher, was the expected Northwest Passage that would carry him triumphantly to the riches of the East and personal wealth and power. He promptly named the waterway Frobisher Strait.

Frobisher sailed sixty miles into the strait, and on August 19 he encountered Inuit hunters in kayaks. The Inuit came aboard the *Gabriel*, explored the ship, received small presents, and departed. The next day Frobisher and some of the crew explored the Inuit village while several of the Natives watched at a distance. Frobisher was suspicious of the Inuit, but he sought to convince one Native to guide him through the straits. It is doubtful that much real communication took place since there was no language in common and virtually no understanding of one another's cultures. Frobisher sent a skiff with five men to convey the Native to shore so he might fetch his kayak to lead the way and ordered the men in the skiff to return immediately to the *Gabriel* after landing the Inuit. What happened next is not entirely clear. Three of the men went ashore, and the other two continued to row the skiff out of sight. Frobisher assumed they had been kidnaped by the Inuit, but perhaps at least initially they hoped to do some trading of their own, or they may have been seeking the company of Inuit women. It is even conceivable that they decided to take their chances on this cold foreign shore rather than remain with the *Gabriel* and under Frobisher's discipline. In any event, they disappeared and were never seen again. This left Frobisher with only thirteen men. The next day a number of the Inuit rowed in their kayaks out to the *Gabriel*. Frobisher lured one man close enough to capture him and tried to indicate to the others that he would release his captive when his five men were returned to him. Again, it is doubtful that much real communication took place. The other Inuit paddled away.

Frobisher reluctantly decided to turn back to England. The loss of the five men left him with barely enough to manage the ship. On the return, the depleted crew again had to fight their way through a major storm, but they survived to arrive in London in early October. Objectively, they had little to show for their voyage—just the kidnaped Inuit and the curiously heavy black stone, now all but forgotten. The Inuit was a sensation in London, but he quickly fell ill and died, like so many others a victim of European pathogens to which he had no immunity. The expedition had brought back no profitable goods, and the expenses totaled far more than the capital raised from the initial investors. Frobisher, however, sought to make up these deficits with enthusiasm and promises. He had explored new coasts far to the northwest, and he proudly proclaimed that he had discovered the western mouth and explored a considerable portion of the fabled Northwest Passage. He was even sure that the land forming the northern shore of Frobisher Strait was a portion of Asia and that the exit into the northern Pacific, from which it would be a short and easy voyage to the wealth of the Orient, lay only a little beyond where he was forced by circumstances to turn back. A new expedition would surely bring success and rich returns to the investors.

Second Exploration and Mining

On his own initiative, Michael Lok proposed to the queen that she grant a charter to establish a new organization to be called the Company of Cathay, which would have the right to seek out the Northwest Passage, claim new lands and trade routes, and hold a monopoly on trade stemming from these discoveries. Frobisher and Lok were each to receive a royalty of 1 percent on this trade. In the immediate future, this company of subscribers would manage Frobisher's next expedition and all the benefits expected to flow from it. The proposal also outlined the conditions under which new investors could join the company. At the same time, Frobisher made a secret proposal to the queen that would have cut Lok out of any role and profits in the anticipated discoveries. He sought for himself the titles of high admiral and governor of newly discovered lands, 5 percent of the profits on cargoes shipped from those lands, and 1 percent on cargoes shipped from England to those lands.

The queen had her own ideas, which promised to be much more profitable for her. She did not grant a charter to Lok's proposed company, although she would allow it to use the name Cathay Company, nor did she grant Frobisher extravagant titles and profits. Rather, she virtually assumed control of the venture. Elizabeth invested £500 and appointed six commissioners, one of whom was Lok, to supervise outfitting for the new voyage. She also lent the expedition a ship, the *Ayde* (*Aid* in modern spelling). The ship was of good size, two hundred tons, but it was at least fifteen years old, a considerable age for a wooden sailing vessel. Moreover, Elizabeth insisted that the ship be listed as an additional investment of £750, far in excess of its actual value. The queen's backing, Frobisher's assurances that he had discovered the Northwest Passage, and Lok's enthusiasm all attracted additional investors, and other developments would soon attract even greater attention.

On returning to England, Frobisher had turned over to Lok the heavy black rock that a sailor had picked up on a small island. The stone intrigued Lok, who broke off several fragments, which he gave to three responsible and respected English assayers, including the chief assayer of the Royal Mint in London. All three reported that the stone contained nothing of value, but Lok was not satisfied: the rock was so heavy and looked metallic. In the sixteenth century, assaying was not a simple process, and assayers varied in techniques and skill. Continental practitioners enjoyed better reputations than English assayers, and Lok thought that perhaps a foreign expert could find what the English assayers had not. He approached Giovanni Battista Agnello, a metallurgist and alchemist from Venice. Why Lok turned to this particular man is not clear, as Agnello does not seem to have been particularly distinguished or even of particularly good repute. In any event, he reported finding gold in the specimen and in two more subsequent assays of fragments of the stone.

Lok did not inform Frobisher of the discovery immediately but did approach Francis Walsingham, Elizabeth's spymaster and an influential member of the Privy Council. Walsingham brought samples of the stone to three new assayers, two of whom reported no gold and only a trace of silver, and the third reported finding nothing of value. Agnello assured Lok that the stone contained a substantial amount of gold and other assayers had not been able to find it because they simply lacked skill. In the meantime, Frobisher had heard rumors that Lok had submitted fragments of the stone to assayers. Lok blandly assured Frobisher that several had found nothing of value, although one had managed to detect tin and a little silver. That seemed valuable enough to have Frobisher load the ships with the ore on the proposed second expedition. Frobisher was justifiably suspicious that Lok was not dealing honestly with him, just as he had acted behind Lok's back.

Lok asked Walsingham to arrange a patent for the second voyage, not to explore the Northwest Passage but rather to mine three hundred tons of the ore, which were expected to yield some £9,000 in gold, a very large sum (more than $2 million today) in an age when the purchasing power of the pound was much greater than today. One third of this sum would pay for the voyage and refining, the queen was to have the second third, and the investors would divide the remaining third. Walsingham remained dubious, but allowed the plan to go forward. Frobisher had to be informed, of course, and while he was delighted at the prospect of riches, his suspicions of Lok were confirmed.

News of the gold ore could not be contained. Soon it was the chief topic of the royal court and potential investors. Some of the assayers had evidently retained fragments of the black stone and passed them on to others, who produced their own analyses. One, Jonas Schutz, sometime assistant to Agnello, maintained that others had not used hot enough furnaces in refining the stone, but he had succeeded and found the true worth of the ore to be twelve times greater than Agnello estimated. Even wilder rumors and claims circulated. Investors clamored to put their money into the expedition. Even the suspicious and cautious spymaster Walsingham invested £200, a considerable sum.

Frobisher was granted the title of captain general and command of three ships, the *Gabriel* and *Michael* from the first expedition and the queen's ship *Ayde*. His commission called for him to employ a maximum of 120 men, although he eventually departed with over 140 on board. His specific instructions were to first establish a mining operation, then search for the five men who went missing on the first expedition (and for more deposits of precious metal at the same time), and then to explore the Northwest Passage to make sure it did indeed connect to the Pacific. Frobisher was also charged with establishing good relations with the Inuit and bringing about half a dozen of them back to England. It is not apparent how he was to balance good relations with kidnaping. Finally, he was to leave several men there to explore the land and observe when the strait was most free of ice and open to navigation. It was anticipated that Frobisher would return to England with the three ships loaded to capacity with gold ore.

The expedition departed in May 1577, and the voyage went smoothly. By early June they were in the Orkneys, by July 4 off the south coast of Greenland (still thought to be Frisland), and by July 17 at the entrance to Frobisher Strait and the island where the black rock was found. It must have come as a shock to Frobisher when an extensive search of the island produced no sign of the heavy black ore he sought, and problems quickly developed with the Inuit. When Frobisher encountered two Native men, he lured them close ostensibly to trade but then seized them. Other Inuit ran to aid their comrades. One escaped as arrows and gunshots were exchanged. At the end of the skirmish, Frobisher had a captive, but the Inuit had received an injury, probably broken ribs, that would eventually prove fatal. Frobisher had been hit in the buttock by an arrow, more humiliated than injured.

For the rest of July, Frobisher and his crews explored the shores of Frobisher Strait, finally locating veins of the black ore on what Frobisher named Countess of Warwick Island. Mining commenced, eventually removing enough rock to leave a cut twenty-four feet deep, fifteen feet wide, and sixty feet long. The men believed they saw the unmistakable glints of gold and silver in the ore. In twenty days, they mined 160 tons of the ore and stowed it aboard the ships. While most of the men were engaged in mining, others investigated the surrounding territory. In an Inuit camp, the English found pieces of clothing that had belonged to the five men who had disappeared on the first expedition, but there was no trace of the men themselves. The next morning the English attacked the Inuit camp, hoping to find the men or at least take captives who might either be exchanged for the missing men or transported back to England. Some of the English moved by land toward the Inuit camp while others advanced in small boats. The Inuit attempted to flee by sea, but the English were able to cut off their retreat and force them ashore on a spit of land bordered in part by cliffs. Here, at what the English later called Bloody Point, a regular battle developed, pitting the Inuit bows against the English crossbows and harquebuses. One sailor and at least half a dozen of the Inuit were wounded. Several of the Inuit men threw themselves over the cliff rather than be taken captive. After the Inuit had been routed, the English captured an Inuit woman with her infant son. Frobisher now had three Natives with whom to bargain or bring back to England.

A few days after the battle at Bloody Point, the Inuit indicated by signs that they wished to parley. In the course of several meetings, Frobisher tried to indicate that he would exchange his three captives for the five men who had gone missing on the first expedition. It is unknown whether the Inuit understood what he wanted, but twice they attempted to ambush the English, probably in the hope of capturing prisoners to exchange for the Inuit held by Frobisher. Finally, all contact was broken and neither the five lost Englishmen nor the three Inuit ever returned home.

The battle at Bloody Point, Frobisher Bay. An early copy of a lost drawing by John White. British Museum number SL5270.12.

The ships, loaded with the black ore, departed for England on August 22, already well into the autumn at this far-northern latitude. The return home was difficult. Storms separated the *Michael* from the other two ships and so battered it that it lost its mainmast. The *Ayde*'s rudder was smashed, and the master of the *Gabriel* was washed overboard and lost. All three ships did, however, survive to reach port at Bristol.

The three Inuit died shortly after arriving in England before they could be presented to Queen Elizabeth, the man probably of the effects of injuries sustained when he was captured and the woman and baby most likely of diseases to which they had no immunity. Frobisher had an audience with the queen, during which he recounted the voyage and presented her with a valuable narwhal tusk. As the tusk had been acquired on the voyage, it actually belonged to the investors, and Frobisher had no authority to give it away, but he felt no compunctions about promoting himself at the expense of the company. The audience went well, and the queen, encouraged by Frobisher's report, was pleased to name the newly found lands Meta Incognita, or Unknown Shore.

Elizabeth tried to keep the details of Frobisher's discovery secret, and she ordered the black ore to be secured in a locked room in Bristol Castle, but her efforts were in vain. Rumor spread that Frobisher had found unimaginable riches. The French ambassador sent reports that

Frobisher had returned with a wealth of gold and suggested that France should send expeditions to the new lands to establish its own claims. The able Spanish ambassador, don Bernardino de Mendoza, dispatched to his king coded reports of Frobisher's activities and actual samples of the black ore, both obtained from a spy who had taken part in assays and had participated in the expedition. Modern researchers Bernard Allaire and Donald Hogarth have made a strong case that the spy was Robert Denham, an assayer who had sailed aboard the *Ayde*. Since Mendoza's reports of the voyage lacked some vital information, it is possible that Denham was unable to communicate freely with Mendoza or even that Denham was a double agent, secretly in the service of Queen Elizabeth.

Jonas Schutz, who had previously assayed a sample of the black rock acquired on the first expedition as containing £240 in gold per ton, was now employed to assay the ore brought back on the second expedition. In his first try he was able to conclude that the ore would yield only £40 per ton but explained the discrepancy as the result of an inadequate furnace. The black ore, he explained, required unusually high temperatures to refine. Michael Lok, filled with enthusiasm, proposed building a "great works" at Dartford to process the ore. This expensive project would consist of two watermills, rock crushers to process the tons of ore, and enormous furnaces to refine the ore. Lok ordered construction begun, but the Cathay Company had no ready funds to meet the expenses or even to pay the wages of the sailors who had served on the second voyage. The Privy Council authorized the Cathy Company to require a surcharge of an additional 20 percent on the original investments. Investors would have to meet this requirement or forfeit their original investment. Soon a second 20 percent surcharge was necessary. Still more money would have to be raised so Frobisher could return to Meta Incognita a third time for a still greater load of the precious ore.

While the building of the great works continued and Lok scrambled for finances to keep the Cathy Company solvent, other problems continued to mount. Schutz's repeated efforts to assay the ore produced inconsistent results. He blamed his failures on technical problems, assuring Lok that the big furnaces of the great works would be much more efficient and productive. Frobisher did not trust either Lok or Schutz and introduced his own assayer, but he ultimately proved to be an incompetent fraud. Lok grew increasingly disillusioned with Frobisher, who never missed an opportunity to promote his self-interests, even at the expense of the company, and whose conceit and arrogance Lok found overwhelming.

The Third Expedition and Colonization

Still, the Cathay Company's plans went forward for a third expedition, and central to the plans was the establishment of a permanent mining colony. The colony initially was to consist of one hundred men. The largest numbers were to be sailors and miners, but other necessary skills were included, such as shipwright, carpenter, tailor, shoemaker, and baker. An extraordinary component of the colony was to be an elaborate, prefabricated building measuring 132 feet by 72 feet and designed to serve as living quarters, administrative center, and fortification. The colonists were to be supplied with eighteen months of supplies and left with several sailing ships. It was anticipated that a fourth expedition would return the summer after the colony was founded to pick up the ore that had been mined by the colonists and resupply them. If for some reason the ships did not arrive, the colonists could load the best of their ore onto ships left at the colony and take it back to England themselves.

Initially, the Cathay Company planned the third expedition to include ten ships, but the enthusiasm ran so high that it prepared a fleet of fifteen ships. Expenses were great, and the Privy Council authorized a 135 percent surcharge on the investors. Queen Elizabeth, who now reckoned her loan of the ship *Ayde* as an investment worth £1,000, required Lok and the other investors to post a bond to cover her surcharge of £1,350. Elizabeth, at least, was guaranteed against all loss.

In early June, the fleet set sail and made a quick crossing, sighting what they still believed to be Frisland in two weeks. After a brief landing, they sailed on, reaching the entrance to Frobisher Strait at the end of June. Progress now slowed, and early in July, floating ice hemmed in the ships. One was sunk by the ice, carrying with it part of the wooden frame for the colony's multipurpose building, but after several days the wind shifted and the ice opened. Still, the situation was difficult. With icebergs, fogs, unfamiliar tides, and unknown currents, it was impossible to keep the fleet together. Moreover, Frobisher disagreed with other navigators about their location and the location of their goal. At one point he sailed with eight ships into Hudson's Bay for several hundred miles before discovering his error. By the time he returned, it was late July.

Ice continued to clog the entrance to Frobisher Strait, and the *Ayde* was nearly sunk when an ice floe rammed a fluke of the ship's anchor through the bow. Morale deteriorated badly, and the men grew increasingly quarrelsome. Frobisher took a pinnace and managed to penetrate to the island where the colony was to be established and there found two of his other ships that had been separated from the main fleet for a month. They had managed to work their way through the ice with great difficulty. Finally, at the beginning of August, the *Ayde* and other ships arrived at the expedition's goal, but some ships were still missing in the ice and fog.

On Countess of Warwick Island (modern Kodlunarn Island) the men built a smithy, a shelter, and an assay shop. Miners excavated ore from a deep trench on the island, and Frobisher found other outcroppings of similar dark stone on other nearby islands and the mainland, where he established other groups of miners. With the mining proceeding, attention turned at last to establishing the colony, but half the frame of the proposed great building had been lost with the ship that sank. Two ships that had not yet been able to reach the island contained many of the provisions for the proposed colony, and another missing ship held half the bricks for the great building. As it was clearly impossible to erect the building as planned and supply it for the long winter, Frobisher and his officers decided to build the best building they could with the available materials but leave no colonists. Instead, they would mine as much ore as possible during the remainder of the short summer and then all sail for home. The expedition would then return the next summer.

As August progressed, the men loaded the ships with well over one thousand tons of ore from Countess Warwick Island and other mines on other small islands and Baffin Island. They erected a small building, twelve feet by fourteen feet, and left provisions in it and buried still more on the island. Toward the end of August, the weather began to deteriorate badly. On August 31, as the ships prepared to set sail for home and Frobisher oversaw the loading of the last of the ore, a tremendous storm struck. Men and officers hurriedly tried to embark on whatever ship was close at hand. Frobisher was unable to get to his flagship, the *Ayde*, and had to board the *Gabriel* instead. Skiffs and ships' boats sank, and on the larger ships ropes gave way, sails split, masts broke or pulled loose and had to be cut away, and men were washed overboard. Anyone not able to get to a ship was left be-

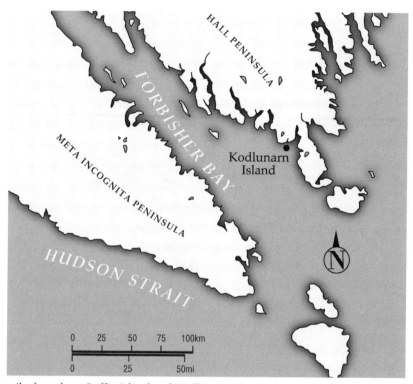

Detail of southern Baffin Island and Kodlunarn Island.

hind. The fleet was largely scattered and only occasionally caught sight of one another on the trip back to England. Despite the damage of the storm, all made it back to England, except one ship that was wrecked on the coast of Ireland.

About 360 of the 400 men who had begun the expedition survived to return to England. At least five had died during the mining, and five others are known to have died aboard the *Ayde* during the return trip. Others were apparently left ashore at Countess Warwick Island during the great storm. The proposed colony had winter residents after all.

When Frobisher arrived in England, he found that the Cathay Company was insolvent. Michael Lok had spent the available funds to build the works at Dartford to refine the ore, but now bills were due for outfitting the expedition, to pay wages of the sailors and miners, to the owners of the vessels for transporting the ore, and more money would soon be required to refine the ore. Queen Elizabeth authorized the Company to raise an additional £6,000.

Jonas Shutz, now chief assayer, produced new, discouraging analyses of the ore, eventually declaring that the ore Frobisher had brought back was worth only £5 a ton, a figure inadequate to pay for refining, much less to settle the outstanding debts of the Cathay Company and repay investors. Frobisher and Lok, long mutually suspicious, berated one another with bitter recriminations and threats.

In December 1578, the Privy Council took charge of the Cathay Company, ordering an audit and removing Lok as treasurer. He survived the audit well, faulted for inconsequential matters only. Lok's successor as treasurer subsequently instigated an audit of Frobisher's accounts that accused him of double billing and overcharging the company for food and supplies and noted that he had exceeded his authorizations in a number of areas. The Privy Council ordered the company to sell its resources to pay its debts, but the resources were in no way adequate. Amid mutual recriminations, the financial collapse of the company, and the discouraging assays, all plans for a subsequent voyage to Meta Incognita were abandoned, and the sailors and miners left behind were forgotten.

Aftermath

Although the audit largely cleared Lok of any fault, his name appeared on the company papers, and for the rest of his life the company's creditors pursued him. They committed him to debtor's prison at least seven times, and one creditor was still pressing a law case as late as 1615, thirty-seven years after the last expedition. Lok never recovered financially and died in obscurity.

Frobisher's future was just as checkered and unpredictable as his past. He helped organize an expedition to the Pacific in 1582, but was rejected as commander or even a captain, probably because he was considered unreliable and uncontrollable. Instead, he was put in charge of purchasing supplies for the expedition, and it appears that he again engaged in fraud, overcharging, and short weighing.

In 1585, however, the famous privateer and naval commander Sir Francis Drake appointed Frobisher his second in command of an expedition that raided the Spanish in South America, the Caribbean, and Florida, and evacuated colonists from the first attempt to establish a colony at Roanoke. The famous "Lost Colony" was the result of a later, second attempt to establish a permanent settlement on the site (chapters 11 and 12). In the battles against the Spanish Armada in

1588, Frobisher made his name and fortune. He commanded the largest English ship, the twenty-four gun *Triumph*, and while he proved himself inept at maneuvering, he fought heroically against heavy odds. The lord high admiral knighted him at sea in the name of the queen. After the death of Frobisher's first wife, he made a financially advantageous second marriage. He was now a knight of the realm and a landed gentleman, but his basic character remained unchanged. While nominally in search of vessels carrying Spanish cargoes in the English Channel, Frobisher was simply a pirate. In 1594, he was back in the service of the English government, commanding the fleet in a combined naval and army expedition to destroy a Spanish fortification erected on a peninsula in Brittany. The expedition captured the fortress, but in the assault Frobisher was shot in the hip. After an operation to remove the bullet, the wound became infected, and Martin Frobisher died at Plymouth on November 22, 1594.

The fate of the sailors and miners left behind at Meta Incognita remained unknown for almost three centuries. Although Frobisher's maps left no doubt of the general area of the colony and the mines, the exact location of it remained lost until the early 1860s. Then an eccentric American explorer, Charles Francis Hall, traveled to the arctic in search of evidence of the lost expedition of John Franklin. The Franklin expedition had departed from England in 1845 to search for the Northwest Passage and soon disappeared. Actually, the mystery had already been solved by the time Hall became involved. Inuit accounts told of the death of the Franklin party after it had to abandon its icebound ships, and in 1859, an expedition recovered physical evidence of the fate of at least a portion of the expedition. Hall, however, thought it possible some of Franklin's men might remain alive, and although a complete novice to the arctic, he managed to raise enough capital to journey north on a whaling ship in search of survivors. Whalers put him in touch with Inuit, with whom he lived and traveled for some time.

The Inuit told Hall stories about visits of white men to the region long ago, and Hall recorded these accounts exactly as they were told to him. The tales had no exact fixed form and frequently varied in details from one telling to the next, but Hall was able to gather that long ago white men had come to an island in the area on three occasions, once with just a single ship, the second time with several, and finally with many. The Inuit remembered that the strangers had killed some of their people but indicated that five of them had lived with the Inuit for several seasons and had eventually built a boat and sailed away. The Inuit also remembered the island, and they took Hall there. On the island that the Inuit called Kodlunarn, or White Man's Island (formerly Countess of Warwick Island), Hall found indisputable evidence of Frobisher's activity, including the foundations of the house, coal, bricks, tiles, and remnants of wood that seemed to indicate to Hall that a small boat had been built there. The Inuit stories obviously contained real memories of the Frobisher expeditions. While it is possible that the Inuit confused memories of the five men who disappeared during the first expedition or even memories of later confrontations with Europeans with events of Frobisher's third expedition, the Inuit traditions provide the best evidence of the fate of the abandoned sailors and miners. They seem to have survived for some time with the aid of the Inuit and then attempted unsuccessfully to return to England in a small boat. Thus ended England's first attempt to establish a colony in the New World.

In the 1990s, an archaeological expedition examined Kodlunarn Island and neighboring sites in detail. In addition to the foundation of the main building, still fairly well preserved, the archaeologists were able to distinguish traces of more lightly built structures that had served the miners that summer. Three were probably workshops and a fourth a barracks or storehouse. In addition to the predictable iron nails, charcoal, coal, flints, bricks, tile fragments, and bits of wood, archaeologists uncovered the cache of provisions Frobisher had hidden on the island, including still recognizable sea biscuits and English peas. Fragments of wood and iron from the main trench are consistent with the attempt to build or repair a small boat.

Lok's Great Works have long disappeared, but in the English town of Dartford where they once stood one can still see a stone wall erected a few years after Frobisher's third expedition. Much of the wall is constructed from local gray ragstone, but scattered through it are heavy black stones unlike anything occurring near Dartford. They are from Kodlunarn Island, and the first assayers were correct. They are just heavy, black stones, hornblende, utterly worthless. The glints of gold and silver are only mica inclusions.

Frobisher's Strait proved equally disappointing. It was not the key to the fabled Northwest Passage and the wealth of the Orient, but merely the entrance to an insignificant, rocky, icy bay, now called Frobisher Bay, on the coast of Baffin Island. Meta Incognita was based on a mistake and a delusion. It was a proposed mining colony where there was nothing to mine and a false entrance to the fabled Northwest Passage. It would not be the last colony based on misconceptions. Those who sought to colonize the New World had great ambitions but little knowledge, and that was particularly true of Frobisher's attempt.

Sources

Of all the early English colonizing ventures, Meta Incognita is the best documented. Frobisher's voyages attracted great attention, and participants wrote a number of accounts, the most comprehensive of which is by George Best, *A true discourse of the late voyages of discouerie, for the finding of a passage to Cathaya, by the Northvveast, vnder the conduct of Martin Frobisher Generall: deuided into three bookes. In the first wherof is shewed, his first voyage . . . Also, there are annexed certayne reasons, to proue all partes of the worlde habitable, with a generall mappe adioyned. In the second, is set out his second voyage . . . In the thirde, is declared the strange fortunes which hapned in the third voyage . . . VVith a particular card therevnto adioyned of Meta Incognita* (London: Henry Bynnyman, 1578). Best took part in Frobisher's second and third expeditions and certainly knew those who participated in the first. He was killed in a duel in 1584.

Dionyse Settle took part in Frobisher's second voyage, and his account appeared in the same year as the expedition's return to England: *A true reporte of the laste voyage into the west and Northwest regions, c. 1577: worthily atchieued by Capteine Frobisher of the sayde voyage, the first finder and generall: with a description of the people there inhabiting and other cirumstances notable* (London: Henrie Middleton, 1577).

Thomas Ellis, who participated in Frobisher's third expedition, published *A true report of the third and last voyage into Meta incognita: atchieued by the worthie Capteine, M. Martine Frobisher Esquire. Anno. 1578. Written by Thomas Ellis sailer and one of the companie* (London: At the three Cranes in the Vintree, by Thomas Dawson, 1578).

Richard Hakluyt, the famous compiler of documents of the age of exploration, reprinted these three works in *The Third and Last Volume of the Voyages, Navigations, Traffiques, and Discoueries of the English Nation* (London: George Bishop, and Ralfe Newberie, and Robert Barker, 1600). Hakluyt occasionally edited the accounts he reprinted.

For instance, he omitted some passages in Best's narrative and suppressed a statement that indicated Frobisher was more interested in finding mines than in exploring for the Northwest Passage, an objective dear to Hakluyt's heart. In addition to the main narratives, Hakluyt included several short documents concerning Frobisher's expeditions to Meta Incognita: Christopher Hall, "The first Voyage of M. Martine Frobisher, to the Northwest, for the search of the straight or passage to China, written by Christopher Hall, Master in the Gabriel, and made in the yeere of our Lord 1576," 29-32, is a seaman's account, filled with technical sailing information about the voyage but little about what Frobisher did at Meta Incognita. "The report of Thomas Wiars passenger in the *Emanuel*, otherwise called the *Busse of Bridgewater*, wherein Iames Leech was Master, one of the ships in the last Voyage of Master Martin Frobisher 1578. Concerning the discouerie of a great Island on the way homeward the 12 of September," 44, is a short account of the sighting of what was believed to be an island but was actually an illusion. Hakluyt's interest in and hopes for the discovery of the Northwest Passage are evident in "Notes framed by M. Richard Hakluyt of the middle Temple Esquire, giuen to certaine Gentlemen that went with M. Frobisher in his Northwest discouerie, for their directions: And not vnfit to be committed to print, considering the same may stirre vp considerations of these and of such other things, not vnmeete in such new voyages as may be attempted hereafter," 45-47.

The many lawsuits that occupied Michael Lok for the rest of his long life provide much information about the finances, schemes, and intrigues in England involving the expeditions. Christopher Hall's discovery of the location of Meta Incognita and record of the Inuit traditions, important to the understanding of Frobisher's expeditions and plans, are published in *Life with the Esquimaux*, 2 vols. (London: Sampson Low, 1864), and in the United States as *Arctic Researches and Life Among the Esquimaux* (New York: Harper & Brothers, 1865). The modern archaeological work begun in the 1990s, Thomas H. B. Symons, ed., *Meta Incognita: A Discourse of Discovery*, 2 vols. (Hull: Canadian Museum of Civilization, 1999), has elucidated the nature of the attempted colony and given credence to the Inuit traditions.

ELEVEN

The English in North Carolina: The First Roanoke Colony (1585–1586)

Background

For much of the sixteenth century, England was preoccupied with matters other than colonization. In 1533, King Henry VIII unilaterally annulled his marriage to Catherine of Aragon, leading ultimately though not immediately to a break with the Catholic Church. Political and trade relations between England and Spain, close in the first third of the century, deteriorated as England moved farther from the church, and Spain emerged as the champion of radically conservative Catholicism. During the brief reign of Edward VI (1547–1553), the English church shifted increasingly away from traditional Catholic practices. Mary Tudor sought to reverse that trend during her reign (1553–1558), but her marriage to Philip II of Spain and the burning at the stake of nearly three hundred religious dissidents in England served only to alienate the English further from Spain and Catholicism. The deterioration of relations continued at an increasing pace under Elizabeth, who followed Mary to the throne. In 1570, the pope declared Elizabeth illegitimate, a heretic, and excommunicated her, exacerbating relations with Catholics in England and complicating relations with Scotland, France, and particularly Spain. Philip II, king of Spain since

1556, increasingly worked to subvert Elizabeth's rule and even sponsored plots to assassinate her in the hopes of returning England to Catholicism. In turn, Elizabeth provided aid to the Netherlands during the long, intractable struggle against Spanish rule and allowed and even supported English buccaneers who raided Spanish shipping and towns, particularly in the Caribbean. In 1585, open hostilities broke out between Spain and England that continued until 1604, after the death of Elizabeth.

Ireland and Scotland also demanded the attention of the English monarchy throughout the century. Henry VIII greatly expanded English activity in Ireland, declared himself king of Ireland, dissolved the Irish monasteries, and reduced the independent power of Irish chieftains. Mary and later Elizabeth encouraged British colonization of Ireland, and Irish groups rebelled at the extension of English dominance, particularly during Elizabeth's long reign. Struggles to establish English enclaves in Ireland and the military activity required to stifle Irish resistance absorbed much of the effort that might otherwise have gone into the establishment of English colonies in North America. The strong alliance between Scotland and France also presented a threat to England during much of the century, and the growth of Calvinism in Scotland led to religious conflict with Catholic elements within the country and tensions with England. Forces foreign and domestic saw the feckless, impulsive Mary Queen of Scots as a useful rival to Elizabeth, and even after Mary was forced to abdicate in Scotland and fled to England, she continued to serve as a pawn in plots against Elizabeth, who finally and reluctantly had her executed. Elizabeth did not acknowledge Mary's son, James VI of Scotland, as her successor until she was on her deathbed. As James I of England, he championed the concept of absolute monarchy, presaging future conflicts.

Despite all the European political, religious, and military concerns, there were good reasons for England to establish colonies in North America. English colonists, like other colonists, sought to discover precious metals and the elusive Northwest Passage to the Orient, but there were other important motives. In case of war, a strong English presence in North America could threaten Spanish holdings in the Caribbean and force Spain to divide its attention and resources between Europe and the New World. Also, it was generally believed at the time that lands on the same latitude must have similar climates and could produce similar products. Thus Richard Hakluyt reasoned in *Discourse of Western Plantings* (1585) that areas on the east coast of North America could produce such typically Spanish products as olive oil and wine, then obtainable in England only with difficulty and expense. English colonies could also serve to check French ambitions in the area and even procure for England domination over the northern cod fisheries.

In 1577, Martin Frobisher made the first attempt to establish an English colony in the New World, a mining venture in the far north near Baffin Island that failed before it was truly established (chapter 10). In 1583, Humphrey Gilbert sailed to North America intending to seek the Northwest Passage and establish a colony from which other explorations could be launched, but the expedition ended in shipwreck and death for Gilbert and others without any enduring achievement. Gilbert was a half-brother of Walter Raleigh's and a cousin of Richard Grenville's, both of whom shared his interest in the New World and played important roles in the founding of the colony at Roanoke.

Exploration, 1584

Despite Humphrey Gilbert's failure, there was growing interest in the establishment of an English colony in North America. Several men were interested in renewing the effort, but Walter Raleigh obtained the queen's letters patent to do so. Gilbert's attempt had been well publicized, but the growing hostility between England and Spain dictated that Raleigh sought to keep his initial exploration discreet. Nevertheless, the extensive Spanish network of spies produced reports of Raleigh's activities from their outset, although those reports contained the usual mixture of accurate information, exaggeration, and baseless supposition.

Raleigh outfitted two small ships for an initial voyage of exploration. The larger ship was commanded by Philip Amadas, a member of a prominent merchant family from Plymouth that, like many contemporary wealthy families, invested capital in land and so were regarded as gentry. The smaller ship was commanded by Arthur Barlowe, who had served under Raleigh while he commanded a company of foot for Queen Elizabeth in Ireland in 1580–1581. Little is known of his background except that he had earlier made at least one voyage to the eastern Mediterranean and showed himself to be an able captain. Simão Fernandes, known to the English as Simon Fernandez or Ferdinando, served as pilot. Born in Portugal, Fernandez was trained in navigation

Sir Walter Raleigh, left, from the first page of his, *The Historie of the World in Five Bookes* (London: William Stansby, 1614). Richard Grenville, right, from Henry Holland, *Herwologia Anglica* (Arnhemiensis, 1620).

in Spain before becoming a pirate in the 1570s. He was captured and condemned to hang but spared by Elizabeth's spymaster, Sir Francis Walsingham, whereupon Fernandez converted to English Protestantism and swore allegance to the queen. He may have made an earlier voyage to North America and demonstrated familiarity with its coast on the expedition. Fernandez was probably also confidentially reporting to Walsingham and Elizabeth.

The two ships set sail in late April 1584, proceeding south to the Canaries and then west. They touched briefly at Puerto Rico, where they took on fresh water and food and then sailed north, arriving in early July among the Outer Banks, a string of barrier islands along the coasts of what today are North Carolina and southern Virginia. The barrier islands were then largely covered with cedars and much wider than their current denuded and eroded state. Finding their way between the barrier islands, the Englishmen explored Roanoke Island and other islands in Roanoke Sound, where they assumed that the abundant plant and animal life indicated the soil was fertile. The indigenous people of Roanoke, headed by a chief named Wingina, seemed gentle and obliging. After a stay of only about a month, Barlowe was ready to return to England in the smaller ship, taking with him two Indians: a Roanoke, Wanchese, and a Croatoan, Manteo.

Typically, there is no indication in the sources whether the two had agreed to go to England or were even asked. Barlowe's return trip was rapid, and he arrived in England in mid-September.

Amadas explored somewhat to the north and then sailed toward Bermuda hoping to prey on Spanish shipping. He found none, survived a storm, and sailed to the Azores, where he cruised for six weeks hunting Spanish ships without success. Short of provisions, he finally returned to England. The object of any voyage sponsored or led by Raleigh was at least in part to hunt Spanish prizes, even in times of nominal peace.

The First Roanoke Colony, 1585–1586

Encouraged by Barlowe's report, Raleigh set to work in England to find support for the planned colony. The Indians whom Barlowe brought to England resided in Raleigh's house, where Thomas Herriot, one of the most remarkable men of the age, taught them English, learned their Algonquian dialect, and even devised a phonetic alphabet to write their language. Herriot, a polymath primarily interested in mathematics and navigation, agreed to take part in the colony to be founded at Roanoke, where he would serve as mapmaker and translator. Information he gleaned from the two Algonquians was incorporated in the surviving revision of Barlowe's account, a work artfully contrived to provide optimistic publicity for the colony.

Raleigh introduced a bill in Parliament nominally to strengthen the queen's letters patent authorizing Raleigh to found the colony but actually to publicize the effort and recruit financial supporters. The bill passed the House of Commons, but the House of Lords took no action, probably considering the queen's approval preempted its authority. In addition, Raleigh and his supporters circulated copies of Richard Hakluyt's essay "A Discourse on Western Planting," which describes the advantages that England could derive from colonies in the New World.

Queen Elizabeth signaled her approval of the colonization effort in early 1585 by knighting Raleigh, allowing him to name the new land Virginia in her honor, as she was known as the Virgin Queen, and appointing him lord and governor of Virginia. The English applied the name Virginia not only to the actual colony but to a vast section of the coast, including much claimed by the Spanish and French. The queen did not contribute financially to Raleigh's project but provided some material support: 2,400 pounds of gunpowder and a medium-sized ship, the *Tiger*, although it is not known whether she lent or rented the ship to Raleigh. Elizabeth was famed for her strict control of royal properties and expenditures.

Raleigh found sufficient resources to launch a substantial effort, involving about six hundred men, roughly half of whom were designated as colonists, hired by Raleigh and his agents for the task. No women were included in this initial effort. The other three hundred men crewed the ships, ranging from the medium-sized *Tiger* of perhaps 160 tons to the *Roebuck* of 140 tons, to the *Red Lion* of 100 tons to the *Elizabeth* and the *Dorothy* of 50 tons each, and two small pinnaces of perhaps 25 tons each, which were anticipated to be useful in the shallow waters between the barrier islands and the mainland. Raleigh did not go on the expedition but appointed a relative, Sir Richard Grenville, as commandant, sailing in the *Tiger* with Simon Fernandez as chief pilot. Plans were also made to send additional colonists in June.

The ships sailed in good order from Plymouth in early April, but off the coast of Portugal a heavy storm scattered the little fleet. One pinnace sank and the other evidentially disappeared in the storm; at least it is not mentioned subsequently in the sources. The captains had been ordered, if separated, to rendezvous on the southwest coast of Puerto Rico, a largely uninhabited area where they might hope the Spanish would not notice them. After the storm, the *Tiger* made a rapid crossing to Puerto Rico, where the men set up a lightly fortified camp and built a new pinnace while awaiting the other ships. Only one, the *Elizabeth*, appeared. Another of the ships approached the uninhabited northern coast of Jamaica, where the captain, running short of provisions, marooned twenty of his men, a few of whom were subsequently captured by the Spanish.

Fearing attack by the Spanish, Grenville, in the *Tiger*, and the *Elizabeth* left Puerto Rico and sailed north. On the way to Roanoke, Grenville captured two small Spanish ships, looted a salt depot on shore, and traded cordially at Hispaniola with the Spanish, who ignored all laws strictly prohibiting such exchanges. Grenville took aboard a variety of domestic animals and a wide variety of Caribbean fruiting plants and vegetables, none of which survived the stress of the voyage and the climate of the Carolina coast—an indication of how little the colonizers knew of their destination.

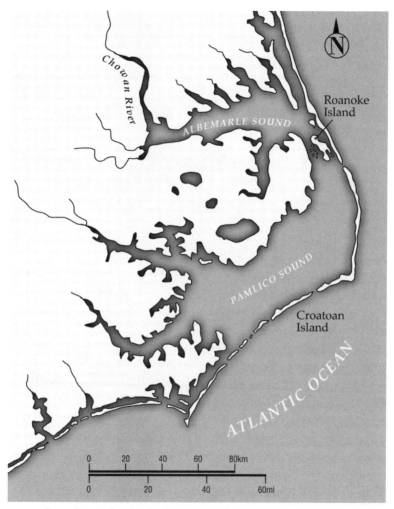

The coast of North Carolina in the late sixteenth century.

During the voyage and afterward, Grenville quarreled with several of the ship captains and a number of the officers and gentlemen, but particularly with Colonel Ralph Lane, who commanded the soldiers on the expedition and was designated to be governor after Grenville returned to England. No details survive about the subject of these disagreements, but Lane complained of Grenville's pride and ambition and drew up a list of grievances he sent back to Raleigh. In all probability the fault did not lie entirely with Grenville. Lane was volatile and vain.

The *Tiger*, the *Elizabeth*, the two captured Spanish prizes, and the newly built pinnace proceeded to the Outer Banks, where Fernandez, navigating through a narrow channel in heavy seas, accidently grounded the *Tiger* on a shoal. The ship was damaged but saved and repaired, although many of the provisions for the colony were lost. After their arrival, the men spent several weeks exploring the vicinity. They were pleased to encounter the *Roebuck* and *Dorothy* nearby, but the captain of the *Red Lion* marooned about thirty colonists on Croatoan Island and then sailed off to loot the Newfoundland fishing fleet. The stranded colonists were fortunate to be discovered and rescued by their comrades.

While exploring, Grenville and his men visited an indigenous village, Aquascogoc, on the Pamlico River. Several Indians swam out to the English boats, and one stole a silver cup. Several days later after discovering the theft, Grenville sent men to demand the return of the cup. When it was not immediately forthcoming, the English attacked, burning the village and the fields of maturing corn. This disproportionate response may have been intended as a demonstration of force to ensure the respect of the Native population, but it marked the beginning of suspicion and hostility toward the English.

The colonists slowly came to realize that all was not as promising as Barlowe's report had indicated. Exploration discovered no gold, silver, or even lead. The indigenous people had some copper, apparently obtained by trade, but the colonists did not find any local source of the metal. The only exportable crop of which they could be certain was sassafras, and while the Native Americans were eager to trade, they had little of value to the English other than food, some skins, and pearls, mainly from fresh-water mussels. Navigation in the shallow waters within the Banks was difficult and dangerous, and Roanoke Island was small, much of it swampy, and there was too little farmable area on the island to accommodate the projected number of settlers. Many of the surrounding islands and much of the adjacent mainland were marshes, forest swamps, or sandy and infertile. The Indians were also an unknown factor. They were numerous and occupied nearly all the productive land in the region. The Roanoke were initially friendly, but their future reactions to English behavior and the permanent occupation of their land could not be predicted. Yet in these early days there was still much optimism. There was much territory not yet explored, and the colonists thought that mineral wealth and herbs of pharmaceutical value still might well be found. Perhaps a Northwest Passage might be discovered somewhere or a short land route to the Pacific, assumed to be not far to the west, and the colony could possibly develop into a strong base from which raids might be launched against rich Spanish shipping.

Rather than the planned 300, Grenville decided to leave just 109 men on Roanoke. The colonists are conventionally referred to as English, but in addition to the English component there were men whose names indicate different origins: Irish, French, German, Portuguese, Spanish, and even a Prague master metallurgist who was Jewish, Joachim Granz. Most of the colonists who were not of English origin seem to have been long resident in England. Notable among the colonists were John White and Thomas Herriot. White had earlier accompanied Martin Frobisher on his unsuccessful attempt to establish a mining colony in the far north (chapter 10), where he drew and painted the land and people. A talented artist, White painted the flora, the fauna, and the Indians both as individuals and in the context of their villages and daily activities. He also aided Herriot, who was charged with mapping the area and acted as a translator. The two Indians brought back to England in 1584 returned along with the colonists and were also supposed to serve as translators, but one, Wanchese, quickly withdrew from the English and had nothing further to do with them. The other, Manteo, acted as intermediary between the colonists and Indians.

On Roanoke, the colonists threw up a basic fortification consisting of a trench and bank, difficult to make formidable in the sandy soil of the island, and built shelters described as "cottages" and work areas. This first settlement must have been rudimentary, built in less than a month during August and early September. The ships unloaded all the provisions they could spare, and the first departed for England on August 5. Other ships left in late August, and the final ship sailed on September 8. On the return trip, Grenville captured a straggler from the Spanish treasure fleet, the loot from which fully repaid the investors in the Roanoke venture.

Little specific is known of the colonists' activities during the autumn and winter. There was some exploration during the autumn, mainly in the vicinity of Roanoke Island and Albemarle and Pamlico Sounds, and one expedition penetrated the southern reaches of Chesapeake Bay and spent a considerable time there. Chesapeake Bay offered sheltered deep-water anchorages, much better than the shallow waters around Roanoke, and there were large tracts of unoccupied fertile land, unlike Roanoke and the immediately adjacent territory.

Many of the provisions brought from England had been lost when the *Tiger* had run aground, so during the autumn and winter the colonists sought to trade with the Indians for corn and venison. The Native economy never produced a large food surplus, and tree-ring evidence indicates Roanoke and the surrounding area were in the midst of a drought, the worst in eight hundred years, which must have further limited availability. Moreover, many of the indigenous people left their villages during the winter for their usual hunt. The colonists survived throughout the winter and spring without starvation, although their rations were short and their diet dull and repetitious. Food was particularly scarce in the spring and early summer before any new crops matured.

By spring, relations between the colonists and the indigenous Roanoke band and other bands farther away had begun to deteriorate significantly. It is difficult to identify the root of these troubles, but several factors seem to have contributed. The colonists' frequent importuning demands for more food had clearly begun to provoke the Roanoke, especially since the colonists seemed prepared to back their requests with force. The English had already demonstrated their willingness to resort to violence with little provocation. Welcomed initially as trading partners, the English seemed much less desirable as neighbors. Despite the linguistic efforts of Herriot and Manteo, communication between the two profoundly different cultures must have been at times difficult, motives and intentions particularly subject to misunderstanding. Colonel Lane, the English commandant, seems to have grown increasingly mistrustful.

In the spring, Lane decided to make an expedition up the Chowan River, a black water river emptying into the Albemarle Sound, to visit the local tribe. Wingina provided Lane with three guides, but Lane claimed there was a vast conspiracy at work. He reported that Wingina sent word to Menatonon, leader of the Chowan people, that the English were coming and that later Menatonon revealed that Wingina warned that the English intended to attack and destroy the Chowan. Lane also claimed that Wingina stated that Menatonon was assembling a vast force of three thousand men to attack the English. None of these claims were substantiated by later events, and Lane's own actions cannot be reconciled with them. It seems likely that Lane's allegations were little more than excuses for his subsequent behavior.

Lane and his men proceeded to the Chowan village in just one pinnace and two small boats. They could have hardly numbered more than forty, no match for the supposed three thousand hostile warriors. When Lane arrived he found no preparations for war and no indication he was expected. He and his men rushed into the village and took Menatonon prisoner. The chief seems to have accepted the fait accompli with equanimity and spent the next two days in conversation with Lane, explaining to him that there was wealth to be found—elsewhere. Menatonon told of a powerful chief to the north along the coast of what must be the Chesapeake Bay who had ropes of pearls to trade; of the Man-

Portrait of a Native American man by John White, ca. 1585. British Museum item 1906, 0509.1.12.

goaks—a pejorative term that the Algonquian-speaking coastal tribes applied to the Iroquoian-speaking tribes of the interior, particularly the Tuscarora—who were rich in copper; and of an even more distant place, Chaunis Temoatan, where there was an abundance of a metal paler and softer than copper. It required little imagination to suppose this might be gold. As in many other instances, Native Americans bedazzled European imaginations with accounts of wealth at a distance. Lane freed Menatonon for an unspecified ransom but took Menatonon's son Skiko as a hostage.

Lane then sent the pinnace with a small crew and Skiko back to Roanoke while he and thirty men packed into the two small boats and attempted to row up the Roanoke River to reach the Mangoaks and perhaps even the mysterious Chaunis Temoatan. Lane began the expedition with few provisions, intending to get food from the Moratuc, an Algonquian people who lived along the lower reaches of the river, but the Moratuc deserted their villages, taking all their food with them. They even fired a volley of arrows from the shore at the English boats on the river, hurting no one, and then retreated into the forest when the English landed. Out of food, Lane abandoned the effort within a few days. Unwilling to acknowledge his foolish decision to undertake an expedition without preparation and with virtually no provisions, Lane blamed the failure on Wingina, whom he claimed had turned the Moratuc against him.

Meantime at Roanoke, conditions grew worse. The relief expedition supposed to arrive by Easter did not appear, and the colonists grew increasingly disgruntled. Basic supplies, even clothing, were close to exhaustion, and food was barely adequate. The colonists insistently demanded food from Wingina's people, but the Roanoke had no substantial reserves beyond their own needs. The Roanoke planted corn on the island and constructed fish weirs for the colonists, but the new crop was far from mature and the old harvest largely consumed. Food became so scarce in the colony that Lane sent some of his men to other islands and the mainland to forage. Wingina, apparently in response to the insistent demands, removed his people from Roanoke Island to a village, Dasemunkepeuc, on the mainland, and assumed a new name, Permisapan, perhaps indicating his role as a war leader. Lane, growing increasingly apprehensive, was convinced that Wingina and his allies intended to attack the colony and so decided to act to forestall any hostile action.

The first part of Lane's plan miscarried. He had his men attempt to seize canoes from the Indians. It is not apparent whether this was an attempt to prevent word reaching Wingina about Lane's preparations or if it was simply an attempt to reduce the Roanoke mobility and increase his own. The Roanoke resisted, several were killed, and the village was alerted. The English landed, and the Roanoke withdrew to the surrounding forest. The next morning, Lane and twenty-seven men boldly went by boat to Dasemunkepeuc, where he demanded to see Wingina/Permisapan. The chief, surrounded by his leading supporters, met with Lane, who sought to blame the events of the preceding evening on the Roanoke. When Lane suddenly gave a prearranged signal, "Christ our Victory," the English pulled their pistols and shot down Wingina and his companions. The chief was only wounded in the first volley and attempted to flee. Lane handed a pistol to his Irish servant, who shot Wingina a second time, but he still managed to disappear into the woods. One of Lane's men followed and soon returned with Wingina's head. Their leaders murdered, the rest of the tribe sub-

mitted—at least for the moment. Lane maintained he had averted imminent danger to the colony, but the animosity between the surrounding people and the English was now firmly established.

In Europe, relations between Spain and England continued to deteriorate. In 1584, the Spanish king, Philip II, signed the Treaty of
Joinville by which he agreed to finance the radical Catholic League in
France. If the league thus strengthened took control of France, England
would face a radical Catholic alliance of the two strongest continental
powers. As a countermove, in 1585, Queen Elizabeth signed the Treaty
of Nonsuch, providing financial and military aid to the Dutch rebellion
against Spanish rule. Despite long-standing political and religious disagreements that caused contraction of commerce between England and
Spain, every spring English ships still sailed to Spain to trade. In 1585,
Philip II seized all English ships in Spanish ports, and in retaliation
Queen Elizabeth issued letters of marque authorizing English privateers to capture Spanish ships. This act merely put a legal veneer on
the English piracy that had taken place for years. The ships previously
designated to bring provisions and more settlers to Roanoke were ordered instead to sail to the Newfoundland fishery to seize Spanish and
Portuguese fishing vessels and to warn English fishing vessels not to
sail to Spain or Portugal to sell their catch.

The Spanish intelligence service was widespread, active, and deeply
interested in all foreign activity in the New World, and it regularly produced reports ranging from accurate to fantasy, and frequently there
was no way to distinguish adequately among them. Reports of the
1584 voyage and Grenville's colonization expedition reached Spain
even before he departed from England, and Spanish reports from the
Caribbean provided more information about Grenville's movements
and intention to found a colony, although uncertainty remained about
his destination. Little was done, however, to oppose the English expedition. Other matters were of much greater moment. In Spain, the
growing hostility with England was of utmost concern, while the Spanish Caribbean was convulsed by Sir Francis Drake's great raid.

In England, Drake amassed a fleet of about twenty-four ships and
eight pinnaces, financed by the queen, by Drake himself, and by a variety of gentlemen and merchants. Preparing and equipping the ships
proceeded slowly, the political uncertainties continually threatening to
cancel the expedition before it began. Drake and the fleet, with about
two thousand men onboard, finally set sail in mid-September 1585,

and even then the ships were not completely provisioned. Drake struck first at the Spanish town of Bayona at the mouth of the Virgo River in northwestern Spain, where the Spanish held the impounded English ships and seamen. After some negotiations, Drake attacked and looted Bayona and the major port of Virgo upriver. He next sailed to the Canary Islands, where cannonade from the chief fortress at Palma encouraged him to sail on to the Cape Verde islands. There the fleet captured and looted the town of São Tiago, taking provisions for the fleet. Before leaving the Canaries, Drake put the towns of São Tiago, São Domingos, and Porto Praya to the torch.

Drake next set sail toward the Caribbean, but his crews had brought aboard an epidemic from the Canaries, perhaps the pneumonic variety of the black plague. Accounts of the number who died while crossing the Atlantic vary from a low of two hundred or three hundred to five hundred or more. On the first day of 1586, even as the disease continued to ravage his crews, Drake captured the town of Santo Domingo on the island of Hispaniola, where his men followed the usual pattern, looting and destroying much of the town, taking the better ships in the harbor, and burning the rest. Afterward Drake recruited Spanish renegades, black slaves, and escaped galley slaves to make up for the losses among his crews. Drake next sailed to Cartagena in Colombia, which he also took and treated in a similar manner, but discontent was growing in his fleet.

Drake's favoritism toward his personal friends offended many of his subordinates, and the loot was much less than promised. His forces weakened by disease, Drake made no attempt to capture Havana, the most important Spanish port in the Caribbean, but rather sailed north along the Florida coast to St. Augustine. There the Spanish offered token resistance before withdrawing to the countryside. Before burning the town, Drake thoroughly looted it, taking even tools and hardware from the houses, intending to give such plunder to the colonists at Roanoke. Sailing farther north, Drake intended to take the Spanish settlement at Santa Elena, but the combination of unknown shallows and adverse winds led him to bypass that Spanish colony.

Drake arrived at Roanoke in early June. The anchorage within the Outer Banks was much too shallow for his ships, so he anchored in the deeper but unprotected waters outside the banks. He had departed from England before news arrived there from Roanoke, and he must have expected to find a colony of at least two hundred or three hun-

dred men and perhaps as many as six hundred, if the planned midsummer reinforcements had arrived. Instead Drake found
about one hundred men discouraged by
the failure to discover any source of
wealth, short of food and supplies of every
sort, and surrounded by hostile Indians.
Drake was ready to provide the colonists
with food, clothing, cannons, small arms,
ammunition, hardware, and tools taken
from St. Augustine, perhaps even black
slaves, as well as pinnaces and smaller
boats, but his account of recent events
could only have discouraged the colonists.
The growing hostilities between England

Sir Francis Drake, detail, engraved by Jodocus Hondiusca,
ca. 1583.

and Spain made future shipments of food and supplies doubtful, and
Drake's own raid in the Caribbean and destruction of St. Augustine
meant that the Spanish would likely mount an expedition against
Roanoke, one that could hardly be resisted by the small colony.

Lane recognized that the continued occupation of Roanoke was not
feasible unless the promised reinforcements, long overdue, finally arrived from England. If they did not appear, he hoped to achieve at least
a worthwhile exploration of Chesapeake Bay before evacuation of the
colony became unavoidable. Drake offered to carry a number of ill
and weakened colonists back to England and leave a number of skilled
navigators and sailors with Lane and even loan him the *Francis*, a ship
of seventy tons, with which to make the exploration. Preparations
were well underway, and a number of Lane's officers and leading men
were aboard the *Francis* preparing for the voyage when a strong storm,
probably a hurricane, struck. Pinnaces and small boats were smashed
against the shore. The larger ships, many with cables broken and anchors lost, put to sea to avoid shipwreck on the coast.

After the storm abated, those ships that could returned to the coast
near Roanoke. Ships that lost all their cables and anchors had no
choice but to sail for England. Among these was the *Francis*, with the
provisions for the exploration and Lane's men on board. That was the
end for the first occupation of Roanoke. Lane accepted Drake's offer
to transport all the colonists back to England. The sea was still rough
and threatening, and the colonists embarked on Drake's ships hur-

riedly, abandoning much at the colony, and sailors had to dump still more goods overboard from the small boats conveying them to the ships. Among the material lost were some of John White's drawings, important charts and maps, and even a considerable quantity of valuable pearls. Three men on a mission inland, perhaps returning the hostage Skiko to his father Menatonon, were simply abandoned and never heard of again. Drake's ships sailed less than two weeks after their arrival.

A few days after Drake sailed, the long-overdue supply ship arrived from England to find the colony deserted, and so it returned to England. About two weeks later, six more ships under the command of Richard Grenville bearing settlers intended to reinforce the Roanoke colony also arrived. Grenville had made a slow voyage from England, apparently more in the hope of encountering Spanish ships to loot than attending to the business of reinforcing the colony.

Apparently ignorant of the Indians' hostility, Grenville left a token group of fifteen men on Roanoke along with a supply of provisions in order to maintain some English presence. It was a foolish and fatal decision. When the English returned to Roanoke in 1587, they found a single skeleton. Manteo, who had gone back to England with Lane and returned to Roanoke with the new contingent of colonists, learned from his fellow Croatoan tribesmen that the Roanoke and several allied groups attacked the Englishmen, killing several. The rest managed to get to a small boat in which they sailed away to oblivion.

Aftermath

Simon Fernandez, who captained one of the ships during the initial exploration before the establishment of the colony, was also the pilot during the second attempt to establish a colony at Roanoke. John White blamed Fernandez for much of the disaster that followed, but we lack Fernandez's view of events. He participated ably in the battle against the Spanish Armada in 1588 and also sailed with the subsequent English expedition to the Azores, but he was not mentioned after 1590. He probably died or was killed during that expedition. The original Portuguese form of his name was Simão Fernandes, and in England he usually signed his name as Simão Fernandez, but others rendered his name in many forms, such as Fernandes, Fernand, Fernando, Ferdinando, and Fardinando. The *Lost Colony* play presented on Roanoke since 1937 depicts Fernandez as a scheming villain.

Thomas Herriot (whose name was also spelled Harriott, Hariot, and Heriot) learned the Algonquian language of the Roanoke and served as translator during the first colonization effort. Afterward he returned to England and played no role in the second colonization of Roanoke. He continued his mathematical studies and late in life became deeply interested in astronomy. Herriot was unfortunate in his patrons. Raleigh was executed, and Henry Percy, Earl of Northumberland, was imprisoned in the Tower of London for sixteen years at the king's pleasure on suspicion of involvement in the Gunpowder Plot. Herriot continued to live with friends and pursued his studies until his death in 1621.

After returning to England, Ralph Lane became a professional military bureaucrat. He served in a camp in Essex in 1588, preparing for the expected Spanish invasion, and as muster master on the English expedition to Spain and Portugal in 1589 commanded by Sir John Norris and Drake, after which Lane was highly critical of Drake's leadership. In 1592, Lane became muster master general and clerk of the check for the garrison in Ireland, and the lord deputy of Ireland knighted him in 1594. He was severely wounded in an Irish rebellion that year, and although he continued in his Irish office, he never fully recovered and remained an invalid until his death in 1603.

Sir Francis Drake has been the hero for generations of English schoolboys, but in recent decades historians have taken a critical look at his character and actions, and the image they portray is much less attractive. He was undoubtedly brave and talented at handling a single ship, but he was negligent in planning and inept in organizing and controlling fleets and campaigns. Personally, he could be charming, sought respect, and for years was a favorite of the queen, but he was also intensely disliked by many of his contemporaries, such as Grenville and Raleigh. He was undoubtedly ruthless and grasping, dishonest even, when dealing with close friends, relatives, and comrades in arms, and above all concerned with accumulating personal wealth.

After returning from Roanoke, Drake led an expedition against the Atlantic coasts of Spain and Portugal in 1587. He successfully looted shipping in the harbor at Cadiz, and the raid may have delayed the attack of the Armada for a year, but predictably, Drake was involved in controversy about accounting and division of the plunder. In 1588, Lord Howard served as admiral of the English fleet opposing the Spanish Armada, and Drake was vice admiral. Despite his impressive title,

Drake played a modest role in the conflict, and even then his perpetual pursuit of personal gain took precedence. He broke off pursuit of the main Spanish fleet to plunder a Spanish pay ship. In 1589, Sir John Norris and Drake sailed out with a fleet to attack and destroy ships of the Spanish fleet, support dom António's attempt to take the Portuguese throne, and sail to the Azores to capture the islands, or at least intercept the Spanish treasure fleet. All miscarried, and Drake, out of favor with the queen, spent the next few years in relative obscurity.

In 1595, Drake and Sir John Hawkins raised a fleet to attack the Spanish in South America. The cocommanders were ill suited for the role. Drake, as ever, was impulsive and poorly organized, while the elderly Hawkins had become plodding and inflexible. The expedition did little but burn a number of small Spanish settlements. Hawkins died on the coast of Puerto Rico, and Drake succumbed near the Isthmus of Panama early in 1596.

Sir Richard Grenville detested Drake and refused to serve under him against the armada. Instead he became the deputy lieutenant of the West Country, where he organized defenses against the expected Spanish invasion. In 1591, as vice admiral of the English fleet under Thomas Howard, Grenville patrolled the Azores, hoping to intercept the South American treasure fleet sailing to Spain. When confronted by a much larger Spanish fleet of fifty-three ships, Howard and the rest of the English prudently retreated, but Grenville ordered his vessel, the *Revenge*, to attack the entire Spanish fleet alone. Grenville was already shorthanded with nearly a hundred men ill, but nonetheless he fought the Spanish for twelve hours until he was virtually out of ammunition, forty of his men were dead, and most of the rest, including Grenville, were wounded. Grenville ordered his ship scuttled, but the sailors refused and surrendered. Grenville died of his wounds a few days later, reportedly raging at the surrender and calling his men traitors and dogs. Soon after, the Spanish fleet was caught in a hurricane. Fifteen Spanish ships and the *Revenge* were lost, along with the Spanish prize-crew and the English prisoners. Although the attack on the Spanish has been long celebrated as an act of supreme honor and bravery, Grenville essentially committed suicide and callously doomed his crew to the same fate.

TWELVE

The English *in* North Carolina: The Second Roanoke Colony (1587–?)

The Colonization Effort

In England, many disgruntled colonists complained of the poverty and hardships during the first attempt to colonize Roanoke, regretted having gone to Virginia, and wished to have nothing to do with any further effort there. Leaders and prominent members of the first effort were, however, less negative. Thomas Herriot wrote an account of the Roanoke venture maintaining that Virginia still offered great unexamined potential. Ralph Lane's report, surviving only in excerpts published by Richard Hakluyt, sought primarily to defend his actions at Roanoke, but he also generally portrayed Virginia positively, although he finally concluded that only the discovery of a good mine of precious metal, the Northwest Passage, or a short land passage to the Pacific could make a Roanoke colony economically viable. He saw that resources such as sassafras and other botanicals might be of some economic significance but were not by themselves enough to support a colony. John White, whose paintings and drawings captured vividly the plant, animal, and human inhabitants of Roanoke and the surrounding area, felt strongly that a new colony at a better location on Chesapeake Bay could succeed.

White approached Raleigh with a proposal to found a self-sufficient agricultural colony deep in Chesapeake Bay where it would be difficult for the Spanish to locate. The new colony, to be named "the Citie of Ralegh," would, of course, also continue to seek elusive sources of wealth and could potentially (and lucratively) serve as a port and re-supply center for privateers preying on Spanish shipping and settlements. There was some talk of establishing a separate fortress some distance from the main colony for the accommodation and protection of privateers while provisioning. Raleigh was occupied with governmental responsibilities in England and efforts to establish a strong English colony in Ireland, but he still held the queen's appointment as lord and governor of Virginia. He would not finance a new colony in the absence of significant proved resources, but he was willing to provide a basis of formal organization, some shipping, and some armaments. Raleigh granted by contract an area of Virginia to a syndicate of which he was the titular head, aided by John White and twelve assistants. White was designated to be the governor of the Citie of Ralegh, and Raleigh paid to have each of the assistants awarded a coat of arms. That entitled them to be considered gentlemen, a status above commoners and appropriate for colonial leaders and officials.

Unlike the first Virginia colony, which consisted entirely of men, the new effort, modeled largely on the contemporary English colonization efforts in Ireland, included whole families, men, women, and children, and unmarried individuals. White recruited colonists mainly from London, chiefly smallholders whose recent experience in raising crops was largely limited to domestic gardens. White seems to have raised some funds for the colony from the assistants, and apparently the colonists themselves provided funds and goods for the venture, either by selling or mortgaging their holdings in England or raising contributions from friends and families. Few men who had been on the first voyage to establish a colony agreed to go on the second, but White believed in the new effort so much that he brought his family, consisting of his pregnant daughter and her husband.

White began recruiting people as early as December of 1586, intending to include about 150 individuals in the colony, but fewer than 120 embarked for Virginia on May 8, 1587. That late date was ominous for a colony that was supposed to be agriculturally self-sufficient. The colonists would arrive in America too late to plant crops that year and could not expect to grow any substantial amount of food until well into 1588. The expedition consisted of the *Lion*, a medium-sized vessel of 160 tons; a flyboat (a bulk carrier loaded with many of the supplies for the colony); and a pinnace.

The only source for the voyage and establishment of the colony is White's inadequate report, which focuses largely on self-justifications and complaints. The target of White's bitter and often unfair criticisms was Simon Fernandez, who had served as pilot on the 1584 exploration and was now one of the twelve assistants. White blames Fernandez for abandoning the flyboat but provides no details other than it was "distressed." It is apparent that the flyboat soon rejoined the expedition, and it was present at Roanoke. He also blames Fernandez for saying that an island was uninhabited where the colonists saw some natives, who gave them no trouble. White similarly complains that Fernandez failed to find salt and sheep where he thought they would be available and did not stop at Hispaniola, where Fernandez said that Raleigh told him a friendly merchant was no longer in place. None of these incidents were of great significance and no more than the usual uncertainties of a sixteenth-century expedition.

Some modern historians have assumed that White was also overall captain of the three ships as well as the designated governor of the colony, but that is not explicitly stated anywhere, and White's behavior is incomprehensible if it were true. Although White complained repeatedly about Fernandez's decisions, he never recorded any act on his part to oppose or overrule Fernandez. The expedition of 1585 that established the first colony offers an instructive parallel. At that time, Richard Grenville was commander of the ships, and Robert Lane was designated as governor of the colony. The two quarreled, but Grenville prevailed as Lane had no authority until the colonists landed. The expedition that founded Jamestown was also organized in exactly the same manner. Christopher Newport had sole command at sea, and Edward Maria Wingfield only became the leader after the colonists landed. It is likely that Fernandez's position was similar, and White did nothing about his disagreements with Fernandez because he lacked authority at sea.

White's account of events at Roanoke Island reveals the source of his hostility toward Fernandez. White maintains that Raleigh had ordered the expedition to stop at Roanoke Island to confer with the men Grenville had left there before continuing on to Chesapeake Bay. On July 22, White and forty of his men went ashore, but, if White's account may be believed, Fernandez refused to let them reembark on the ship, stating that the summer was so far advanced that he would carry them no farther. So the colonists were unloaded on Roanoke Island rather than in Chesapeake Bay. The usual explanation is that Fernandez was eager to leave because the season for profitable privateering was quickly passing, but that does not agree with his actual conduct. Fernandez showed no haste to depart, tarrying for over a month before finally setting sail on August 27. It is likely that White's superficial and biased account conceals factors of which we are now not aware. We cannot even be certain that Fernandez was solely responsible for embarking the colonists on Roanoke; we have only White's claim for that. Fernandez died soon after returning to England without leaving his account of events, and none of the other colonists ever returned to England.

Even though the original intention was to plant a colony in Chesapeake Bay, there were reasons for Fernandez and even White to accept Roanoke at least temporarily. No specific site had been chosen in Chesapeake Bay, and scouting for a suitable location would have consumed time. Fernandez and his ship would have had to search the bay and then lie at anchor during unloading at the height of the hurricane season. Even Fernandez's time at Roanoke lasting until late August put his ships and men at peril, and his primary responsibility was their safety. Moreover, at Chesapeake, the colonists would have had to unload the ship, clear land, and build shelters, activities that likely would have extended into the late autumn and early winter, while at Roanoke the colonists found the cottages built by the previous colonists largely intact and quickly rendered habitable.

On Roanoke it soon became apparent that the Indians had not forgotten or forgiven the actions of Lane and the earlier colonists. Only six days after the first landing, George Howe, one of the twelve assistants, was catching crabs some distance from the others when the Roanoke ambushed him. They left him with his skull broken and pierced by sixteen arrows. Manteo, who had gone to England with Lane and returned to Virginia with White, now went with White to Croatoan Island, where Manteo's family lived. The Croatoans greeted the colonists in a friendly manner, and White requested that the Croatoans arrange a peace conference between the colonists and the other neighboring villages. The Croatoans made the effort, but none of the other villages sent representatives.

The Croatoans told White that the Roanoke, now residing at the village of Dasemunkepeuc on the mainland, were responsible for the attack on the men that Grenville had left on Roanoke and the death of George Howe. White resolved to extract revenge, and a group of the colonists went by night and attacked a group of Natives sitting around a fire at the village, wounding at least one severely before the colonists discovered they were friendly Croatoans. The Roanoke had left the village, and the Croatoans had come to harvest the abandoned crops. White wrote that the Croatoans readily forgave the incident, but the affair can only have enhanced the colonists' reputation for violence.

On August 18, 1587, John White's daughter, Elenora Dare, gave birth to a daughter named Virginia, the first English colonial birth in America. The birth of Virginia Dare has become a central feature in the modern romantic account of the Lost Colony, even though there were earlier Spanish births in North America, and, of course, Native women had been giving birth for thousands of years.

Although the colonists had just arrived, they already faced a food shortage. They probably had enough to feed themselves through the winter but certainly not enough to last until they could grow substantial crops in 1588. Roanoke lacked abundant natural resources that could support the colony, and there was little prospect of any substantial food aid from the neighboring Indians. Someone had to return to England to arrange provisions to be sent promptly and in sufficient quantity to ensure the survival of the colonists. After considerable discussion and disagreement, the colonists insisted that White should return. He departed on the flyboat at the time same time Fernandez set sail on the *Lion*, August 27. White had spent just a month and five days at Roanoke, and he left behind about 117 colonists, among whom 17 were women and 11 children. White's voyage back to England was beset with difficulties. Two accidents severely injured a number of sailors and left the ship badly undermanned. A strong storm blew the ship far off course, and by the time it finally made port in Ireland on October 16, a number of the crew had died and the rest were in great need of food and water.

White found England preparing for the Spanish Armada. Grenville intended to send a strong privateering squadron to the Caribbean that could also carry supplies to the colony, but the queen and her council ordered all suitable ships to sail to Plymouth to join in the defense against the Spanish fleet. Grenville was left with only two small ships judged unsuitable for naval combat, a bark of thirty tons, and a pinnace of twenty-five tons, and the tiny ships would have to sail through a maritime war zone to reach Roanoke. They set out on April 22, 1588, carrying a dozen colonists, probably mainly family members of those already at Roanoke, in addition to a cargo of food. The captains of the two ships quickly showed themselves much more interested in the potential profits of piracy than relieving the colonists. They chased, captured, and looted several other small vessels of various nationalities until near Madera a French ship boarded the bark, and during the fight White was wounded three times. The French prevailed, and the looted bark crept back to England. The pinnace also returned to England a few weeks later without reaching North America. There would be no relief for the colonists in 1588.

In England, White recovered from his wounds. Raleigh, occupied with court, governmental duties, and his ongoing effort in Ireland, seems to have turned the Virginia matter over to colleagues who formed a syndicate, pledging funds and material support for the colony in exchange for assurances of future trading rights within Raleigh's claim in North America. Still, no relief effort set sail for Virginia in 1589. The royal quarantine on shipping was still in effect, although it was not difficult to gain exemptions. More significantly, all large ships in England were gathered together at Plymouth, where they were armed and manned for an expedition against Spain. The English fleet sought to cripple the Spanish navy, overthrow Spanish control of Portugal, install the pretender dom António as king there, and intercept the Spanish treasure fleet in the Azores, all of which failed. It was also a difficult and dangerous time for ships, particularly small ships, to sail without strong escorts, which were still not available.

In 1590, Raleigh was finally able to arrange that three privateering ships on a raid to the Caribbean would accompany a cargo ship of eighty tons to bring relief to the colony. The relief ship could not carry all that was needed, so the flagship of the privateers was to carry John White, some artillery for the colony, and some settlers who were to go to the colony. At the last minute before sailing, the captain of the flagship refused to board the would-be colonists and their gear, but accepted White as a passenger. It is likely the captain decided the settlers and their equipage would unacceptably reduce the efficiency of what was in reality a fighting ship. The privateers set sail in late March

1590, but the supply ship had not appeared at the time and seems not to have left England until May, when it was escorted across the Atlantic by another privateer. The ships rendezvoused on the northern coast of Hispaniola and attacked Spanish shipping in the Caribbean with mixed success, after which the flagship and the cargo ship sailed up the Florida coast, where they survived a hurricane before arriving at Roanoke. The sea, still rough from the hurricane, overset a boat attempting to land on the island, and the captain of the flagship and six others drowned.

Despite discouragement, White and others landed at Roanoke, where they saw a tree engraved with the letters "CRO." Coming to the settlement itself, they saw that the houses had been pulled down and an area fortified with a palisade. At the right side of the entrance, the word "CROATOAN" was cut into a post but without a cross that White had told the colonists to add to any message as a sign of "distress." White's account of the expedition contains a famous and ambiguous passage, "at my comming away they [the colonists] were prepared to remoue from Roanoak 50 miles into the maine." Some have taken "maine" to refer to the mainland, indicating that the colonists were going to move from the island up the Albemarle Sound to the mainland, while others have taken the "maine" to refer to the sea, as in the phrase "the Spanish main," indicating that the colonists were preparing to move north to the Chesapeake or even south to Croatoan, the distance "50 miles" a rough approximation in either case. The colonists left behind some unworked iron bars, two lead ingots, and several light artillery pieces, and nearby five chests had been buried but dug up and looted, presumably by the Roanoke Indians. Before they could make any extensive search for the colonists or even sail the relatively short distance to Croatoan Island, a damaging storm arose, and the cargo ship, leaking, low on provisions, and shorthanded, set sail for the Azores. The storm continued, and the flagship also sailed for the Azores. There was talk of returning to search for the colonists, but the loss of the captain and other men from the flagship and the deteriorating condition of both ships led them to return to England.

No further expeditions were mounted from England specifically to search for the missing colonists, though the question of their fate and the possibility that some might have survived remained intriguing. The establishment of the Jamestown colony and related activities produced a number of reports and rumors about the fate of the Roanoke colonists, though little was done to investigate the accounts and locate any surviving colonists, perhaps not surprising considering the terrible challenges faced by the Jamestown colonists. The reports share much in common with rumors in other colonies about gold and silver mines, wealthy tribes, and ways to the western ocean. The location of the objects of desire was always somewhat vague and just out of current reach, yet close enough to encourage hopes for the future. All, like the whereabouts of the Roanoke refugees, proved ultimately elusive.

The second occupation of Roanoke Island was a dubious scheme from its beginning, poorly supported and inadequately supplied. The colonists were largely from London and knew little about their new surroundings, and it may be doubted that many had the skills necessary to prosper or even survive as farmers in Virginia. The colonists, if White is to be believed, intended to go to Chesapeake Bay, but they landed at Roanoke, a much inferior location, far too late to plant crops, and it was immediately apparent that their supply of provisions was inadequate. They had enough food for winter 1588, but by the spring their European provisions would have been depleted, little could be grown and harvested until well into the summer, and the Roanoke and their allies were irredeemably hostile. Driven by such circumstances, the colonists abandoned Roanoke Island. There is no indication they perished there.

It is doubtful that any tribes in the region produced sufficient surplus food to support an influx of a large number of at least initially unproductive English settlers. The colonists most likely had to split up into small groups seeking refuge in several places. Perhaps one group remained behind on Roanoke waiting for the long-delayed aid from England, and when it could no longer hold out there, it may have moved or attempted to move to Croatoan Island, leaving behind the famous carved word. The Croatoan remained friendly, but their island was not very productive. If all the colonists had moved there, they soon would have become an unsupportable burden. The Chesapeake and other tribes on the north shore and by the head of Albemarle Sound and on the Chowan River were generally friendly, at least when the English first appeared, and traded with them, but one can only speculate how these groups might have reacted to the permanent intrusion of many hungry, probably demanding English settlers into their territory.

The situation the Roanoke colonists faced was strikingly similar to that of the colonists who founded Jamestown in 1607. Despite three shipments from England bringing supplies, provisions, and reinforcements, by 1610 over 80 percent of the Jamestown settlers were dead, victims of famine, disease, accident, and warfare with Native Americans. There is no reason to suppose that survivors of the Roanoke colony, lacking any support from England, fared better. The thought that the Roanoke refugees found solace among friendly Indians and there long remained, mingling their cultures and fortunes, is appealing and romantic, but less than likely. Most were probably dead within a year or two. But even this is a theory, and theories abound; all that can be said for certain is the colonists abandoned Roanoke Island and disappeared without leaving behind certain knowledge of their fate.

Aftermath

Sir Walter Raleigh played an important role in the English naval battle against the Spanish Armada, but in 1591 he lost the favor of Queen Elizabeth when he married a lady-in-waiting without royal permission. The breach with the queen was never fully repaired and was worsened by Raleigh's continuing feud with another of the queen's favorites, Robert Devereux, Earl of Essex. In 1594, Raleigh, entranced by the Spanish legend of El Dorado, sailed to northern South America. There, after attacking Spanish holdings in Trinidad, he sailed up the Orinoco River, intending to locate El Dorado and to establish an English base for further attacks on the Spanish Caribbean. He found nothing, and the expedition was a failure. In 1596, Raleigh sailed as part of an English attack on Cadiz, during which he was painfully wounded. He also took part in a subsequent expedition to attack the Spanish port of Ferrol that was also a failure.

In 1603, Queen Elizabeth died, and King James VI of Scotland became King James I of England. Raleigh had once unwisely questioned James's right of succession and now was far out of royal favor. There were several plots against James I during the early years of his reign, and the Privy Council accused Raleigh of complicity in several. He was convicted of treason in a grotesquely dishonest trial and initially sentenced to be hanged, drawn, and quartered, but the king suspended the sentence and imprisoned Raleigh in the Tower of London, where he remained for almost thirteen years. In 1615, James I, persuaded by courtiers, desperate for money, and intrigued by tales of wealth on the

Orinoco River, released Raleigh from the tower to command an expedition to penetrate far up the river, where Raleigh insisted there were rich deposits of gold and silver. The king ordered Raleigh on pain of death to do no injury to any Spanish subject. Raleigh intended to locate and mine the deposit, load the ships with high-grade ore, and sail back to England. The plan was ridiculous, a disaster from the beginning. Raleigh fell ill and could not lead the expedition up the Oronoco himself. Despite orders to his subordinates, a battle broke out between the English and the Spanish, which the English won, but the search for the mine found nothing. The expedition disintegrated, ships slipping away. Raleigh had no choice but to return to England, where he was arrested. Spain's King Philip III demanded justice, and James I had no reason to show mercy. He rescinded the suspension of Raleigh's conviction for treason, and Raleigh was beheaded in 1618.

Little is known about John White after his return to England in 1590. There is no indication he instigated another search for the lost colony and his family. He lacked personal resources to do so, England was too deeply involved in hostilities with Spain to pay attention to the lost colonists, and Roanoke had not produced profits to attract new investors. The last certain mention of White was in 1593, and it is thought he died about that time or shortly thereafter, either in Plymouth or in Ireland where he had a house. White was certainly an acute observer and an artist of talent, but his ability as a leader of a colonial effort may be doubted. *The Lost Colony* play idealizes White as a kindly, concerned, and tragic leader.

Today there is great public interest in the Lost Colony. The paucity and ambiguity of evidence about the fate of the colonists invite a variety of theories, which have proliferated in such numbers that it would require a substantial volume merely to catalogue and summarize them. A number of organizations are dedicated to the study of Roanoke and the lost colonists, distinguished mainly by different methodologies and assumptions: the First Colony Foundation, Croatoan Archaeological Society, Roanoke Island Historical Association, and Lost Colony Center for Science and Research. Many books, articles, and websites claim to have solved the mystery of the colonists' fate, but too often the claims consist of a long string of conjectures, each possible but none certain, and often even one false conjecture would invalidate the entire argument. Some focus entirely or nearly so on one fraction of the evidence, ignoring others that seem to indicate different conclusions. Differing, mutually exclusive theories range from reasonable to bizarre, and none presents convincing evidence. None can be proven definitely correct or have even achieved general acceptance.

Maps depict the Roanoke colonists' knowledge of the region and possible places they may have sought refuge, but no map, of course, shows where the Roanoke colonists went. Investigators evaluate differently the information provided by various maps, maintaining they support different and contradictory hypotheses about the fate of the colonists. Evidence that can be cited to support contradictory hypotheses can never be decisive for any. In recent years, however, new map discoveries have produced some intriguing preliminary indications of where the colonists may have gone, and further discoveries are eagerly awaited.

Archaeologically recovered European artifacts can only rarely be attributed with certainty to the Roanoke colonists rather than to other Europeans, and even if individual items can be connected to the Roanoke colonists, their significance is often unclear. A sixteenth-century artifact does not prove the existence of a Roanoke refugee settlement. Indigenous groups traded with one another, passing along European items. The discovery of architectural remains definitely attributable to the refugees would be of greater importance, but none yet discovered rise to that level. Archaeology is ultimately of greater importance to the understanding of the indigenous cultural contexts into which colonists intruded and effect on the Native peoples of those intrusions. The fascination with the lost colonists helps promote and fund these broader archaeological concerns.

Since 1894, the Roanoke Colony Memorial Association has celebrated Virginia Dare's birthday, August 18, and now several organizations sponsor a festival, the Virginia Dare Faire and Virginia Dare Night, on the same date. The Fort Raleigh National Historic Site features an attractive visitor center and bookstore. A play, *The Lost Colony*, has been presented on Roanoke every summer since 1937. Currently, the drama is performed in a specially constructed amphitheater nightly from Monday through Saturday from May through August. It is estimated that over three million people have seen the production. More or less related tourist attractions, restaurants, and motels proliferate in the area. The Lost Colony is big business.

Sources

David Beers Quinn (1909–2002) was the dominant figure in studies of the Roanoke colony during his lifetime, and his works remain of fundamental importance. *The Roanoke Voyages, 1584–1590*, 2 vols. (London: University Press, Cambridge, for the Hakluyt Society, 1955) contains almost all of the known contemporary accounts—Arthur Barlowe's narrative of the 1584 exploration voyage, Thomas Herriot's report on Virginia, Ralph Lane's account of the first colony, John White's narrative of the 1590 voyage—and has a wealth of short sources such as governmental documents, letters, and legal proceedings relevant to both Roanoke colonies. Quinn's volumes also include a large section of Spanish sources relevant to the Roanoke colonies and information about the language of the Carolina tribes and the archaeology of the Roanoke settlements. The few documents discovered subsequently are mainly of marginal significance. David B. Quinn, ed., *New American World: A Documentary History of North America to 1612*, vol. 3 (New York: Arno Press, 1979), 265-340, contains a selection of the English documents and several of the Spanish documents, and William P. Cumming, R. A. Skelton, and David B. Quinn, *The Discovery of North America* (New York: Heritage Press, 1972) contains reproductions of important English, Spanish, and French maps. Quinn's *Set Fair for Roanoke: Voyages and Colonies, 1584–1606* (Chapel Hill: University of North Carolina Press, 1985) presents an able overview of the Roanoke colonies and a good summary of Quinn's views, and Paul E. Hoffman, *Spain and the Roanoke Voyages* (Raleigh: North Carolina Department of Cultural Resources, 1987) provides a succinct analysis of the ineffective Spanish responses to the English efforts at Roanoke.

THIRTEEN

The Sagadahoc *or* Popham Colony: Fort St. George (1607–1608)

Background

In 1606, King James I signed a charter permitting the establishment of two colonies in North America. The southern colony, Jamestown in Virginia, survived, though at the cost of much suffering and loss of life. The northern colony was founded on the coast of Maine, a geographic term of uncertain origin already in use in the seventeenth century. It was generally known as either the Sagadahoc Colony, after its location by the mouth of the Sagadahoc (now the Kennebec) River, or the Popham Colony, after the name of two of the leaders of the venture, and it did not survive.

By the time the northern colony was established in 1607, the basic form of the eastern coast of North America was fairly well known. Numerous Spanish, Portuguese, Basque, Breton, French, and English fishermen had operated along the coast for a century, often going ashore to dry their catch. Others traded with the coastal tribes for furs and hides. Some passed on information about their voyages, but they did not explore and chart the coast systematically. French explorers examined the coast and islands methodically from north of Newfoundland to just beyond Cape Cod, but they were not enthusiastic about what they saw there and only planted several short-lived colonies to the north along the coast of Acadia (chapter 7).

Formal English exploration began with John Cabot, who sailed to New England in 1497. Subsequently, England was deeply involved in conflicts at home and abroad, and there were few English expeditions until the late sixteenth century. In 1566, Humphrey Gilbert, the half-brother of Sir Walter Raleigh, wrote an essay on the possibility of finding a Northwest Passage to the Orient. First circulated in manuscript copies, it was finally published, perhaps without Gilbert's permission, as *A discourse of a discoverie for a new passage to Cataia* (London: Jhones, 1576). The word "Cataia" in the title is more usually spelled Cathay, today's China. Gilbert's essay helped promote the idea of an English colony in the northern part of North America, and in 1583, Gilbert himself set out to establish such a colony and find the Northwest Passage.

Gilbert left Plymouth in England with five ships, one of which soon turned back, many of the crew having fallen ill, but the remaining four reached Newfoundland. There Gilbert found thirty-six fishing vessels from various nations in St. Johns harbor, where many fishermen dried their catch. Gilbert formally claimed Newfoundland for England, but dissension and illness among his crews led him to dispatch another ship back to England carrying the malcontents and sick. From Newfoundland, Gilbert intended to follow the coast of North America south, searching for the Northwest Passage and a good location for a colony that would serve as a base for further exploration, but his largest ship went aground on the shoals by Sable Island and sank with significant loss of life. The men of the last two ships, demoralized and short of supplies, abandoned the voyage and turned back toward England. On the return voyage, Gilbert insisted on sailing on the smaller ship, a tiny ketch, which sank in a fierce storm with all hands. The last ship survived to return to England. Gilbert's written work and even his failed voyage further excited English interest in establishing colonies, and the following years saw a flurry of English activity along the eastern coast of America.

In 1585, Raleigh attempted to establish a colony on Roanoke Island in what is now North Carolina, the most famous colonial failure (chapters 11 and 12). In 1602, Bartholomew Gosnold attempted to colonize Cape Cod, but the attempt was quickly abandoned, and in that same year George Waymouth searched for the Northwest Passage along the coast of New England. In 1603, Englishman Martin Pring explored much of the New England coast, and in 1605, Waymouth was active along the coast of Maine, where he kidnapped five Indians and carried them back to England.

Colonization

In 1606, King James I chartered the London and Plymouth Companies, two similar combinations of merchants and wealthy gentlemen intending to establish colonies. The London Company founded the southern colony, Jamestown, in the next year. The effort to establish the northern colony began well. The two most prominent leaders of the Plymouth Company were Sir Ferdinando Gorges, a renowned soldier and governor of the fort at Plymouth, and Sir John Popham, the wealthy lord chief justice of England. In 1606, they sent out two ships to reconnoiter the coast of Maine. Before they reached North America, the Spanish captured one ship and dealt harshly with the crew, but the second ship was able to survey the coastline in detail. The colonizers, unlike many others before, would know well where they were going. In 1607, two ships, the *Gift of God* and the *Mary and John*, set sail from Plymouth carrying the colonists and their supplies. The ships became separated during the voyage, but both arrived safely.

The commanding officer of the colonizing venture, termed the president, was George Popham, the son of the elder brother of John Popham. On December 3, 1607, Gorges wrote a letter to Robert Cecil, Earl of Salisbury, in which he described George Popham: "For firste the President himselfe is an honest man, but ould, and of unwildy body, and timerously fearfull to offende or conteste with those that will or do oppose him, but otherways a discreete carefull man." Second in command was Raleigh Gilbert, the son of Humphrey Gilbert who perished at sea and the nephew of Sir Walter Raleigh. Gilbert, a much younger man than Popham, was undoubtedly able and energetic, but Gorges, in the same letter, reported negative aspects of Gilbert's personality: "Captaine Gilberte is described to mee from thense to bee desirous of supremacy, and rule, a loose life, prompte to sensuality, litle zeale in Religion, humerouse, head stronge, and of small judgment and experience, other wayes valiant inough." In an ideal situation, the better qualities of each leader would have compensated for the weaknesses of the other, but actually, each seems to have brought out the worst in the other.

The colonists numbered about 120. Little is known about their recruitment, but in addition to a number of gentlemen, people with practical skills such as farmers, carpenters, blacksmiths, shipwrights, coopers, and sailors took part in the colony. The most numerous single group was a contingent of soldiers who provided protection and unskilled labor.

Long before the colonists arrived, Indians in the area were accustomed to trade furs and hides for items of European manufacture such as iron tools, brass kettles, and even boats. Not all exchanges were peaceful, however, and explorers almost routinely kidnapped Natives and brought them back to their home countries, where most soon succumbed to European diseases. Few lived to return and serve as interpreters. The Sagadahoc colonizers brought with them Skitwarres, a member of the Etchemin tribe, kidnapped by Waymouth in 1605. Even before choosing the exact site for the colony, a small group went along with Skitwarres to assure the local Etchemin of their peaceful intentions. Skitwarres used the occasion to leave the English and return to live with his people, although he occasionally continued to act as an intermediary between the two groups, but now representing Etchemin interests to the English rather than the other way around.

On August 18, 1607, the leaders selected the precise location for the colony, a small peninsula near the mouth of the Kennebec River. On August 19, the colonists staked out the projected colony, and the next day they began actual construction. They named the settlement Fort Saint George, but the colony was actually a civilian community surrounded by a defensive earthwork and ditch rather than a true military installation. The first projects were the earthwork and storehouse, followed by other buildings. The colonists also built a pinnace, the *Virginia*, about fifty feet long and about thirty tons.

A plan of the colony, dated October 8, 1607, survives in the Spanish Archivo General de Simancas. Don Pedro de Zuñiga, the Spanish ambassador to England, acquired it apparently through his extensive network of spies and sent it to the Spanish king, Philip III. It is a fascinating work, at once surprisingly accurate and wildly imaginative. It is clear that the plan did not represent the status of the colony at the time it was drawn but rather future intentions. The plan shows the perimeter fortification as built of cut stone or brick, but at the time it was just an earthwork. The plan also shows purely imaginary elaborate masonry gates and a number of buildings that the colonists had

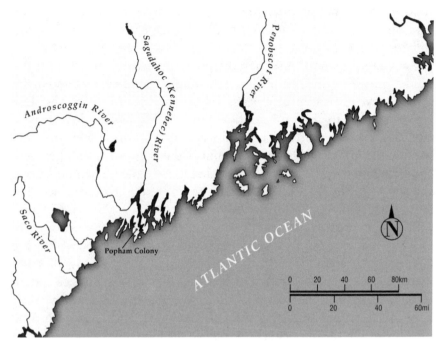

The coast of Maine, showing the location of the Popham Colony.

not yet constructed—and never would. Yet archaeological work has proved that the plan was the result of a precise survey and those buildings that the colonists built were accurately located and depicted.

The exaggerations depicted in the plan of the colony are also apparent in George Popham's letter of December 13, 1607, to King James I. Popham overstated the riches of Maine, which he claimed included nutmeg, cinnamon, Brazilian cochineal, and even ambergris. He also wrote that the Indians were eager to become subjects of the king and wished to convert to Christianity, and that the western ocean was only seven days' journey from the colony.

Troubles and Abandonment

While the great majority of the colonists labored to construct shelter before winter, some went on expeditions to explore the nearby coasts and rivers and met with the Etchemin in the neighborhood. The leaders of the colony, despite years-long access to captives from the area, had virtually no understanding of their culture and regarded them as simple savages, inferior in every sense. George Popham attempted to establish good relations, but he offended Indians when he led armed colonists who blundered into villages without advance notice, causing alarm. Gilbert, predictably, was even more inept at dealing with Indians.

As winter began to close in, more problems arose. The colonists depended almost entirely on provisions brought from England, and much was destroyed when the colony's storehouse accidently burnt. They had arrived too late to grow substantial crops, and the few gardens they established produced little. The southern colony, Jamestown, survived because the Indians provided corn, but in the north such supplies were not forthcoming. The colonists had antagonized the Etchemin, who in any event had little surplus. Maine was less fertile than Virginia, and during the winter most of the Natives left the coast to hunt inland, while the few remaining near the coast were themselves short of food.

The *Mary and John* sailed for England in early October, while the *Gift of God* remained with the colony as a protection against any seaborne attack by the French or Spanish. As winter set in, ice endangered the ship, and the leaders of the colony decided in late November or early December 1607 that the *Gift of God* should sail for England too. They took the opportunity to relieve the food crisis to some degree by sending about forty-five men back to England in the ship. The colonists could not provision the ship for the entire voyage, so they loaded thirty masts they had prepared, a cannon, and other items to sell in the Azores to buy food to finish the voyage.

The *Mary and John* arrived in England on December 1, 1607, and the *Gift of God* on February 7. They brought word of the food shortage in the colony, but two ships bearing supplies for the colony did not sail until the first half of March. During the seventeenth century, Europe was in the midst of what modern climatologists call the Little Ice Age, and winter 1607–08 was the coldest of that cold century. Weather probably delayed the dispatch of the relief ships.

Winter on the coast of Maine is intimidating, and winter 1607–08 was exceptionally brutal. For months the colonists subsisted on short rations, scarcely able to stir from their cramped, cold quarters, hemmed in by ice, snow, dark, and storms. The conditions proved fertile ground for the growth of factionalism, and Raleigh Gilbert was at the center of it. His father had received a patent from the king to establish a colony that long predated the Plymouth Company's charter of 1606. Gilbert claimed the earlier grant was still valid and that as his father's heir he was entitled to authority over the colony. Gilbert

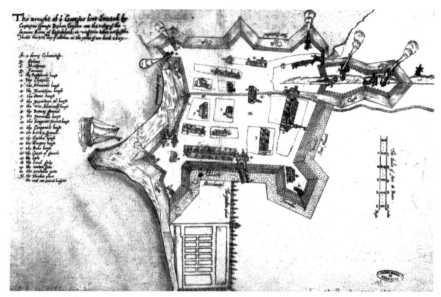

Plan of the Popham colony by John Hunt, October 7, 1607, Archivo General de Simancas.

even sent messages on the *Gift of God* to friends in England urging them to join him in the colony to support his claims. Gorges and the other investors in England were able to quash Gilbert's pretensions, but Gilbert nevertheless became the de facto leader of the colony when George Popham died on February 5, 1608.

The two supply ships arrived at the mouth of the Sagadahoc River probably in May 1608. Along with food they brought alarming news: Sir John Popham, the lord chief justice and most important investor in the colony, had died on June 10, 1607, almost a year previously and less than two weeks after the colonists had departed from England. His death deprived the colonial venture of a powerful voice at the royal court and his support of £500 a year, by far the largest investment in the colony.

The sources are unclear whether an additional one or two supply vessels sailed to the colony during summer 1608, but at least one left England in mid-July and arrived at the colony in September, bringing word of another important death in England: Sir John Gilbert, the elder brother of Raleigh Gilbert, had died in early July. That left Raleigh Gilbert the heir to the family lands, and he decided to return to England. The economic survival of an aristocratic family required vigilant, direct management of family lands. The head of the family had to collected rents, adjudicate disputes among tenants, and protect property against encroachments. Many estates were heavily mortgaged, and the head of the family had to manage finances carefully to avoid foreclosure and ruin. Whatever Raleigh Gilbert's other faults, his abandonment of the colony ought not to be attributed to timidity or selfishness. It was his duty to his family to return. In October 1608, as the first signs of impending winter became apparent, Gilbert and the remaining colonists abandoned the colony at Sagadahoc, sailing for England on the relief ship and the pinnace *Virginia*.

Aftermath

The Popham Colony began with many advantages lacked by other colonies, even colonies that succeeded. Investors in the project were wealthy and well connected to the English court. The coast of Maine was well mapped in preparation for the establishment of the colony, the settlement was quickly fortified, and the colonists erected substantial buildings, with plans for many more structures. All of these advantages were not enough to overcome a host of problems. Neither George Popham nor Raleigh Gilbert was an ideal leader, and their contrasting styles led to factionalism. The colonists had embarked with no adequate appreciation of the challenges presented by the coast of Maine, and they were unfortunate that winter 1607–08 was extraordinarily severe. The provisions they brought from England were inadequate. They arrived too late to grow crops, their storehouse burned, and the Etchemin did not supply substantial amounts of food.

Perhaps more importantly, the colony lacked any real economic basis. Initially the investors had high hopes that colonists would find rich mines, establish a strong trade in furs, find exotic spices and medicinal herbs, perhaps discover the Northwest Passage, and project British claims in North America. The colonists found no gold or silver, and, nearly as disappointing, they also failed to find copper and zinc. In addition to Sir John Popham's role as the lord chief justice, he was a major investor in the Society of Mineral and Battery Works and Society of Mines Royal, which exercised copper and brass monopolies in England. Brass was crucial for defense and the economy, the material of ship's cannons and wool carding combs, but the English, using high-sulphur coal, failed to produce quality brass. England had to import the vital metal at high expense.

The fur trade offered perhaps the best opportunity for economic viability, but it too proved disappointing. The leaders of the colony failed to establish mutual confidence and cordial personal relationships with the Etchemin and other neighboring tribes essential to active trade, and the Popham Colony was not the only source of trade goods. The French were not distant, and traders of several nations frequently operated along the coast. William Strachey, writing between about 1615 and 1620, stated that the colonists traded for many kinds of furs, but the colony seems to have returned only a small quantity of furs to England. Despite George Popham's enthusiastic claim that tropical spices grew in Maine, probably based on overly imaginative interpretations of plants of vaguely similar appearance, there was no botanic cornucopia. The Northwest Passage was an illusion, and the tiny colony was a poor effort at projecting British imperial ambitions.

The loss of leadership also played a factor in the failure. Seventeenth-century society was hierarchical: aristocrats led, commoners followed. Popham's death and Gilbert's decision to return to England left the colonists leaderless, a condition for which they had no experience or preparation, and they must have realized that wealthy gentlemen and rich merchants in England would not continue to support the remaining commoners.

Later in the seventeenth and eighteenth centuries, visitors to the site remarked on the scant discernable ruins of the colony, and even those had disappeared by the twentieth century. In 1962 and 1964, Wendell S. Hadlock dug at what was thought to be the site of the Popham Colony at Sabino Head but found little, just a few artifacts and some evidence of burning. He concluded that the site might be correctly identified but that erosion and disturbances had largely destroyed any remains.

In 1994, Jeffrey P. Brain reexamined the site. He established the correct orientation of the 1607 map to the local topography, and over the next years he and his team were able to verify the accuracy of the map in regard to buildings that had actually been constructed before the colony was abandoned. Brain's careful, skilled excavation team was able to identify specific buildings depicted on the plan and reveal the construction technique: posts were planted in the ground, and the area between the posts was walled with wattle and daub, and the building roofed with thatch. They also recovered hundreds of artifacts left behind by the colonists. Brain's work has elucidated the written sources and added new dimensions to the understanding of the colony, recovering, for example, goods brought from England for trade to the Etchemin. Much of the colony remains unexcavated. Some of it lies under a road and parking lot, while other areas, including the chapel where it is likely that George Popham was buried, are on private land and the owners have refused permission to excavate.

Sources

The most important single source for the Popham Colony is "The Relation of a Voyage unto New England," an account of the colony found among the papers of Sir Ferdinando Gorges after his death, published in Henry O. Thayer, *The Sagadahoc Colony* (Portland, ME: Gorges Society, 1892; repr. New York: Research Reprints, 1970). "The Relation" is incompletely preserved. There may be a page or two missing at the beginning, and certainly several are missing at the end. The name of the author is also missing on the manuscript, but internal evidence indicates it was written by James Davies, pilot of the *Mary and John* and later sargent major of the colony. The work originally ended on September 26, 1607, when Davies sailed on the *Mary and John* back to England. The lost pages at the end of the work were utilized in William Strachey's account of the colony, written about a decade after the failure of the colony (see below).

Sir Ferdinando Gorges wrote an account of the colony long after the events, apparently relying on memory rather than documents. The account is short of specifics and contains some demonstrable errors, but it provides a valuable perspective and a few important facts. It was first printed eleven years after his death as Sir Ferdinando Gorges, *A Brief Narration of the Originall Undertakings of the Advancement of Plantations into the Parts of America, especially showing the Beginning, Progress and Continuance of that of New England* (Corn-Hill, England: Printed by E. Brudenell for Nath. Brook, 1658).

George Popham wrote to King James I on December 13, 1607. The letter grossly exaggerates the success and future prospects of the colony and addresses the king in the most sycophantic terms imaginable. Letters from Sir Ferdinando Gorges to Robert Cecil, Earl of Salisbury, contain trenchant observations of the characters of George Popham and Raleigh Gilbert. Various other letters at least touch on the colony, occasionally bearing some relevant information. All of these sources and a variety of lesser documents touching on the history of the colony are conveniently gathered and republished in Thayer, *Sagadahoc Colony*.

Don Pedro de Zuñiga, the Spanish ambassador to England, acquired the detailed "Plan of St. George's Fort," dated October 8, 1607, apparently from his extensive network of spies. He sent it to King Philip III, and after the colony was abandoned, the map was sent to the Archivo General de Simancas, where it is today. A researcher employed by J. L. M. Curry, US minister plenipotentiary to the Court of Spain, discovered the map in 1888, and it was first published in A. Brown, *The Genesis of the United States* (Boston: Houghton Mifflin, 1890), 190, along with scattered references to the colony from elsewhere in the archive. The map is also printed in Thayer, *Sagadahoc Colony*.

Also important is an account of early English colonization written by William Strachey between about 1615 and 1620 and preserved in several manuscripts. It was first printed in 1849 as William Strachey, *Historie of Travaile into Virginia Brittania* (London: Haklukt Society, 1849). Strachey was the secretary of the Jamestown Colony but took no part in the Popham Colony. He based his account chiefly on "The Relation" attributed to James Davies, but he also included some specific information about sailing and navigation apparently from lost logbooks or memoranda. Strachey used a copy of "The Relation" that contained a few more pages than now exist, and he continued his account further from various other sources.

The archaeological investigations of Jeffrey P. Brain that have done much to reveal the colony are published in a series of exemplary reports: "The John Hunt Map of the First English Colony in New England," *Northeast Historical Archaeology* 37, no. 1 (2008): article 6, http://digitalcommons.buffalostate.edu/neha/vol37/iss1/6; "The Popham Colony: An Historical and Archaeological Brief," *Maine Archaeological Society Bulletin* 43 (2002): 1-28; *Fort St. George: Archaeological Investigation of the 1607–1608 Popham Colony on the Kennebec River in Maine* (Salem, MA: Peabody Essex Museum, 1995; repr. Augusta: Maine State Museum, Maine Historic Preservation Commission, and Maine Archaeological Society, 2007); *Fort St. George II: Additional Archaeological Investigation of the 1607–1608 Popham Colony on the Kennebec River in Maine*, new ed. (Augusta, ME: Maine Archaeological Society, 2016); *Fort St. George III–XV*

(Salem, MA: Peabody Essex Museum, 1998–2012). His work has shown the accuracy of the 1607 plan of the fort, located specific buildings, recovered examples of the trade goods brought from England and relics of the daily lives of the colonists, and brought life to the documents.

A Final Note

THE SIXTEENTH-CENTURY HISTORIAN Gonzalo Fernández de Oviedo y Valdés, writing specifically about the failure of the San Miguel de Gualdape colony, described a basic flaw that was characteristic of all colonies, both those that failed and those that survived: ignorance. Oviedo explained that ignorance led to inappropriate preparation. Colonists set out with little real knowledge of the conditions they would face, usually based on overly optimistic reports of explorers seeking fortune in the New World that relied on superficial impressions made during brief visits. Colonial expeditions many times could not leave Europe until spring brought favorable sailing weather, and the long passage across the Atlantic meant that colonists arrived too late to plant crops during their first year of residence. In addition, colonies were often poorly financed because investors and settlers sought immediate wealth, sometimes at the expense of critical basic needs, such as seed and tools for raising crops. As a result, the supplies they carried with them frequently proved inadequate, and colonial organizers in Europe were often not able to produce and send provisions promptly and of sufficient quality and quantity to support nascent colonies. European technology and religious exclusivity led colonists to regard themselves as inherently superior to Indians, whom they dismissed as simple savages. Colonists made little or no effort to understand or respect the culture and attitudes of the people already inhabiting the land. Failing to comprehend the reality of Indian economies, colonists thought erroneously that the Native peoples would be able to support them, and they were ready to try to force them to do so. With leadership seldom able to adequately address all challenges, colonists too often resorted to violence that ultimately failed to provide any real solution to problems and frequently made matters worse.

The wealth of Aztec Mexico and Inca Peru fired European imaginations, ambitions, and greed. Colonists, merchants, aristocrats, and national monarchies all sought the sort of New World riches that drove Spain's empire. Even failing discovery of instant treasure, however, a successful colony might produce valuable resources, trade, and markets, all of which could build wealth, and competition encouraged rapid commitment and conflict over locations in North America. Ignorance and haste, however, often combined to foster disaster. Consideration of the multitude of factors that caused a colony to fail leads to a deeper appreciation of dangers and hardships faced by all colonists, and an overview of the behavior of colonists, both successful and unsuccessful, leads to understanding and sympathy for the Native Americans who had to interact with them.

Further Reading

Chapter 1

Cameron, Guy E. *San Miguel De Gualdape: The Failed 1526 Settlement Attempt and the First Freed Africans in America* (e-book). www.amazon.com/San-Miguel-Gualdape-Settlement-Africans-ebook/dp/B015C1YVII.

Cameron, Guy, and Stephen Vermette. "The Role of Extreme Cold in the Failure of the San Miguel de Gualdape Colony." *Georgia Historical Quarterly* 96, no. 3 (Fall 2012): 291-307.

Hernández de Biedman, Luís. "Relación de la isla de la Florida." In *Colección de varios documentos para la historia de la Florida y tierras adyacentes*, vol. 1, edited by Thomas Buckingham Smith, 46-64. London: En la casa de Trubner y Compania, 1857.

Lowery, Woodbury. *The Spanish Settlements within the Present Limits of the United States 1513–1561*. New York and London: G. P. Putnam's Sons, 1901.

Peck, Douglas T. "Lucas Vásquez de Ayllón's Doomed Colony of San Miguel de Gualdape." *Georgia Historical Quarterly* 85, no. 2 (Summer 2001): 183-198.

Pickett, Margaret F., and Dwayne W. Pickett. *The European Struggle to Settle North America: Colonizing Attempts by England, France and Spain, 1521–1608*. Jefferson, NC: McFarland, 2011.

Rouse, Irving. *The Tainos: Rise and Decline of the People Who Greeted Columbus*. New Haven, CT: Yale University Press, 1992.

Sauer, Carl Ortwin. *Sixteenth Century North America*. Berkeley: University of California Press, 1971.

Shea, John Gilmary. "Early Florida." In *Narrative and Critical History of America*, edited by Justin Winsor, vol. 2, *Spanish Explorations*, 231-298. Boston: Houghton Mifflin, 1884.

Tesser, Carmen, and Charles Hudson, eds. *The Forgotten Centuries: Indians and Europeans in the American South, 1521–1704*. Athens: University of Georgia Press, 1994.

Wilson, Samuel M. *The Indigenous People of the Caribbean*. Florida Museum of Natural History, Ripley P. Bullen Series. Gainesville: University Press of Florida, 1999.

Chapter 2

Connor, Jeannette Thurber, ed. and trans. *Colonial Records of Spanish Florida: Letters and Reports of Governors and Secular Persons*, vol. 1: 1570–1577. Deland, FL: Florida State Historical Society, 1925.

Hann, John H. *Indians of Central and South Florida, 1513–1763*. Gainesville: University Press of Florida, 2003.

Hudson, Charles M. *The Juan Pardo Expeditions: Exploration of the Carolinas and Tennessee, 1566–1568*. Rev. ed. Tuscaloosa: University of Alabama Press, 2005.

Hudson, Charles M., Marvin T. Smith, Chester B. DePratter, and Emilia Kelley. "The Tristán de Luna Expedition, 1559–1561." *Southeastern Archaeology* 8, no. 1 (1989): 31-45.

Kelton, Paul. *Epidemics and Enslavement*. Lincoln: University of Nebraska Press, 2007.

Kritzler, Edward. *Jewish Pirates of the Caribbean*. New York: Anchor Books, 2008.

Lowery, Woodbury. *The Spanish Settlements within the Present Limits of the United States, 1513–1561*. 3 vols. New York & London: G. P. Putnam's Sons, 1901.

Matter, Robert Alan. *Pre-Seminole Florida: Spanish Soldiers, Friars, and Indian Missions, 1513–1763*. New York: Garland, 1990.

Milanich, Jerald T. *Florida Indians and the Invasion from Europe*. Gainesville: University Press of Florida, 1995.

Priestley, Herbert Ingram. *Tristán de Luna, Conquistador of the Old South: A Study of Spanish Imperial Strategy*. Glendale, CA: A. H. Clark, 1936.

Serrano y Sanz, Manuel. *Documentos Históricos de la Florida y la Luisiana*, siglos XVI al XVIII. Madrid: V. Suarez, 1912.

University of West Florida Division of Anthropology and Archaeology. uwf.edu/cassh/departments/anthropology-and-archaeology/ and links listed there.

Worth, John E. "Documenting Tristan de Luna's Fleet, and the Storm that Destroyed It." *Florida Anthropologist* 62, nos. 3-4 (Sept.-Dec. 2009): 83-92.

———. Faculty homepage. University of West Florida. uwf.edu/jworth/index.htm.

———. "Razing Florida: The Indian Slave Trade and the Devastation of Spanish Florida, 1659–1715." In *Mapping the Mississippian Shatter Zone: The Colonial Indian Slave Trade and Regional Instability in the American South*, edited by Robbie Ethridge and Sheri Shuck-Hall, 295-311. Lincoln: University of Nebraska Press, 2009.

Chapter 3

Bushnell, A. T. "A Land Renowned for War: Florida as a Maritime Marchland." In *La Florida: Five Hundred Years of Hispanic Presence*, edited by Viviana Días Balsera and Rachel A. May, 103-116. Gainesville: University Press of Florida, 2014.

Chang-Rodríguez, Raquel. "On the Trail of Texts from Early Spanish Florida: Garcilaso's *La Florida del Inca* and Oré's *Relación de las mátires*." In *La Florida: Five Hundred Years of Hispanic Presence*, edited by Viviana Días Balsera and Rachel A. May, 83-102. Gainesville: University Press of Florida, 2014.

Cotgrave, Randal. *A Dictionarie of the French and English Tongues*. London: Adam Islip, 1611.

Lyon, Eugene. "The Captives of Florida." *Florida Historical Quarterly* 50, no. 1 (July 1971): 1-24.

———. "Santa Elena: A Brief History of the Colony, 1566–1587." *Research Manuscript Series*. Book 185 (1984). Accessed May 5, 2020. scholarcommons.sc.edu/archanth_books/185.

McGrath, John T. *The French in Early Florida: In the Eye of the Hurricane*. Gainesville: University Press of Florida, 2000.

Milanich, Jerald T. "The Devil in the Details," *Archaeology* (May/June 2005): 27–31.

Sutherland, N. M. *The Huguenot Struggle for Recognition*. New Haven, CT: Yale University Press, 1980.

Chapter 4

Francis, John Michael, and Kathleen M. Kol. *Murder and Martyrdom in Spanish Florida: Don Juan and the Guale Uprising of 1597*. New York: American Museum of Natural History, 2011.

Gradie, C. M. "Spanish Jesuits in Virginia: The Mission That Failed." *Virginia Magazine of History and Biography* 96, no. 2 (April 1988): 131–156.

Hann, John H., and Jerald T. Milanich. *A History of the Timucua Indians and Missions*. Gainesville: University Press of Florida, 1996.

Hoffman, Paul E. *Florida's Frontiers*. Bloomington: Indiana University Press, 2002.

———. *A New Andalucia and a Way to the Orient*. Baton Rouge: Louisiana State University Press, 1990.

Jones, Katharine M. *Port Royal under Six Flags*. Indianapolis: Bobbs-Merrill, [1960].

Mallios, Seth. *The Deadly Politics of Giving: Exchange and Violence at Ajacan, Roanoke, and Jamestown*. Tuscaloosa: University of Alabama Press, 2006.

Marotti, Frank, Jr. "Juan Baptista de Segura and the Failure of the Florida Jesuit Mission, 1566–1572." *Florida Historical Quarterly* 63, no. 3 (January 1985): 267–279.

Milanich, Jerald T. *Laboring in the Fields of the Lord: Spanish Missions and Southeastern Indians*. Washington, DC: Smithsonian Institution Press, 1999.

Sacchino, R. P. Francisco. *Historiae Societatis Iesu pars tertia siue Borgia*. Rome: Typis Manelfi Manelfii, 1649.

Townsend, Camilla, ed. *American Indian History: A Documentary Reader*. Malden, MA: Wiley-Blackwell, 2009.

———. "Mutual Appraisals: The Shifting Paradigms of the English, Spanish, and Powhatans in Tsenacomoco, 1560–1622." In *Early Modern Virginia: Reconsidering the Old Dominion*, edited by Douglas Bradburn and John C. Coombs, 57–89. Charlottesville: University Press of Virginia, 2011.

Wolfe, Brendan. "Don Luís de Velasco/Paquiquineo (fl. 1561–1571)." *Encyclopedia Virginia*. Accessed May 9, 2020. www.encyclopediavirginia.org/Don_LuA.

Worth, John E. *The Timucuan Chiefdoms of Spanish Florida*. Vol. 1, *Assimilation*. Gainesville: University Press of Florida, 1998.

Chapter 5

Bowne, Eric E. "The Rise and Fall of the Westo Indians." *Early Georgia* 28, no. 1 (2000): 56-78.

———. *The Westo Indians: Slave Traders of the Early Colonial South.* Tuscaloosa: University of Alabama Press, 2005.

Boyd, Mark Frederick, Hale Gilliam Smith, and John W. Griffin. *Here They Once Stood: The Tragic End of the Apalachee Missions.* Gainesville: University Press of Florida, 1951.

Días Balsera, Viviana, and Rachel A. May, eds. *La Florida: Five Hundred Years of Hispanic Presence.* Gainesville: University Press of Florida, 2014.

Gray, Saber. "'I Do Not Know How to Fulfill These Demands': Rethinking Jesuit Missionary Efforts in La Florida, 1566–1572." MA thesis, University of South Florida St. Petersburg, 2014.

Hann, John H. *A History of the Timucua Indians and Missions.* Gainesville: University Press of Florida, 1996.

Kelton, Paul. *Epidemics and Enslavement.* Lincoln: University of Nebraska Press, 2007.

Martin, Joel W. "Southeastern Indians and the English Trade in Skins and Slaves." In *The Forgotten Centuries: Indians and Europeans in the American South, 1521–1704*, edited by Charles Hudson and Carmen Chaves Tesser, 304-324. Athens: University of Georgia Press, 1994.

Milanich, Jerald T. "Franciscan Missions and Native People in Spanish Florida." In *The Forgotten Centuries: Indians and Europeans in the American South, 1521–1704*, edited by Charles Hudson and Carmen Chaves Tesser, 276-303. Athens: University of Georgia Press, 1994.

Oatis, S. J. *A Colonial Complex: South Carolina's Frontiers in the Era of the Yamasee War, 1680–1730.* Lincoln: University of Nebraska Press, 2008.

Rock, C. "The San Pedro Mission Village on Cumberland Island, Georgia." *Journal of Global Initiatives* 5, no. 1 (2010): 87-98.

Chapter 6

Bruseth, James E., and Toni S. Turner. *From a Watery Grave: The Discovery and Excavation of La Salle's Shipwreck, La Belle.* College Station: Texas A&M University Press, 2005.

Dunn, William Edward. *Spanish and French Rivalry in the Gulf Region of the United States, 1678-1702, the Beginnings of Texas and Pensacola.* Austin: University of Texas, 1917.

Folmer, Henry. *Franco-Spanish Rivalry in North America, 1524–1763.* Glendale, CA: A. H. Clark, 1953.

Foster, William C. *Spanish Expeditions into Texas, 1680–1768.* Austin: University of Texas Press, 1995.

Gilmore, Kathleen. "Treachery and Tragedy in the Texas Wilderness: The Adventures of Jean L'Archeveque in Texas (a Member of La Salle's Colony)." *Bulletin of the Texas Archeological Society* 69 (1998): 35-46.

Leprohon, Pierre. *Cavelier de La Salle, fondateur de la Louisiane.* Paris: Denoë, 1942. Reprinted Paris: André Bonne, 1984.

Sobel, Dava. *Longitude: The True Story of a Lone Genius Who Solved the Greatest Scientific Problem of His Time.* New York: Walker, 1995.

Weddle, Robert S. *The French Thorn: Rival Explorers in the Spanish Sea, 1682–1762.* College Station: Texas A & M University Press, 1991.

———. "Talon Children." *Handbook of Texas Online.* Accessed May 5, 2020. http://www.tshaonline.org/ handbook/online/articles/fta60.

———. *The Wreck of the Belle, the Ruin of La Salle.* College Station: Texas A & M University Press, 2001.

Chapter 7

Barbeau, Michel. "Cartier Inspired Rabelais." *Canadian Geographical Journal* 9 (1934): 113–25.

Bideaux, Michel. *Jacques Cartier Relations.* Montréal: Le Presses de l'Université de Montréal, 1986.

Biggar, Henry Percival. *The Early Trading Companies of New France. A Contribution to the History of Commerce and Discovery in North America.* Toronto: University of Toronto, 1901.

Dedek, N. *La cosmographie de Jean Alfonse de Saintonge: représentation du monde et de l'État à la Renaissance.* Montréal: Université du Québec à Montréal, 2000.

La Roque de Roquebrune, Robert. "La Rocque de Roberval, Jean-François de." *Dictionary of Canadian Biography.* Vol. 1. University of Toronto/Université Laval, 2003–. http://www.biographi.ca/en/bio /la_rocque_de_roberval_jean_ francois_de_1E.html.

Marichal, R. "Les compagnons de Roberval." *Humanisme et Renaissance* 1 (1934): 51-122.

Schlesinger, R., and A. P. Stabler, eds. *André Thevet's North America: A Sixteenth-Century View.* Kingston and Montréal: McGill-Queen's University Press, 1986.

Turgeon, Laurier. Une histoire de la Nouvelle-France: Français et Amérindiens au XVIe siècle. Paris: Belin, 2019.

Chapter 8

Armstrong, Bruce. *Sable Island, Nova Scotia's Mysterious Island of Sand.* Halifax, NS: Formac, 1987.

Bourel de La Roncière, Charles-Germain-Marie. *Histoire de la Maritime française.* Vol. 4: *En quete d'un empire colonial.* Paris: E. Plon, Nourrit et Cie, 1910.

Byrne, M.-L., and S. B. McCann. "The Dunescape of Sable Island." *Canadian Geographer* 39, no. 4 (1995): 363-368.

———. "The Internal Structure of Vegetated Coastal Sand Dunes, Sable Island, Nova Scotia." *Sedimentary Geology* 84 (1993): 199-218.

Jansen, Olaf U. "A Reader's Guide to the History of Newfoundland and Labrador to 1869." Olaf U. Jensen website, Grenfell campus, Memorial University of Newfoundland. Accessed May 5, 2020. www2.grenfell.mun.ca /nfld_history/index.htm.

Kurlansky, Mark. *Cod: A Biography of the Fish That Changed the World.* Toronto: Vintage Canada, 2011.

Lanctôt, Gustave. "La Roche de Mesgouez, Troilus de." In *Dictionary of Canadian Biography.* Vol. 1. University of Toronto/Université Laval, 2003. Accessed May 5, 2020. http://www.biographi.ca/en/bio/la_roche_de_ mesgouez_ troilus_ de_1E.html.

McCann, S. B., and Mary-Louise Byrne. "Dune Morphology and the Evolution of Sable Island, Nova Scotia." *Physical Geography* 15, no. 4 (1994): 342-357.

Villiers, Marq de, and Shiela Hirtle. *Sable Island: The Strange Origins and Curious History of a Dune Adrift in the Atlantic.* New York: Walker, 2004.

Chapter 10

Allaire, Bernard, and Donald Hogarth. "Martin Frobisher, the Spaniards and a Sixteenth-Century Northern Spy." *Terrae Incognitae* 28 (1996): 46-57.

Auger, R., et al. *Material Evidence from the Frobisher Voyages: Anglo-Inuit Contact in the North American Arctic in the Late Sixteenth Century.* British Museum Occasional Paper 109. London: British Museum, 1995.

Collinson, Richard. *The Three Voyages of Martin Frobisher: In Search of a Passage to Cathaia and India by the North-west, A.D. 1576–8.* London: Hakluyt Society, 1867.

Fitzhugh, William W., and Jacqueline S. Olin, eds. *Archeology of the Frobisher Voyages.* Washington, DC: Smithsonian Institution Press, 1993.

Hogarth, D. D., Peter W. Boreham, and John G. Mitchell. *Martin Frobisher's Northwest Venture, 1576–1581: Mines, Minerals & Metallurgy.* Hull, QC: Canadian Museum of Civilization, 1994.

Hulton, Paul. *The Watercolor Drawings of John White from the British Museum.* Washington, DC: National Gallery of Art, 1965.

Jones, Frank. *The Life of Sir Martin Frobisher, knight: containing a narrative of the Spanish Armada.* London: Longmans, Green, 1878.

McDermott, James. "The Account Books of Michael Lok, Relating to the Northwest Voyages of Martin Frobisher, 1576–1578." MPhil thesis, University of Hull, Quebec, 1984.

McFee, William. *The Life of Sir Martin Frobisher.* New York: Harper & Bros., 1928.

McGhee, R. *The Arctic Voyages of Martin Frobisher: An Elizabethan Adventure.* Montréal: McGill-Queen's University Press, 2014.

Ruby, Robert. *Unknown Shore: The Lost History of England's Arctic Colony.* New York: Henry Holt, 2001.

Chapters 11 & 12

The bibliography concerning the Roanoke colony is immense, and this list is highly selective and tries to represent a variety of approaches and conclusions. Many of the books and articles listed below contain additional bibliography.

Barbour, Philip L. *The Complete Works of Captain John Smith (1580–1631).* 3 vols. Chapel Hill: University of North Carolina Press, 1986.

Connor, Robert D. W. *The Beginnings of English America: Sir Walter Raleigh's Settlements on Roanoke Island, 1584–1587* (Raleigh, NC: North Carolina Historical Commission, 1907).

Cumming, William Patterson. "The Identity of John White, Governor of Roanoke, and John White, the Artist." *North Carolina Historical Review* 15 (1938): 197-203.

Durant, David N. *Ralegh's Lost Colony*. New York: Atheneum, 1981.

Foss, Michael. *Undreamed Shores: England's Wasted Empire in America*. New York: Book Club Associates, 1974.

Gardiner, Samuel Rawson. *History of England from the Accession of James I to the Outbreak of the Civil War*. 3 vols. London: Longmans, Green, 1882–1884.

Grassl, Gary Carl. *The Search for the First English Settlement in America: America's First Science Center*. Foreword by Ivor Noël Hume. Bloomington, IN: Author House, 2006.

Hoffman, Paul E. *Spain and the Roanoke Voyages*. Raleigh, NC: North Carolina Department of Cultural Resources, 1987.

Horn, James. *A Kingdom Strange: The Brief and Tragic History of the Lost Colony of Roanoke*. New York: Basic Books, 2010.

Hulton, Paul. *America 1585: The Complete Drawings of John White*. Chapel Hill: University of North Carolina Press, 1984.

Hulton, Paul, and David B. Quinn. *The American Drawings of John White, 1577–1590*. 2 vols. London: Chapel Hill, 1964.

Humber, John L. *Backgrounds and Preparations for the Roanoke Voyages, 1584–1590*. Raleigh, NC: America's Four Hundredth Anniversary Committee, North Carolina Department of Cultural Resources, 1986.

Kelsey, Harry. *Sir Francis Drake: The Queen's Pirate*. New Haven, CT: Yale University Press, 1998.

Kupperman, Karen Ordahl. *Roanoke: The Abandoned Colony*. 2nd ed. Lanham, MD: Rowman & Littlefield, 2007.

Lorant, Stefan, ed. *The New World: The First Pictures of America*. Revised edition. New York: Duell, Sloan, & Pearce, 1965.

Moran, Michael G. *Inventing Virginia: Sir Walter Raleigh and the Rhetoric of Colonization, 1584–1590*. New York: Peter Lang, 2007.

Parks, George Bruner. *Richard Hakluyt and the English Voyages*. New York: F. Ungar, 1961.

Quinn, David B., and Alison M. Quinn. *Virginia Voyages from Hakluyt*. London: Oxford University Press, 1973.

Rowse, Alfred L. *The Elizabethans and America*. New York: Harper, 1959.

———. *The Expansion of Elizabethan England*. 2nd ed. Foreword by Michael Portillo. Basingstoke, UK: Palgrave Macmillan, 2003.

Rukeyser, Muriel. *The Traces of Thomas Hariot*. London: Gollancz, 1971.

Saucer, Carol Ortwin. *Sixteenth Century North America: The Land and the People as Seen by the Europeans*. Berkeley: University of California Press, 1975.

Stick, David. *Roanoke Island: The Beginnings of English America*. Chapel Hill: University of North Carolina Press, 1983.

Strachey, William. *The Historie of Travell into Virginia Britania*. Edited by Louis B. Wright and Virginia Freund. London: Hakluyt Society, 1953.

Trevelyan, Raleigh. *Sir Walter Raleigh*. New York: Henry Holt, 2004.

Wilson, Samuel M. *The Indigenous People of the Caribbean*. Florida Museum of Natural History, Ripley P. Bullen Series. Gainesville: University Press of Florida, 1999.

Wright, Louis Booker. *The Elizabethans' America: A Collection of Early Reports by Englishmen on the New World*. Cambridge, MA: Harvard University Press, 1965.

Additional select reading relevant to the fate of the lost colonists, including works ranging from responsible research to bizarre and fraudulent:

Ambers, Janet, Joanna Russell, David Saunders, and Alice Rugheimer. "Examination of Patches on a Map of the East Coast of North America by John White ('La Virginea Pars'; 1906,0509.1.3)." CSR Analytical Request No. AE2012-21, British Museum. Accessed May 4, 2020. www.firstcolonyfoundation.org/documents/british_museum_findings.pdf.

Brenau University. "The Dare Stones." Accessed May 5, 2020. www.brenau.edu/darestones/.

Cobb, Collier. "Early English Survivals on Hatteras Island." *University of North Carolina Magazine* (February 1910), Old Ser. 40, no. 3, New Ser. 27, no. 3: 3-10.

Howe, C. K. *Solving the Riddle of the Lost Colony*. Beaufort, NC: M. P. Skarren, 1947.

La Vere, David. *The Lost Rocks: The Dare Stones and the Unsolved Mystery of Sir Walter Raleigh's Lost Colony*. Wilmington, NC: Burnt Mill Press, 2011.

———. "The 1937 Chowan River 'Dare Stone': A Re-Evaluation." *North Carolina Historical Review* 86, no. 3 (July 2009): 251-281.

Lawler, Andrew. "The Mystery of Roanoke Endures Yet Another Cruel Twist." *Smithsonian Magazine*. Accessed May 5, 2020.

https://www.smithsonianmag.com/history/mystery-roanoke-endures-yet-another-cruel-twist-180962837/.
———. "The Search for the Lost Colony." *National Geographic* 233, no. 6 (June 2018): 128-141.
———. *The Secret Token: Myth, Obsession, and the Search for the Lost Colony of Roanoke.* New York: Doubleday, 2018.
Lloyd, Nathaniel. "The Lost Colony and the Dare Stones, Part One." *Historical Blindness,* Dec. 23, 2016. Podcast. Accessed May 5, 2020. www.historicalblindness.com/blogandpodcast//the-lost-colony-and-the-dare-stones-part-one.
———. "The Lost Colony and the Dare Stones, Part Two." *Historical Blindness,* Jan. 22, 2017. Podcast. Accessed May 5, 2020. www.historicalblindness.com/blogandpodcast//the-lost-colony-and-the-dare-stones-part-two.
Lost Colony DNA Project, Lost Colony Center for Science and Research. Accessed May 5, 2020. www.lost-colony.com/DNAproj.html.
MacMillan, Hamilton. *Sir Walter Raleigh's Lost Colony: An Historical Sketch of the Attempts of Sir Walter Raleigh to Establish a Colony in Virginia, with the Traditions of an Indian Tribe in North Carolina. Indicating the Fate of the Colony of Englishmen Left on Roanoke Island in 1587.* Wilson, NC: Advance Press, 1888.
McMullan, Philip S., Jr. *Beechland and the Lost Colony.* Nags Head, NC: Pamlico & Albemarle, 2014.
Miller, Lee. *Roanoke: Solving the Mystery of the Lost Colony.* London: Penguin, 2002.
Quinn, David Beers. *The Lost Colonists: Their Fortune and Probable Fate.* Raleigh, NC: America's Four Hundredth Anniversary Committee, North Carolina Department of Cultural Resources, 1984.
Robinson, Melvin. *Riddle of the Lost Colony.* New Bern, NC: Owen G. Dunn, [1946].
Sparkes, Boyden. "Writ on Rocke: Has America's First Murder Mystery Been Solved?." *Saturday Evening Post,* April 26, 1941, 9-11, 118, 120-122.
Stahle, David W., Malcolm K. Cleaveland, Dennis B. Blanton, Matthew D. Therrell, and David A. Gay. "The Lost Colony and Jamestown Droughts." *Science* 280 (April 24, 1998): 564-567.
White, Robert. *A Witness for Eleanor Dare: The Final Chapter in a 400 Year Old Mystery.* San Francisco: Lexikos, 1991.

Chapter 13

Baxter, Jeffrey P. *Sir Ferdinando Gorges and his Province of Maine.* Vol. 3. Boston: Prince Society, 1890.

Brown, Alexander, ed. *The Genesis of the United States.* Boston: Houghton Mifflin, 1890.

Cormack, Lesley B. "Britannia Rules the Waves?: Images of Empire in Elizabethan England." In *Literature, Mapping, and the Politics of Space in Early Modern Britain*, edited by Andrew Gordon and Bernhard Klein, 1-20. Cambridge: Cambridge University Press, 2001.

Cumming, William Patterson, R. A. Skelton, and David B. Quinn. *The Discovery of North America.* Toronto: McClelland and Stewart, 1971.

Harvey, P. D. A. *Maps in Tudor England.* Chicago: University of Chicago Press, 1993.

Hill, W. Scott. "The Site of Fort Saint George, Erected by Captain George Popham, in 1607." *Kennebec Journal* (1891): 1-5.

Hindle, Brian Paul. *Maps for Historians.* Chichester, UK: Phillimore, 1998.

Mancall, Peter C. "Introduction: English Promotion and Settlement of the Americas." In *Envisioning America: English Plans for the Colonization of North America, 1580–1640*, edited by Peter C. Mancall. Boston: Bedford Books of St. Martin's Press, 1995.

Pagden, Anthony. "The Struggle for Legitimacy and the Image of Empire in the Atlantic to c. 1700." In *The Oxford History of the British Empire.* Vol. 1: *The Origins of Empire*, edited by Nicholas Canny and Alaine Low, 34-54. Oxford: Oxford University Press, 1998.

Pollak, Martha D. *Military Architecture, Cartography and the Representation of the Early Modern European City: A Checklist of Treatises on Fortification in the Newberry Library.* Chicago: Newberry Library, 1991.

Quinn, David B. *The Voyages and Colonising Enterprises of Sir Humphrey Gilbert.* 2 vols. London: Hakluyt Society, 1940.

Quinn, David B., and Alison M. Quinn, eds. *The English New England Voyages, 1602–1608.* London: Hakluyt Society, 1983.

Acknowledgments

WE THANK MILNER LIBRARY of the Illinois State University at Normal, and particularly Joshua Layden of the Interlibrary Loan Department. The University of Illinois at Urbana-Champaign has also been a valuable resource. The Internet Archive (archive.org), Google Books (books.google.com), and the Hathi Trust Digital Library (www.hathi trust.org) are of fundamental importance to research. They have made it easier, through digital scanning, to obtain a copy of a book published in 1580 than one published in 1980.

We particularly acknowledge the work of our editor Ron Silverman, of Paul Rossmann who improved the presentation of our maps greatly, and of Trudi Gershenov for the evocative cover. And we thank our publisher, Bruce H. Franklin, always knowledgeable, courteous, and helpful. Remaining infelicities and errors are our own responsibility.

David MacDonald
Raine Waters

Index